FINLAND – A NATION OF OPERA

19 essays about contemporary opera

Elke Albrecht & Eeva-Taina Forsius-Schibli (eds.)

FINLAND – A NATION OF OPERA

19 essays about contemporary opera

Translation into English by Jaakko Mäntyjärvi

Muusakirjat

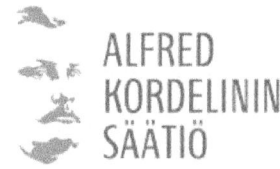
ALFRED
KORDELININ
SÄÄTIÖ

This translation was supported by the Alfred Kordelin Foundation.

© for the English edition:
Elke Albrecht, Eeva-Taina Forsius-Schibli & Muusakirjat, Helsinki, 2015
Original edition: *Olemme oopperamaa. Suomalaisen nykyoopperan synty ja kohtalo.* Helsinki: Vehrä, 2014.
German edition: *Finnland – Land der Oper. 19 Essays zur zeitgenössischen Oper.* Helsinki: Muusakirjat, 2014.
Translation into English: Jaakko Mäntyjärvi
Language editor: Peter Kislinger

Cover, illustrations & layout: Elke Albrecht
Photos: Elke Albrecht, Pekka Hako, Maarit Kytöharju

Publisher: Muusakirjat, Helsinki, Finland
Printed in Germany by BoD – Books on Demand, Norderstedt

ISBN: 978-952-68244-5-1

Content

Foreword

JORMA SILVASTI

I first came into contact with opera when singing in the Savonlinna Opera Festival Choir at the age of 15–16. The year was 1975 and the occasion was the premiere of *Ratsumies* (The Horseman) by Aulis Sallinen, which also marked the celebration of the 500th anniversary of Olavinlinna Castle, the festival venue. Afterwards, we the performers were euphoric: although we could have no inkling of what was about to unfold, we did feel we were part of something larger, an emerging process that would eventually come to be called the Finnish opera boom. For myself, this experience in the summer of 1975 inspired me to take singing lessons.

At that time, Olavinlinna Castle in the town of Savonlinna in Eastern Finland was the only large-scale opera performance venue in Finland, and the opera boom that the festival launched can now be seen as an important boost for the project to build a new Opera House in Helsinki. After many twists and turns, the new Opera House was inaugurated in 1993, marking the ascent of the Finnish National Opera to international prominence. This achievement is a tribute to the status of Finnish contemporary opera and by extension elevates our national self-esteem.

Gradually, a broad range of new works emerged that enabled musicians, particularly singers, to perform opera in their native language. Composers explored today's society, Finnish history and folk poetry as sources for opera librettos. The entire production community – directors, singers, musicians – engaged in experiments in form, style, composition technique and new approaches. These new departures had a way of attracting new audiences too.

To my mind, all this was put into words most aptly by Aulis Sallinen in an interview: "Do you really imagine that central European provincialism is somehow more universal than Finnish provincialism?"

World premieres have always attracted much attention in Finland, yet revitalising the repertoire remains a major current challenge in our field. There is an incredible range of operas out there, a true embarrassment of riches for opera producers to choose from. The Savonlinna Opera Festival aims to make an effort to contribute to a renewal of the core repertoire as far as a summer festival can within its resources, but the stated mission of the Finnish National Opera to produce works of Finnish national significance is also an important part of cherishing our national culture.

Savonlinna, nestled amidst the gorgeous scenery of the Finnish lakeland, is an excellent and unique venue for both traditional and contemporary opera, for both grand dramatic productions and intimate performances for the whole family. These help the next generation, our future audiences, to enter and explore the mysterious and wonderful world of opera.

The writers contributing to this compendium form a significant part of the unique phenomenon of Finnish opera, as indeed do many other composers not featured here. In their music and their writings, they enshrine the multitude of nuances and variations that may be found in this field. However different they may be in approach and style, they have all written works that provide audiences with unforgettable opera experiences and contribute for their part to the continuation of this grand tradition.

Jorma Silvasti
Artistic Director of the Savonlinna Opera Festival
Savonlinna, August 2015

Foreword by the editors

ELKE ALBRECHT & EEVA-TAINA FORSIUS-SCHIBLI

Finland's two leading opera institutions recently celebrated their 100th anniversary: the Finnish National Opera in 2011 and the Savonlinna Opera Festival in 2012. In the run-up to these celebrations, in summer 2010 to be precise, we conceived the idea of publishing a collection of essays by Finnish composers discussing their opera output. We already knew that Finland would be the guest of honour at the Frankfurt Book Fair in autumn 2014, and as a multi-national and bilingual editing team we naturally had an interest in this. This was why the plan was to translate the book into German first and into English later. Recent decades have seen Finnish operas transcending our national borders, and the Finnish opera boom that started in 1975 is an acknowledged phenomenon among international cognoscenti. As Atso Almila and Jukka Linkola perceptively write in their respective essays, "we are a nation of opera" (this quotation was the title of the original edition) and "we cannot live in a museum".

What we wanted to offer Finnish opera composers – the heart, soul and driving force of a unique phenomenon – was an open forum for writing about what it is like to be an opera composer in this day and age. Not everyone whom we approached agreed to contribute. Some felt that a composer should only express himself in his music. Others simply did not have the time to write an essay by the deadline, which was dictated by the timetable of the Frankfurt Book Fair. Still others said that they wanted to think about it a bit longer, saying they may return to the subject at some point in the future.

What we wanted to offer opera lovers was an opportunity to understand what it means for the creator of a work to be at the centre of a gigantic production process and what all that involves.

The only limitation we imposed on our contributors was that their essay had to be principally about opera, but in all other respects they were free to write in any style or with any approach they chose, from systematic analysis to humorous anecdotes. We wanted to gain a highly diverse and colourful documentation of the work of an opera composer working in Finland, with all of its positive as well as negative aspects and feelings. Discussion of opera as an art form and how it has changed, and of the status of opera in the past and the present, were also welcomed. It was of crucial importance for us to preserve the authenticity, colour and style of the essays we received, and for this reason we only performed minimal editing on them, mainly to correct typographical errors and punctuation, and so on.

We sent our contributors a list of questions to get them started in the process of thinking about their essay. It goes without saying that they were at liberty to ignore it completely if they chose. Its purpose was to point out that even the tiniest practical details may be interesting to an outsider. As we read the essays that came in, we found that many of our questions were reflected in the texts, sometimes even as structural elements. We therefore decided that the reader too should know the questions.

- Why write an opera in this day and age?
- For whom do you write music?
- What are your influences?
- How do you find ideas or inspiration?
- How do you choose a topic?
- What is your relationship to the *Kalevala* and other national subjects?
- What dramaturgical concepts do you employ, or favour?
- Where do your librettos come from?
- Do you write your own librettos?
- How does your composition process work in practice? Do you use pencil and paper, or a computer?
- How do you technically prepare for the process of composing an opera?
- Do you collaborate with singers and other musicians? If so, how?
- What is the status of opera in Finland today? Is contemporary music in general, and contemporary opera in particular, somehow special in Finland?
- What is it like to write an opera to a commission?
- Do you collaborate with cultural authorities and (foreign) opera houses?
- What happens after a world premiere? Are your works performed in other productions in Finland and/or abroad?

- How has writing an opera affected how you write other works? Has it had any stylistic influence?
- How do you see the future of opera?

For the benefit of readers not familiar with Finnish history and culture, we have provided a glossary of names and terms.

We would like to extend our special thanks to Jorma Silvasti, the current Director of the Savonlinna Opera Festival, for contributing a foreword; Tiina Lehtoranta and Johanna Pitkänen from the Finnish Literature Exchange (FILI) for their ongoing support and advice; Rainer Oesch, our legal counsel; Sigfried Schibli for much practical advice; Claus Carlsen for kindly letting us have his camera; Pekka Hako and Maarit Kytöharju for letting us have some photos; Kiti Häkinen, Katja Kuuramaa and the cultural-co-operative Vehrä, the Finnish publisher of the original edition, for giving us permission to use and edit one of the original covers; our translator into English, Jaakko Mäntyjärvi; our language editor, Peter Kislinger; Alfred Kordelin Foundation for financially supporting the translations; and, finally, Pro Musica Foundation for endowing the editor with a research grant.

Last but not least, we would like to thank the most important people of all: the composers who wrote us an essay. Without them, this book would not exist.

Elke Albrecht & Eeva-Taina Forsius-Schibli
Helsinki & Basel, August 2015

Is it all over for opera?

KALEVI AHO

In 1967, composer and conductor Pierre Boulez declared in the now notorious provocative interview for the German *Der Spiegel* magazine: "Blow up the opera houses!"[1] As far as Boulez was concerned, the history of opera ended with Alban Berg's *Wozzeck* and *Lulu* – he said that not a single proper opera worth mentioning had been written since then. Boulez considered even the quite successful modernist operas of Hans Werner Henze to be old-fashioned rubbish and compared Henze to Charles de Gaulle, the then President of France, quipping that he could produce any kind of crap because he thought he would be king forever. Mauricio Kagel and György Ligeti lacked a sufficiently broad expertise of theatre, Boulez went on, and he derided Boris Blacher's recent opera *Zwischenfälle bei einer Notlandung* (Incidents after a crash landing) as being nothing more than film music.

Boulez was irritated by the fact that all the opera houses of the world programmed the same narrow core repertoire. He considered Paris to be an especially provincial opera city; he felt that the Paris Opera was full of dust and shit – a threadbare museum that catered mainly to tourists.

However, all this in no way prevented Boulez from conducting *Parsifal* at Bayreuth, which is a museum to Wagner if anything, in 1967. His view was that *Parsifal* was to a great extent absolute music that simply needed to be cleansed of all the late Romantic layers mistakenly imposed on it.

---

[1] 'Sprengt die Opernhäuser in die Luft', interview with Boulez by Felix Schmidt and Jürgen Hohmeyer, *Der Spiegel* 40/1967 (25 September 1967).

So is it all over for opera? Even today, the repertoire of the world's opera houses consists largely of the same 20 to 30 works as in the 1960s: Mozart, Rossini, Verdi, Wagner, Puccini, Strauss... Contemporary operas are being written all the time, and Finland has enjoyed a particularly remarkable opera boom, but they never seem to have staying power. However impressive and successful a new opera may seem, it is almost axiomatic that after a couple of productions it will remain on the shelf gathering dust. When opera houses wish to revitalise their repertoire, they usually go for an obscure 19th-century work rather than anything more recent.

Finland is a fortunate exception in that a handful of contemporary operas have indeed established themselves in the core repertoire. The most successful Finnish opera of all time is *Viimeiset kiusaukset* (The Last Temptations) by Joonas Kokkonen, premièred in 1975. Operas by composers such as Sallinen, Rautavaara and Ilkka Kuusisto are also staged more or less regularly.

Having said that, the default is still that once a new opera has been premièred, it will sink into obscurity. Despite this apparently depressing fact, most composers still dream of writing an opera. Why is that?

For me, the answer is simple: opera is an art form with a unique fascination that stimulates the imagination and fires up the emotions. Also, an opera has both words and music. In opera, you can clearly express things that you cannot express with music alone.

This is why I have written five operas. The most important element for me is the libretto. It has to be something that I can identify with and can use to convey something important to viewers and listeners. A libretto has to be dramaturgically feasible, specifically in the context of opera. I was never interested in writing operas where the text is chopped up into tiny bits, obscuring the meaning of the text. My purpose in opera has always been to communicate directly to the viewer-listener, while in instrumental music my approach is more abstract.

For an opera to work in the way the composer intended, it must be directed and staged in a way that does justice to the work and enhances its core nature. The kind of *Regietheater* that has become increasingly common since the 1960s is quite the opposite, with the director superimposing a new and modern staging on an old work while retaining the original words and music. This may have the effect of rendering the story unrecognisable and incomprehensible for the audience.

Modernised stagings of old operas can be impressive when the director has confidence in the underlying narrative and the music. As an example, I might mention Patrice Chéreau's production of Wagner's *Ring*, which was booed at its premiere in 1976 but given a standing ovation with bravos lasting 45 minutes at its final performance in 1980. I also enjoyed the imaginative production of Rossini's *Il viaggio a Reims* directed by Dario

Fo at the Finnish National Opera in 2012, where Fo managed to propel the rather uninteresting story to fantastic heights on the strength of its bubbly music. Far more often, however, one gets the unfortunate feeling that neither the director nor the production designers have faith in the opera they are directing or in its music. In such a case, a modern production may turn out so artificial and awkward that it practically destroys the entire opera.

For me, the most impressive opera experiences are those in which the focus is not on the narcissistic visions of the director and set designer but on a seamless blend of music, directing and staging so that the directing itself becomes practically invisible: with this kind of blend, the entire production will seem natural, compelling and meaningful. Good productions do not need to be explained or justified in the programme book.

Writing an opera is such a huge undertaking that there is no point in doing it just for your own enjoyment. At the very least, you need to know that the work will be performed, and ideally it should be commissioned – as indeed has been the case with all of my operas.

My first opera, a dramatic monologue entitled *Avain* (The Key, 1977–1978), was written for the studio stage of the Finnish National Opera as it then was, a tiny venue in Hakaniemi in Helsinki in the late 1970s. In the event, it was premièred in the chamber music hall of Finlandia Hall on 4 September 1979. The only vocal role was taken by Matti Lehtinen, the production was directed by Hannu Heikinheimo, and the 13-member orchestra was conducted by Hannu Bister.

Finding a libretto for this project was a difficult process. To be sure, director Hannu Heikinheimo suggested Juha Mannerkorpi's *Avain* as a libretto at the very start, but having read it I felt that it would be insurmountably difficult to set to music. I then read some three dozen plays and short stories before coming back to *Avain*. This time it no longer seemed quite so impossible, and I prepared the libretto myself – I say prepared, not wrote, because all I did was remove bits of Mannerkorpi's text. I changed nothing of what remained. Mannerkorpi approved of my abridged version, and at my request also rewrote the final scene as poetic prose to make it easier to set to music.

As I took the opportunity to adapt the libretto for *Avain* myself, I also had control over its musical pacing from the start. Opera librettos do not necessarily work well as literature. Good librettos give the appearance of already incorporating or allowing for the music. Scenes where things happen fast may need a lot of text, while slower scenes need very little. There is also a lot you can do with just music, without text. It is generally a good idea to leave some room for pure music in an opera; if there is too much text, the composer has to keep churning it out until it becomes tedious for the listener. A libretto can thus seem out of balance when read as text yet work wonderfully when combined with music in the opera.

Many librettists have made the mistake of attempting to write a libretto that is a grand drama in its own right, without giving thought to the music. Jealous of their creation, they may also refuse outright to make a single change to their text to conform to the demands of music theatre. Aulis Sallinen, for instance, encountered this problem when he adapted librettos to his operas *Ratsumies* (The Horseman) and *Kuningas lähtee Ranskaan* (The King Goes Forth to France) from plays by Paavo Haavikko. The playwright had difficulty accepting Sallinen's deletions that were necessary to fashion a libretto whose dramaturgy would work in an opera.

It was a great help to me in writing *Avain* that at the very start of the process Matti Lehtinen, the soloist at the premiere, read the entire libretto out loud to me like an actor. I made notes of his stresses and emphases, his tempo, pacing and pauses, and the melodic contours of his voice. Without this assistance, the project might have failed.

The process of writing the music, then, was more or less the same that it subsequently was for my other operas. Because the libretto gave a ready-made structural framework for the composition, I made no overall sketches of the shape of the work. Actually, I rarely make sketches anyway; I start at the beginning, writing in full score by hand, and go on until I come to the end. Long after writing *Avain*, I did learn the basics of the music writing programs Finale and Sibelius, but I never started using either of them regularly. For me, handicraft is an important part of composing, writing something down on paper with my own hands. Somehow I feel that when music is written in an individual handwriting, the music itself becomes more personal and has more character than if the score were printed out from a computer.

Because the comprehensibility of the words was of prime importance in *Avain*, the vocal writing was based on the prosody of the Finnish language. I read the text out loud to myself many times, as if acting it, with various types of interpretation, giving thought to which word or which syllable should be emphasised. After settling on a final approach, I began to exaggerate its profile to convert it into melodic shapes. I was inspired to do this by Matti Lehtinen's original reading of the text to me. The vocal part in *Avain* contains both speech and singing and various kinds of expression between the two. There is a great deal of *Sprechgesang*, or speech-singing, where the pitches do not matter so much but the rhythm must be precise.

When *Avain* was performed in the small auditorium of the Hamburg State Opera in 1982 and 1984 (with Toni Blankenheim in the only role), the conductor, Klauspeter Seibel, noted that its aesthetical approach was remarkably similar to that of the operas of Leoš Janáček. This inspired me to take a closer look at Janáček's operas: I borrowed scores, bought recordings and read Janáček's writings on music that had been translated into German. In 1984, I translated some of his writing into Finnish and wrote an essay on the aesthetics of his operas. Indeed, Janáček became one of my most important influences as an opera composer, and I was pleased that I had arrived at my approach independently, before being aware of what he was doing.

For Janáček, as for myself, the idea is that words alone do not always tell the truth of what the speaker is thinking. The tone of the voice is also important. I can say "I love you" so that I really mean what I say. But I can set that sentence to music in a way that will make it actually mean "I don't love you any more" or even "I hate you". All this is possible in opera, and the setting of the text can be underlined by the orchestral scoring.

In *Avain* as in my other operas, there are situations where a person says one thing but thinks another, and this unspoken level – unconscious, if you will – is often reflected in the orchestra. There are endless ways of setting a text to music, and in its rich variety of expression opera as an art form trumps literature and even drama.

In 1981, the Finnish National Opera gave guest performances of *Avain* in Warsaw and Poznań in Poland. The meaning and content of the work were crystal clear to Polish audiences even though Matti Lehtinen's wonderful performance was in Finnish. It was on that tour that I overheard Keijo Kupiainen, the production manager, talk to Simo Tavaste, the financial manager, about a play named *Insect Life* by Josef and Karel Čapek where all the characters were insects.

I pricked up my ears, because I was already on the lookout for a libretto for a new opera after *Avain.* Above all, I wanted to write a satirical opera with a strong social message. After we returned home, Kupiainen gave me an English translation of *Insect Life* and later a Finnish translation of the play. I wrote my first draft for the libretto in 1982 and also wrote some music for the opening.

In winter 1983, I went to talk about my insect opera with Juhani Raiskinen, General Director of the Finnish National Opera. He was not enthusiastic about the idea, and so I stopped working on the score because I had no idea as to where the opera might be performed.

In 1985, the Town of Savonlinna organised an invited composition competition. The composers invited were Einojuhani Rautavaara, Paavo Heininen and myself. The idea was to perform the winning opera at the Savonlinna Opera Festival to celebrate the 350th anniversary of the founding of the town in 1989. I already had a libretto almost finished and some music too, so I dusted off the project and completed *Hyönteiselämää* (Insect Life) after two years of work in July 1987.

Two aspects of the Čapek brothers' play fascinated me. Firstly, the play was excellent for music theatre: it was funny, its structure was clear and it matured towards the end, where comedy morphed into tragedy. The insect characters practically invited musical characterisation. Secondly, the text incorporated caustic social criticism of the kind that I had been trying to find. There is no psychological drama; the insect characters are rather one-dimensional and marionette-like representatives of human stereotypes. The play holds up a mirror to modern social phenomena such as selfish hedonism, materialism and militarism. But when you look into the mirror, everything is back-to-front: what was self-evident becomes doubtful.

In adapting the libretto for *Hyönteiselämää*, I took considerable liberties with the play, which had been premièred in 1921. To sustain the attention of an opera audience, I telescoped the original three acts into two. This allows only one interval for the audience to distance themselves from the performance. In the scene where the ants prepare for war, I added quotes from politicians' speeches in the 1980s describing situations where war might be justified. The ants thus motivate their warfare of total destruction with the words of Ronald Reagan, Alexander Haig and other prominent politicians of the time. I myself wrote the lyrics for the grasshoppers' lullaby for the unborn child and other aria-like numbers, and for the ants' working music and war music.

The music has an important dramaturgical function in *Hyönteiselämää*. It sets up expectations for the listener. These are sometimes fulfilled but sometimes confounded, with the listener being thrown from one emotional extreme to another. The music and absence of music serve to take the listener away from the real world and then back again. The music paces the action on stage so that variety is preserved and boredom avoided. When the ants' war progresses to its culmination, the music disappears altogether, and all we hear under the spoken lines is the electronically created horrible, ear-piercing sound of the war machine, the 'peacemaker'.

The pluralism of musical styles in *Hyönteiselämää* represents a collection of stereotypes much like the insect characters represent human stereotypes of our day. Every type of insect has its own music. The orchestral score is quite independent of the vocal lines at times, and in the event the singers were given facial mikes to avoid their voices being drowned by the orchestra.

Hyönteiselämää was not performed in Savonlinna in 1989, the selected opera being Heininen's *Veitsi* (The Knife). Rautavaara's competition entry, *Vincent*, was performed at the old Opera House in the following year, 1990, but *Hyönteiselämää* had to wait nine years for its premiere. In the end, it all turned out for the best, because the premiere on 27 September 1996 was staged in the new Opera House, where the production was more impressive than could have ever been achieved in Savonlinna. Directed by Jussi Tapola and conducted by Pertti Pekkanen, the opera proved a success: all performances were sold out and, due to popular demand, the Finnish National Opera put on six further performances in 1997.

The opera was also recorded for TV. It was decided that the sets would be kept so that the production could be revived at some point in the mid-2000s. However, in the 2000s the management of the Finnish National Opera was replaced a couple of times, and the new artistic directors were no longer interested in this satirical opera. As far as I know, the sets were destroyed.

Hyönteiselämää piqued the interest of some foreign dramaturges and directors. There were plans to stage the opera in Washington DC in 2001 and in Prague or Brno in the Czech Republic at about the same time. The Washington project fell apart due to a failure to obtain sponsorship, while in Prague it was apparently the conservative and cautious programming policy of the city's two opera houses that scuppered the idea. In Brno, the theatre was quite simply too small for an opera on this scale.

Hyönteiselämää had a considerable impact on my subsequent music. When it became apparent in early 1988 that it would not be performed in Savonlinna, I wrote my Seventh Symphony and sub-titled it the *Insect Symphony*, as it was based on material from the opera. It was with this that I found a wholly new approach to the symphony genre, and after that I found it much easier to write symphonies.

My Thirteenth Symphony (*Symphonic Character Studies*), completed in 2005, is also based on an opera, *Salaisuuksien kirja* (The Book of Secrets, 1998). This was the concluding opera in the trilogy *Aika ja uni* (The Age of Dreams), the monumental project conceived by the Savonlinna Opera Festival for the year 2000. It consisted of three separate operas by three composers, opening with the non-narrative choral opera *...nunc et semper...* by Herman Rechberger followed by *Marian rakkaus* (Maria's Love) by Olli Kortekangas, the most realistic and plot-driven of the three. My 75-minute *Salaisuuksien kirja* concluded the trilogy. The libretto was written by Paavo Rintala, but all three composers played rather fast and loose with his text. The three operas shared an outside commentator character named Bertrand, whose monologues bridged the gaps between the operas. I was asked to compose these monologues and found myself writing the lyrics as well, following Rintala's ideas as far as possible. Paavo Rintala himself was in the terminal stage of Parkinson's disease and was unable to write anything any more. He died on 8 August 1999, almost one year before the premiere of *Aika ja uni* directed by Jussi Tapola and conducted by Osmo Vänskä in Savonlinna on 15 July 2000.

Salaisuuksien kirja proved to be the most problematic element in the trilogy. This part of the libretto opens in Jerzal (Jerusalem) in the early years of the Christian era, where the actions of a religious rabble-rouser named Chrestus and his subsequent cruci-fixion spark a great riot. We then follow a trial convened in Rome to establish what ex-actly happened in Jerzal two years earlier. The text finds parallels in the modern world, the powder keg of Palestine and the Middle East and today's superpower politics. From Rome, we move to 15th-century Paris, where the Mad King (Chrestus was also described as the Mad King a few times) causes confusion. He discovers a book called the *Book of Secrets*, which contains ultimate truths about the universe, and begins to read it. But no one can understand anything of his incoherent speech, and eventually the book is re-vealed to contain nothing but empty pages.

The libretto for *Salaisuuksien kirja* began life as a radio play, and when Rintala sent me the draft libretto in autumn 1997, it was very obviously unfinished, almost wholly lacking in dramaturgy. It was hugely too long, and much of the trial scene and the story of the Mad King consisted of philosophical train-of-thought ruminations. At the same time, there was an immensely powerful vision in it. Because of Rintala's advanced illness, I was obliged to edit the libretto myself. I had to rewrite much more than with *Hyönteis-elämää*, but I never departed from Rintala's original ideas, and eventually I was quite pleased with the result. This is the most philosophical opera I have written to date, and after all the trouble with the libretto was over, I wrote the music in a state of great inspiration.

As in *Hyönteiselämää,* the orchestra plays a vital role in *Salaisuuksien kirja*; it is the orchestra that keeps the story together and shapes the dramaturgy of the work. In the trial scene, I tried to paint musical portraits of the various witnesses, and these became the 'character studies' in my Thirteenth Symphony. The Mad King scene is a narrative sustained by the orchestra.

Even before *Salaisuuksien kirja,* I had begun to work on an opera based on the radio play *Ennen kuin me kaikki olemme hukkuneet* (Before We All Have Drowned) by Juha Man-nerkorpi. I had first come across this play in 1977, reading through the collected works of Mannerkorpi while working on *Avain.* I already decided back then that I would also set this compelling, elegiac radio play to music. Whereas *Avain* has only a single male role (baritone), *Ennen kuin me kaikki olemme hukkuneet* has a dominant female role (mezzo-soprano), a nurse named Maija Salminen. At the beginning of the opera, lonely and burned out from her work, she drowns herself in the river. The remainder is a sequence of flashbacks interspersed with dream-like scenes where the drowned woman describes what she is feeling and observes the efforts to find her body.

In a couple of scenes, the dead woman makes contact with the living: with Göran, a surgeon with whom she had an affair that ended badly, and Saku, the son of her colleague Mrs Järvinen. Saku has the ambition of inventing a radar that would find people who are about to drown before they actually die – like a torch that would illuminate drowning people as soon as you shine it on the water. In the final scene, when the police have already found Maija's body and lifted it out of the water, Saku points his torch at the water in search of other drowned people.

Drowning is used as a metaphor to depict mental drowning. The only 'radar' that would save someone from that is another person's sense that something is wrong. The only way to achieve that is to teach people to listen, as the main character tells Saku at the end: "Listen so that you will learn how to hear and to save us, before we are all drowned."

Ennen kuin me kaikki olemme hukkuneet deals with problematic core issues of human life, but instead of spreading despair the drowned woman radiates great sensitivity, warmth and light. The character of Maija Salminen prompts great empathy; indeed, to my mind she is one of the most effective and profound female characters in all of Finnish literature.

In April 1986, Sakari Puurunen – a stage director who had been a close friend of Mannerkorpi (the author having died in 1980) and who had liked my *Avain* – unexpectedly sent me his draft libretto for this opera. I read it, but surprisingly I found myself disliking it. In the original radio play, the entire action seemed to be played out from the bottom of the river. The real-time action only covers the time from when the little boys Saku and Roto find the abandoned bicycle of the drowned woman to the time when the police finally drag her body from the river and bring it to land. This straightforward sequence of events is interrupted by various flashbacks.

By contrast, Sakari Puurunen's draft libretto was set mainly in an operating theatre. Puurunen also included a choir, he had three policemen searching for the body instead of the two in the original play, and he added yet another character, Mikko. He is Saku's father, a ship's mate who had drowned some years earlier when his ship sank in a storm. Saku's drowned father is alluded to in the original play, but he does not himself appear. Puurunen's libretto thus had two people commenting on the action from the hereafter.

Sakari Puurunen wrote his libretto with the large auditorium of the Finnish National Opera in mind, but I preferred a more intimate and smaller-scale work, with no choir. I decided that when I started work on the opera, I would adapt the libretto from Mannerkorpi's play myself.

In autumn 1990, this project began to come into shape. Walton Grönroos, the General Director of the Finnish National Opera, wanted to commission an opera from me for the studio stage (later to be named Almi Hall) of the new Opera House, then under construction. Eeva-Liisa Saarinen was pencilled in for the leading role. After some delay, the commissioning agreement was signed in August 1994, and the premiere was scheduled for the 1996–1997 season. Osmo Vänskä would conduct the production. In September 1994, I adapted the libretto, condensing and simplifying the original play.

In late February 1995, I started work on the music. In the course of the year, however, it turned out that the Finnish National Opera was in serious financial trouble. One of the cost-cutting measures decided on by the management was to cancel all premieres for the following two years. This affected not only *Ennen kuin me kaikki olemme hukkuneet* but also *Hyönteiselämää*, whose premiere was scheduled for September 1996 and which thus also faced the axe. I was so shaken by the Finnish National Opera's plans that I stopped writing the new opera.

Then the Director General of the Culture Department at the Ministry of Education, Irmeli Niemi, intervened. She made it a condition of the Finnish National Opera receiving its central government grant for 1996 that the Finnish premieres were not cancelled. The budget cuts would have to be found elsewhere. And so *Hyönteiselämää* was premièred on 27 September 1996 after all.

In spring 1997, Juhani Raiskinen was again appointed General Director of the Finnish National Opera, and I agreed with him that once I had completed *Salaisuuksien kirja*, which the Savonlinna Opera Festival had commissioned in the meantime, I would finish *Ennen kuin me kaikki olemme hukkuneet*. I returned to this project in April 1999, and the opera was finished six months later, in September 1999. It was premièred in Almi Hall on 8 February 2001, with Riikka Rantanen giving a magnificent performance in the lead role. The production was directed by Janne Lehmusvuo and conducted by Osmo Vänskä.

The lead had been reassigned to Riikka Rantanen because the tessitura of Eeva-Liisa Saarinen's voice had become somewhat lower in the course of the 1990s, and the role of Maija Salminen was now too high for her.

In rehearsals for the premiere production of *Ennen kuin me kaikki olemme hukkuneet*, a dispute arose with the director. There is a tragic culminating moment in Act II where the main character, the burned-out and suicidal nurse Maija Salminen, encounters a male patient in the night who is quite as desperate as she is, and they go into an adjacent room to seek a moment's love and warmth in one another's company. The scene is underlined with a poignant love theme. The director, however, was determined to stage the scene in such a way that Maija would end up killing the patient. I was quite outraged that the director of a premiere production would blatantly ignore the specifications of the composer and attempt to turn the sympathetic and sensitive main character into a murderer. Such radical and questionable reinterpretations are sadly not unusual in modern, director-centred productions.

The writing of this opera was a longer and more complicated process than that of any other work of mine before or since. It remains one of my favourites in my entire output, and it is a great regret for me that there is no recording of it. The premiere was not broadcast, and a recording project was planned but cancelled – not once but twice. Sinfonia Lahti had been engaged to record the work at Sibelius Hall in Lahti for the BIS label in January 2002, but the singer engaged as Göran demanded a fee so high that the orchestra could not agree; it would have meant raising the fees of all the other vocal soloists accordingly. The budget collapsed, and the project folded.

One year after the premiere, in February 2002, the opera was performed in Lübeck in a German translation. The lead was taken by Angela Nick, one of the greatest stars of the Theater Lübeck. Undaunted by the cancellation in Lahti, the BIS label attempted once more to record the opera, this time in Lübeck in November 2002. This time it was the Lübeck Opera Orchestra that presented outrageous demands. Theater Lübeck refused, and the recording was, predictably, cancelled.

If there is any opera of mine of which I would heartily like to see a new production, it is *Ennen kuin me kaikki olemme hukkuneet.* That would hopefully mean that a decent recording could be made too.

I had already started to think about my next opera in 2000. The initiative for this came from Maritza Núñez, a Peruvian-born playwright, poet and choir conductor resident in Finland. She introduced me to her play *Sueños de una tarde dominical* (Dreams of a Sunday Evening) about painters Frida Kahlo and Diego Rivera and asked me whether I would be interested in setting it to music. The play had received an award for best play in Spanish in 1999.

The play is not only about Frida and Diego but also about their contemporaries in Mexico in 1939–1940: Lev Trotsky, surrealist author André Breton, photographer Tina Modotti, Mexican painter David Alfaro Siqueros, Frida's sister Cristina and Trotsky's wife Natalia. There is also a character called the Other Frida, who in Act I steps out of the painting titled *Two Fridas* and who is present in several scenes as the mental mirror or conscience of the 'real' Frida.

I was attracted by this carnevalistic, somehow dreamlike text, as it invited a new approach to shaping an opera. The characters were also interesting, dramatic and compelling.

I presented the project to the new Director of the Finnish National Opera, Erkki Korhonen, in the early 2000s. He showed an interest, and it was planned that the opera would be jointly produced with the Volksoper in Vienna. That meant composing it in two languages, Finnish and German. Somewhat later, the Director of the Volksoper,

Dominique Mentha, was forced to resign, and the Finnish National Opera lost interest. It seemed that this project was destined to sink without a trace. However, in 2011 it was resurrected as a proposed production at the Sibelius Academy by Maritza's husband, musicologist Alfonso Padilla. The Sibelius Academy decided to commission the opera from Maritza and myself.

Working with Maritza Núñez was very easy. In autumn 2011, she wrote a first draft of the libretto, and we reviewed it critically together. Even this first draft was very much operatic, as well it should be, since it was written by a consummate professional. It was obvious that she had had music in mind when writing the text. I gave input on the length of the libretto (the amount of text) and its shape, i.e. how the scenes were arranged. The final libretto was completed in February 2012, and the opera was entitled *Frida y Diego*. The libretto is in Spanish. I wrote the first measures of music in late February 2012.

The characters in this opera are powerful and dramatic, operatic if you will, and the range of moods extends from the dreamlike opening to the wild carnival parody of Act II. Act III contains heated political debate and incisive parody (Diego mocking Stalin) during which the carnival goes sour as the inebriated Frida and Diego get into an argument. Act IV contains the dramatic high point of the work (the assassination of Trotsky), but the conclusion is again dreamlike and conciliatory. Frida and Diego, divorced for a while, marry again.

The major challenge in writing *Frida y Diego* was the language of the libretto, as I do not speak Spanish. It was an invaluable help that Maritza and Agustín Gutiérrez Canet, the Mexican Ambassador, made a recording of them reading the text. I listened to this constantly while writing the opera to find a musical rhythm for the lines and to get the word stresses right. Maritza also prepared a version of the libretto where she had hyphenated all the words and marked the stresses. Gutiérrez Canet also supplied me with recordings from Mexican radio of the actual voices of Trotsky, Diego and Siqueros, and I chose their voice types on the basis of these samples: Diego is a tenor, Trotsky is a high baritone, and Siqueros is a bass. No recording of Frida speaking could be found in any archive, but according to contemporary descriptions she had a low and husky voice. She is therefore a contralto.

There is a lot of Mexican flavour in the score. Its instruments include a folk harp, which is smaller than a concert harp and has a range of five octaves. It is commonly used in Mexican music. At the beginning of Act I, I quote *La Bamba*, a tune known to every Mexican, and the carnival in Act II includes another Mexican tune, *La Negra.* Later in Act II, a parody of Hitler is underpinned by marches and a foxtrot in German 1930s style. A theremin is used to create an eerie atmosphere in the dream scenes. There is also music of a more 'modern' kind, and musical styles shift all the time. The main characters have their own instruments and *leitmotifs*: Frida is represented by the alto sax, Diego by the tuba, Siqueros by the trombone and Tina Modotti by the oboe. Trotsky's entrances are generally heralded by a martial tune that merges the *Internationale* with the national hymn of the Soviet Union.

Because of this plurality of styles, *Frida y Diego* bears a notional resemblance to *Hyönteiselämää,* but its musical material is very different. Its aesthetic is the 'aesthetic of the impure': purity of style is a secondary consideration for me, as the main thing is to express the content of the work as effectively as possible and to engage the listener. This end justifies all stylistic means.

The premiere of *Frida y Diego* took place at the Helsinki Music Centre (Musiikkitalo) on 17 October 2014, with singers from the Sibelius Academy opera class and the Sibelius Academy Orchestra, in a production directed by Vilppu Kiljunen and conducted by Markus Lehtinen. All performances were sold out.

By writing operas, I have sought for my part to disprove Pierre Boulez's claim that the history of opera came to an end with Berg's *Lulu* in 1935. Opera is such a rich art form that we need not concern ourselves with reports of its demise. New operas are being written all the time, and composers have pushed the envelope of the opera genre in all sorts of new directions. Many of these new operas are works that would deserve to gain a lasting place in the repertoire of opera houses. And considering the number of Finnish operas currently in production, it is safe to say that the Finnish opera boom is far from over.

The problem with opera is, and has always been, not that contemporary operas are bad but that opera houses follow an ultra-conservative and overly cautious programing policy. New operas should be given a chance. If a work proves to be successful in its premiere production, we should not let it disappear; opera houses should be encouraged to see whether it could be a similar success in subsequent productions. This is the only way in which to find new additions to the core repertoire, to extend it beyond the 20 to 30 warhorses that everyone performs all the time. An opera does not have to be by Verdi, Wagner, Puccini or Alban Berg to be effective.

Approaching folk opera

ATSO ALMILA

There is a great paradox about opera in Finland. On the one hand, the art form itself is seen as elitist in the worst sense of the word and regarded by many as completely alien and therefore an unnecessary and futile pursuit – and what is more, one that is paid for with taxpayers' money. But on the other hand, there is also public awareness of the international success story of Finnish opera; names such as Kokkonen, Sallinen, Talvela and Hynninen are most likely familiar even to the most uncultured man in the street. Opera has been a cornerstone of 'Finland's national brand' since long before anyone had even thought of such a term, and hence long before obsessing about our brand became a national pastime.

Considering that opera is the butt of many jokes and the source of silly stereotypes that provide ample material for comedy, and considering that it may be seen as intimidating because it combines several branches of the arts at a highly demanding level, it is scarcely surprising that it takes a lot of effort and audience education to lower the threshold and to dispel the perceived aura of elitism. This does not just mean elite creators and performers, you understand; the perception is that this art form is only attended, enjoyed and appreciated by the elite of our society.

What is the image that the average Finn has of opera? The late Kari Suomalainen, for decades the country's most influential cartoonist in the *Helsingin Sanomat* newspaper, portrayed opera for his readers as a corpulent Wagner soprano in a horned helmet, singing the long and tedious story of the *Ring*, high and loud, with the audience dressed to the nines consisting of culturally enlightened society ladies and their reluctant, yawning husbands.

In the 1970s, the opera *Viimeiset kiusaukset* (The Last Temptations), written by Joonas Kokkonen to a libretto by his cousin Lauri Kokkonen, achieved the near-impossible by reaching out to audiences who did not care for the traditional opera repertoire – which at the time, it must be said, was performed in Finland to a high degree of quality despite modest circumstances, and in Finnish translations as was the practice. The story in *Viimeiset kiusaukset* was Finnish, as indeed had been the case with earlier success stories in Finnish opera, *Pohjalaisia* (The Ostrobothnians) by Leevi Madetoja and the initially unlucky *Juha* by Aarre Merikanto, which had to wait for years for its premiere and eventual success. *Viimeiset kiusaukset* thus had precedent on its side, and being easily accessible it won over quite a remarkable number of people holding deeply held prejudices and resentment against opera. Of course, it then prompted resentment of a wholly different kind, being ridiculed as a 'fur cap opera' by the rather straitlaced young modernist composers of the day.

So what did Kokkonen's fur cap opera achieve? It was the opening salvo in a new triumphal progress of Finnish opera that Aulis Sallinen's similarly accessible and later quite sizeable opera output carried forward. This boom later produced such diverse works as *Silkkirumpu* (The Damask Drum) by Paavo Heininen, which was a considerable success at the Finnish National Opera despite its extremely complex and demanding music, and *Isän tyttö* (Daddy's Girl) by Olli Kortekangas, which was one of the most resoundingly successful Finnish operas of the 2000s at the Savonlinna Opera Festival.

Without these important fur caps we would never have had such energy poured into this genre or arrived at a situation where Finland has a world-class Opera House and internationally famous opera composers such as Kaija Saariaho. We are a nation of opera.

Having said that, I freely admit that I prefer not to engage in conversation with an unknown taxi driver when driving past the Opera House. You can never tell whether they will heartily curse society for shelling out taxpayer money on such idiotic things or turn out to be an opera fan and proud of our culture. At the time of this writing, in 2014, we are living amidst a very strange hostile trend: certain political extremists are demanding that publicly subsidised culture should be confined to historical relics, artworks that they consider reflect the 'Finnish identity' (whatever that is) as defined more than a century ago. But the artists they name as ideals to look to are people like Jean Sibelius and Akseli Gallen-Kallela and their ilk, who were the most cosmopolitan and internationally oriented artists that Finland has ever had!

I have tried to explain that from that golden age more than a century ago, and actually from far earlier than that, we may find the ideal of human growth, which means combining physical and spiritual wellbeing – which, incidentally, are both aspects of 'culture'. Being an 'educated person' today is almost something to be sneered at rather than something to aspire to. Opera is an easy target, being the most expensive art form there is. And yet Finnish opera is a testimony to the high standard of Finnish expertise, and thus it is not so difficult to understand why guests from abroad, whether corporate or political, are often taken to an opera performance. Opera is our showcase to the world. Finnish music remains at the very top of 'Finland's national brand' without any particular efforts to sustain that status. Moreover, opera brings together Finland's finest musicians to tackle its not inconsiderable challenges.

The Association of Finnish Symphony Orchestras is one of the most comprehensive municipal orchestral organisations in the world. Its member orchestras offer live concerts and operas locally in many Finnish cities and towns, some of them quite small. Our provincial opera companies typically operate in towns where there is an orchestra and a favourably disposed local authority. Municipal theatres are naturally roped in because of the expertise they have: sometimes a theatre may have an orchestra pit allowing for performances to be held there; sometimes sets built in a theatre workshop are brought into a concert hall. Provincial opera companies provide emerging singers with invaluable performing opportunities, and I would go so far as to say that the often-belittled genre of operetta has actually taught many singers a lot. Young budding conductors and provincial opera companies have also found a happy, cost-efficient partnership. The availability of fine stage directors has in many cases resulted in a smoothly running master-and-apprentice arrangement.

Many provincial opera companies stage operettas so as to be sure of having a solid box office take. Granted, the audiences will probably consist mostly of elderly ladies. But let's face facts here! Without elderly people in the audience we would soon not have an audience, because the percentage of elderly people in the population is increasing all the time! Anyone and everyone who buys a ticket and attends a performance is worthy of our appreciation, however much they may conform to stereotypes of people who go to listen to classical music. We are glad for their patronage and try to cater to them as best we can.

Operetta is instructional, and because of this it is my firm belief that there are not enough operetta productions for training purposes. Operetta is anything but easy and simple if it is done well. It is an incredibly effective school for clarity of diction for singers, both spoken and sung. And there is no better way to learn how to pace stage action than by having to work with comedic timing, also a must when performing in an operetta. We composers might also venture into this genre more, every now and again.

There are several small opera companies in Finland that are astonishingly broad-minded with regard to their repertoire. Many highly trained singers who have not managed to gain an engagement at a prestigious opera house have gathered up a group of singers in a similar situation, perhaps joined by young enthusiastic choral singers, and hey presto – there's an opera company. This is precisely the sort of initiative that our arts institutions (the famous 'bricks and mortar') should be supporting. Such groups should be given the security of longer-term funding, as with provincial opera companies. How can you plan your operations even a couple of years ahead if there is no certainty of funding? How do you engage musicians, let alone commission new works? I would say that independent ensembles and opera companies that have proven their quality should be given funding for a five-year period at a time so that this important work can be brought onto a stable foundation.

And what about us composers? What could we learn from creating an operetta or even a musical, assuming that trained voices are available? I can let you in on a little secret, dear reader, based on my extensive experience in opera and theatre, as both composer and conductor: if the audience cannot understand the text, 90% of the time it is the composer's fault.

Not being able to understand the text in an opera means that the composer has not set the text sensibly, for instance by not paying attention how vowels fit into the melodic line. There may also be balancing issues if the orchestration is too thick. However, the venue may also be to blame. Sung translations are often problematic because of the great differences between language versions, and these days works are usually performed in their original languages, particularly since the advent of surtitling.

Finnish composers need to find opportunities to try their hand at vocal music for the stage. Collaborating with small ensembles like those described above may help everyone involved present the story in a better a clearer way. So I say go for it – and without microphones if at all possible!

Jorma Panula, Ilkka Kuusisto, Pekka Kostiainen, Uljas Pulkkis, myself and most recently Jaakko Kuusisto share the distinction of writing what are known as 'folk operas' for the Ilmajoki Music Festival. Each of us have had one to four operas performed there. We should note that even a work as distinguished as Leevi Madetoja's *Pohjalaisia* has been performed at the Ilmajoki festival, as the opening production in a guest performance by the Finnish National Opera in the 1970s, no less, and the festival staged its own production in the 2000s. But what exactly is a 'folk opera', then? Folk music, of course, is music that cannot be attributed to any particular creator, whereas the Ilmajoki operas are through-composed musical works that only contain folk music as one element among many, if even that. There is an institution named the Volksoper in Vienna, a theatre that stages musicals, operettas and light operas. Perhaps this would be a more exact analogy for the Ilmajoki festival. We should note that Ilmajoki and many other summer festivals that have followed its lead have fostered a large number of new Finnish operas, and the festival setting appears to have defused whatever prejudices audiences may have had about opera. It is almost as if the festival itself 'guarantees' that audiences will not be faced with anything too complicated. Jorma Panula's pioneering work in particular contributed to this image.

Ilmajoki, Kokkola, Nivala, Åland and many other summer opera happenings produce works that may survive for a season or two or in the best case have some performances elsewhere in Finland in the winter. This network, combined with the activities of provincial opera companies and small groups, is a pathway to the richness of Finnish opera where even the most obstinate opera denier may find something of interest. Our leading institutions, the Finnish National Opera and the Savonlinna Opera Festival, have taken the bold and rewarding step of investing in productions for children. These and the often-demanded adventure stories for teens are featured particularly in collaboration with schools.

Culture comes cheap in Finland. In any given year, the budget for the entire culture department in a city the size of Kuopio, for instance, is only 0.3% of the total budget. But however affordable and cost-effective cultural services may be, they are subjected to the same budget cuts as everyone else. Yet it is something to think about that for a small body like the Joensuu City Orchestra, a cut of 10,000 euros is crippling, while for the local authority it represents a saving that is less than negligible. Would it not be a better idea to invest instead? It would only take a modest increase in public funding to the Finnish National Opera, to the Savonlinna Opera Festival and to smaller groups to lower the threshold decisively for our less advantaged citizens to enjoy opera too: to bring ticket prices down!

Hidden in words and music

MARKUS FAGERUDD

I have been interested in the theatre for as long as I remember. The expression and presence of a live human being is the most fascinating thing I know. I began my career as a professional musician in a theatre, and I still view incidental music for drama as the most challenging type of music there is. Writing music for the stage highlights issues of balance and unconscious influence. My connection to the theatre also affects the way I write an opera. The nature and naturalness of language is the core around which everything else emerges. I am one of those composers who do not write their own librettos. Opera is a collaborative art form where professionals are needed to take care of every parameter. The libretto is of crucial importance: it is a body of text that will fuel my composition process day in and day out, feeding and sustaining the flight of my imagination. My feeling is that my own literary talent would be far too mundane to undertake such a task as writing a libretto. Beautifully written, precise language easily conducts music into sensitive, emotional territory. You can never emphasise emotion too much. If there is too little emotion, the music dies; the more emotion, the longer it lingers in the listener's memory.

I have written five operas for children and adolescents and one chamber opera for 'grown-ups'. I was also the musical coordinator of the community opera *Free Will*, which was premièred at the Savonlinna Opera Festival in summer 2012. This work was created by writers and composers all around the world.

So why write opera for kids and teens? I am not very interested in art whose purpose is to 'teach and educate' the recipient. This is an obvious trap to fall into in any production aimed at children: adults feel it their duty to instruct their young listeners rather than agreeing to be one of the participants with them. Perhaps this is why adult listeners listening to contemporary music often pose questions about the 'accessibility' of the music. There is a wall of expectations blocking experientiality.

Dramaturgy and time are of essence in operas for children. What is the optimum duration? How to balance relationships within the work? These are issues that have to be resolved on a case-by-case basis; there is no standard answer. It is important to understand the age groups for which the work is intended. Sometimes you get lucky and can write music in what could be described as a 'laboratory setting'. This happened to me while writing the opera *Heinähattu, Vilttitossu ja Suuri Pamaus* (Strawhat, Feltslipper and the Big Bang) to a libretto by Sinikka and Tiina Noponen in 2003. This is an opera aimed at children under school age. It features two sisters and their thoughts when a new baby is expected in the family. My own daughters were aged 4 and 6 at the time. By observing how they played, I gained an insight into how to solve certain musical problems in the opera. They adopted roles in their games, each with its own way of saying things. Trying to figure out where children get their influences can be a never-ending quest, but the clarity with which they express things is something that we should strive for in performances, in singing. Trivial as it may seem, immersing myself in my daughters' conversation helped me find key features for the dialogue in the opera. The intuition that I found guiding my composition process was incredibly liberating. It also felt an honour to be part of a team that was exploring the world of young girls, which I believe is an important thing to know about.

Children are not confused by the conventions of opera. Sung dialogue causes no puzzlement or aversion. Perhaps the fascination of the setting comes from its freedom: abrupt transitions, free association, high speed and amplified emotions are some of the tools in my toolbox when writing an opera. I tend to think about music in these terms when writing, and have sometimes described my style as musical nativism. This may manifest itself for instance in the essential equality of all dramaturgical events: the important thing is *when* something happens, not how we get there. This is a consequence of wanting to see the world through a child's eyes, constantly alert to new opportunities and new pathways. And being a participant, not just a creator.

With the chamber opera *Välilasku* (Una espera inesperada, Stopover), based on the fine libretto by Maritza Núñez I had the rare opportunity of writing an opera in Spanish, a language that I do not speak. It is set airside at an international airport where two strangers meet. Both are stranded as a result of the Icelandic ash cloud, and there are no flights to anywhere. A 'suspended state' emerges where the two characters experience an erotic release in a space where there may be no tomorrow.

The composition process was a curious one. After receiving the libretto, it took a long time for me to figure out how to approach it. Eroticism in music is not the easiest sort of thing, especially if you want to avoid the obvious.

Surprisingly, it was the sound of the language that removed the block. Because I do not know Spanish, I could listen just to the intonation of the language in ways that I could not have imagined. *Välilasku* is written in a sort of tango nuevo style, with freetonal influences. The use of language as musical input was a new and liberating experience. I do not believe I would have written that music if the libretto had been in Finnish or in my native language, Swedish. So here is an interesting question: does a language have more properties and tendencies of a given kind than another language? But then, the tango is an erotically charged dance anywhere in the world. Nevertheless, I cannot escape the impression that the Spanish language had a crucial effect on my musical choices. Do similar intuitive choices emerge from Finnish or Swedish? The languages I speak every day? Certainly not in the same way. Perhaps the answer lies in the listening, in listening to the sound of the language rather than its meaning, in receiving information as a phonetics rather than semantics. A language is music before it turns into music. It would be exciting to know what my choices would have been like if the libretto had been in French, German, English or Chinese.

Välilasku was written quickly, in a couple of months. My entire composition process has gone through an upheaval in recent years, becoming an increasingly freeform chain of events. Your mind speaks when you let it wander. This is what I believe today. I do not have a primary goal of being recognisably myself in the music I write: what is important is to let what I observe speak for itself.

Projections

PAAVO HEININEN

What opera is, what language is

Opera is a projection (an operation that relates one set to another, specifically defining the coexistence of two sets P1 and P2 so that each member of P1 corresponds to a member of P2) from the set of music to the set of text, or from the set of fragments of music (or image) to the set of fragments of text.

We may imagine this as two parallel lines of set members with each member joining hands, as it were, with its corresponding member in the other line. Or as the coordination of two two-dimensional layers: a field of flowers over which a field of bees flies, each bee landing on one and only one flower.

How do we know what the aforementioned 'correspondence' might be? This is an issue that can be very distressing; I am acquainted with a composer who does not set texts to music at all because there is no correspondence rigorous enough to be found.

In opera, we are dealing first of all with parallel time structures. An opera (an opera performance, that is) is a public projection of these parallels to our senses and our consciousness (our 'intelligence'). Synchronism – that is the correspondence: the simultaneous focus on music and text moment by moment. This incorporates all elements of music, including motion through time; all elements of the visual staging; and all the phonetic and semantic dimensions of the text.

Why, indeed, is a given item of text paired with a particular item of music? Because the composer decides so. The recipient may consider this a bad decision. But that choice (or indeed the judgment that it is 'bad') cannot be made simply be reference to an *a priori* list of 'correct' correspondences. (That would be tantamount to acknowledging convention or 'naturalness' as an immutable authority, and a composer would not be a composer if he did not defy this.)

But the projection is also a non-temporal one. Examined out of time (in our memory, in our understanding), the musical elements of a work constitute a repertoire, a closed world with its own structure and organisation. The text elements organise themselves in correspondence with the musical structures and elements. (From one list to another: one theme for each character, for instance.) Here, we are not dealing with progression in real time or syntax, but a domain of elements, a set of choices: the vocabulary of a language. The discovery of correspondences begins with understanding the parallels in the performance just heard (once heard, sometimes heard), but now including analysis of the structure of the vocabulary in each set of elements. Appreciation of the whole is what gives us the justification to decide that a particular decision or choice of correspondence was good and consistent while another was bad and incongruous.

Language is a projection of the content of our memory, its stock of images ('the world', 'things') to the set of acoustic objects ('spoken words'). In a coherent conversation, we may understand the set of spoken words to include combinations and structures created using those words: derivatives, syntax, language games.

And what about the set of all things in the world? It is estimated that in the Stone Age there were only 94 'things' in the world, while in Shakespeare's time there were 1,324, and these days maybe 11,099 – but dividing the world into 'things' and tallying them up like this seems more in the realm of TV comedy. Seriously, though, analysing the world as a collection of discrete 'things' is a development that begins in infancy for every human being and is an ongoing process.

By 'set of things', we mean:

- a simplified and organised group of objects processed from the overwhelming sum total of our observations, memories and notions, and
- an even further simplified and structured table of contents of our conscious world distilled from its temporal and spatial vastness.

(These 'things', by the way, also include events – as a notional extension of objects – and therefore linguistic events too.)

The world of sound impulses that we live in is more or less the same for all of us and observable in similar ways, whereas the way in which each of us analyses and understands the world is trapped within our own consciousness and individuality. In practice, however, we have so much in common with other people in the way we understand the world that referring to the common through the unique is possible. In other words, we understand people who speak the same language, and they understand us, even if each utterance is individually different.

Language, then, is the projection of a familiar set (sounds) to an even more familiar set (mind). This projection dictates that anything non-familiar is not language. Non-familiar sounds are only encountered by tourists and ethnographers. An audience listening to Janáček expects to hear non-familiar music pairing hands with a familiar linguistic structure, but this approach breaks down when we hear Janáček's familiar music pairing hands with non-familiar sounds made by human voices that we are told are in the Czech language. However good the intent, it destroys the nexus of familiar and non-familiar.

What this means in practical terms is that opera must be in a language that is familiar to the listener. Otherwise, the text cannot merge with the music and the visual stimuli into a single continuum of multi-dimensional moments in time. A person watching and listening to an opera cannot simultaneously be reading a translation. It is impossible to match a read translation structurally (moment by moment) to music in real time.

Finding, choosing and writing a libretto

We might imagine that choice in this matter means choosing a subject, but there is more to it than that. There are positive and negative criteria at play in choosing a subject. We know and believe we know what the subject of an opera could be and what it should be. We require a subject to be powerful, meaningful and sustainable. This is no different from any other area of human activity, and as in everything else, generalities can be adapted and tweaked depending on the individual and the context. Idea, message, tension of action, cast of colourful characters. The limitations that apply are specific to opera and technical in nature.

But the limitations 'specific to opera' actually begin with the general nature of performances on stage and the general nature of spoken language (*mutatis mutandis,* sung language). A stage work must feature things that can be shown on stage, things the showing of which can be executed within the timetable and resources of a normal theatre production, sentences that can be comprehended when heard, i.e. devoid of the length, argumentation and syntactic meandering that are permissible in written text.

And what about 'specific to music'? There are two sides to this issue: the subject allows for music, or the subject requires music. This is only partly a feature of the subject in itself: a subject may be presented with many words or few words, and the latter is better suited to a musical treatment. But there are subjects that do not lend themselves to being presented with few words. There is no point in writing an opera based on a lecture, or a political memo. An opera based on an essay is a borderline case.

Where is music needed? Distancing from realism is what music does best. But distancing from realism is not at all what happens when the significance of a real entity (a person, an idea, an event) is shown in its inner true meaning. When people compare real life with opera (to the disadvantage of opera), they stretch truth beyond its limit if they seriously claim that they have never encountered a situation where words and phrases are repeated incessantly (sometimes by one, sometimes by many), or voices are pitched or paced so as to seek (and demand, and achieve) maximum effect, or things that remain unsaid are quite as significant as the things that are said. And people actually sometimes do break into song even in real life.

Topicality? Topical relevance?
The issue of topicality in opera comes back to how modern and how political it is.

Unfortunately, the life span of an opera is so long that it is all but impossible for it to remain topical or politically relevant beyond its inception. The potential of a political interest (insofar as there is one) is undermined by the fact that audiences are often unable or unwilling to perceive it. As a case in point, the most explosively revolutionary of all subversive operas, *Le nozze di Figaro*, is understood today (by the director on stage and by the viewers in the audience) as a light-hearted depiction of the historical lifestyle of the upper classes, an apotheosis of escapism.

On the other hand, there is also a tendency to think that a modern subject is not 'suitable' for opera, because it is not romantic or elegant or solemn – it seems too mundane somehow. But this is just superficial: the principal challenge lies with the competence of the creators, although the viewer is of course also required to transcend convention. The guiding principle for the composer is therefore that topicality is not essential, but neither is modernity prohibited. However, we do our entire profession and music as a whole a disservice if we completely avoid subjects from our time and our own experience in the realm of opera – this must not happen.

Within these limitations, the choice of subject is a similar issue in all branches of the arts, literature above all. The world of drama (i.e. spoken theatre) has so many special issues of its own that little support can be found for the theory or practice of opera. We should remember that this was not always the case.

The libretto and how to edit it: What is required of a libretto?
What the creating of music requires from the text it is setting is attraction, expectation and tension. Support for extensive structures would also be nice. And inspiration? Per-

haps, but many composers are quite inventive enough even without a text to inspire them, in instrumental music.

(Is this a paradox? Take Sibelius, about whose imagination there can surely be no doubt. Having listened to his collected piano works and his collected solo songs, I was left with the impression that the songs were better, much better, because the lyrics were so much more impressive. To put it another way: his piano works seem to imply unexpressed words, images and stories that fall far short of those produced by the poets whose texts are featured in the solo songs.)

(And while we are on the subject of paradoxes, consider Sibelius's relationship to opera: he went looking for an opera libretto in the realm of the *Kalevala*, when in fact the only real Sibelian text source for an opera was right there under his nose, in Swedish poetry: a young man and woman at the threshold of emerging love and unspoken promises (*Snöfrid*), a young man and woman plagued by doubts and devastated by partings (*Men min fågel märks dock icke, Långsamt som kvällsskyn*), excluded and lonesome young people beside life-threatening rapids (*Näcken*); but also young couples finding happiness and a positive perspective for reminiscence for those left alone.)

Time structures: Act I to Act III, exposition – argumentation – solution and culmination. Important but not specific to opera. And this, a time span of one, two or three hours, is not the major challenge faced by a dramatist.

The lower levels of hierarchy in the time structure, the details, or clusters of details, are what are crucial and challenging. What this may mean in the context of an act (on the scale of a little over or under one hour):

- understanding the structure of the act, from exposition to realisation and understanding, and
- going from equilibrium to movement in terms of the characters and their actions.

And above all, in the context of a scene (on the scale of one quarter or one third of an hour):

- from illness and fatigue to ecstasy and defiance,
- from hesitation to choice and decision.

Finding such structures does not usually stem directly from the subject chosen; it is a matter for narrative technique and drama strategy, and as such within the domain of the librettist, who must find a narrative approach, a perspective, a time dimension (or compression). The librettist can do this independently or at the composer's request (or demand), assuming that their collaboration allows for this. Wagner is an example of a composer who did all the work himself, while Verdi's dialogue with his librettists is an excellent example of how the process can progress – not to speak of the voluminous corres-pondence between Richard Strauss and Hofmannsthal.

An experienced theatre professional knows a lot about this sort of thing. But only the composer – each individual composer in each individual case – knows how he is able to (and wants to) expand and condense time within the domain of his composition tech-nique.

Three attempts at a miracle

MIKKO HEINIÖ

1. From commission to subject

1.1. Someone must really want that opera...

The history of Finnish music teaches us that if a composer writes an opera just for himself, it generally progresses no further than his own desktop. Even commissioned works may sink without a trace for years, or even permanently, if the commissioning party loses interest. For opera today, a commission is an absolute must. A commission has three dimensions: principle, practice and finance – in this order. By commissioning an opera, a particular body declares that it *wants* to have a work written by a particular composer, commits to having that work performed and agrees to pay a fee for it.

It takes two to three years to write a full-length opera. If the commission fee is, say, 60,000 euros, that works out to perhaps 10 euros per hour, sometimes more depending on the box office royalties. This clearly demonstrates that a composer must have a grant or other income in order to be a full-time opera composer.

Usually the commissioner and the performer are one and the same, but my opera *Eerik XIV* proved an exception to this rule. The work was commissioned by the City of Turku, but its performances were entrusted to the Turku Music Festival and the Turku 2011 Foundation. The final decision to actually stage the work was delayed so far that it proved very difficult to recruit performers – but everything did come together, even better than expected.

1.2 Myth and marketing

Riddaren och draken (The Knight and the Dragon, 2000) was commissioned for the 700th anniversary of Turku Cathedral. It is based on Christian tradition but is not really a religious opera. Bo Carpelan chose the legend of St George as the basis for his libretto. St George was a popular saint in the Nordic countries, with no fewer than two altars dedicated to him in Turku Cathedral in the Middle Ages. Carpelan converted the dragon into a bandit named Drake, represented as one of the many outlaws who plundered the Cathedral and City of Turku many times in the 16th century. The story is familiar and straightforward, yet here the contrast of good and evil is not only highlighted but also questioned. Although the action is set in the indeterminate past, it is infused with the modern notion that our lives are about our choices, our ways of giving meaning to the people and things around us.

With *Käärmeen hetki* (The Hour of the Serpent, 2002–2005), the commission from the Finnish National Opera did not in any way specify a subject, although the Finnish National Opera indicated that they would like to see a major soprano role. Juha Siltanen wrote a period drama set in late 19th-century Helsinki, touching on major innovations of the era such as electricity, motion pictures and psychoanalysis. I was proud of having such a narrative to work with, an original story that did not attempt to capitalise on the publicity value of a well-known person, historical event, novel or play. I should have known better. We did take into account the added value, the aura, that would be lent by casting an international soprano star – a true diva – in the lead role; it was to be not only an opera for her but an opera about her. I should have known better. The soprano star found no such value in the libretto, and very late in the day she backed out of the project. The public lost interest, there were empty seats at the performances, and the production was scrapped after its initial run even though it was of a very high quality in every respect.

Every production of every opera is a learning experience for a composer, whether proactively or reactively. For my third opera, *Eerik XIV*, again with a libretto by Juha Siltanen, I fell back on a historical figure.

King Erik XIV of Sweden (1533–1577) was an exceptionally complex person with a singularly dramatic life: he was deposed and spent 13 months imprisoned in Turku Castle, and his queen, Karin Månsdotter, is buried in Turku Cathedral. This connection alone made it easy for the librettist and myself to sell the idea to the City of Turku when they wanted to commission a grand opera that would be the highlight of Turku's year as the European Capital of Culture in 2011. *Eerik XIV* has a specific focus that can be summarised in a slogan: unique love amidst political turmoil.

People often ask why composers turn to the distant past for subjects instead of finding them in the here and now. Perhaps the 'once upon a time' nature of historical events is particularly suited to the way in which opera creates illusions. However, what is important is not that the characters are historical but that they are *mythical* (whether we understand 'myth' as a symbolic expression, a social construct or a reflection of the unconscious). Even modern characters can acquire mythical stature, but historical figures have had more time in which to achieve this. A mythical character or event may prompt audiences to come and find out what kind of a new artistic interpretation the creators have chosen to put on it. I would imagine that this gives the viewer a much bigger kick than just identifying historical verisimilitude. But regardless which era the subject of a libretto is derived, the choice of subject always implies the claim that this is something that remains relevant to us today.

2. From libretto to composition

2.1. Text that begins to sound like music

While *Riddaren och draken* was written by a poet, *Käärmeen hetki* and *Eerik XIV* are very obviously the work of a dramatist. Having said that, I should note that Juha Siltanen's librettos are more poetic than his plays. My feeling is that the language of spoken drama is ill suited to the kind of reality which is the strength of opera and where it is the most powerful of all art forms. (Comic opera, with deliberate clashes between text and music, is another kind of animal altogether, and one that carries a high risk of falling flat.) Whatever the process is for choosing a text, the listener must be convinced that this is exactly how this text should be set to music – and that it was worth setting to music in the first place.

A libretto means many things to many people, but its significance for the composer is of paramount importance. It guides his work (or at least it should), and he spends more time with it than anyone else, including the librettist. For myself, I am a language hedonist: I can only spend thousands of hours with a text where every line inspires me, from the surface to deeper levels of meaning. I can only use a text if I can literally hear it as music in my mind. I do not subscribe to the conventional view that many good operas have terrible librettos. After all, an opera is not a work of literature-cum-music but a work for the stage. If it works on stage, its libretto cannot, by definition, be terrible (whatever one may think of its literary merit or lack thereof).

I also like to do my bit to uphold Finland's duality of languages by using Swedish on a daily basis in addition to my native Finnish. To simplify, in writing music I feel that Swedish represents sonority, distance, solemnity and the spirit, while Finnish represents semantics, proximity, the mundane and the body. I have set more texts in Swedish than in Finnish, and setting a text in Finnish has always had to have a specific motivation for me, such as an opera project. I had imagined that I would translate the libretto of *Riddaren och draken* into Finnish before beginning to work on the music and do it in a way that would allow me to write the music so that it fit both the Swedish and the Finnish text. But having received the libretto, I immediately abandoned the idea: I had no choice but to tailor my music to Carpelan's incredibly beautiful and poetic text.

Käärmeen hetki, by contrast, was a project wholly in Finnish and an attempt to introduce elements of modern drama to the opera stage. With *Eerik XIV*, Juha Siltanen's initial idea was to create a fully multilingual libretto (with dialogue in Swedish but internal monologues in Finnish), but in the end it turned out to be mostly in Swedish. (This, by the way, was an incredible linguistic *tour de force* by an author whose mother tongue is Finnish and who categorically refuses to speak Swedish in any context.)

2.2. Team working

The procedure for creating *Riddaren och draken* was that Carpelan wrote the text and then our dramaturgical consultant Erik Söderblom and myself held a meeting to talk and to give feedback. This went back and forth, and Carpelan wrote four versions of the libretto in all. When I began writing the music, the libretto was finished; but then, this opera was only going to be 75 minutes long, in one act without an interval.

My following operas were more than two and a half hours long each, taking three years apiece, and with these the libretto was still being written or edited while I was already working on the music. In the innumerable meetings I had with librettist Siltanen and director Söderblom, we talked about what I had written and what new text there was. Sometimes the music influenced the text, especially since we considered the transitions between scenes to be very important. The librettist might say: "Since you ended the previous scene like that, I'm going to have to change the beginning of the next one." The most rewarding moments were those where solving a musical problem also resolved a dramaturgical issue – or vice versa.

These sessions with two experienced experts of the theatre bred inspiring discussions about theatre, cinema and literature. I was soon declaring to everyone who would listen that composers should not attempt to write their own librettos because there was so much to be gained from working with other professionals: sparring partners feeding completely new ideas that would make the resulting work more than the sum of its parts. In other words, music theatre above all things offers a composer the opportunity to think outside the box and step out of his marginalised isolation – mentally, socially and artistically.

Subsequently, I have been less keen to evangelise about this, because working with a librettist does have its disadvantages. The composer may find himself waiting for text or rewrites for a long time just when he would have the time or the inclination to write the music. And because a librettist may easily conceive of stage time passing much faster than the composer would like, a first draft of a libretto is always too long and leaves no room for purely instrumental sections that would offer the listener a chance to catch his metaphorical breath amidst a constant bombardment of information. Unless you allow the thing to blow up into Wagnerian proportions, of course. The libretto may have far too many details and layers of meaning to be useful, however fascinating they may be. Taking just a little off the sides (as opposed to chopping off limbs) may result in a text that is just too dense. But all these practicalities notwithstanding, I have never yet considered writing the libretto for my next opera myself. Assuming that there will be a next one, of course.

I have not had any actual artistic disagreements with my librettist, only one disagreement on principle that has not actually affected the works themselves but does have a bearing on their use. My position is that the libretto is an integral part of the indivisible artwork that we call an opera. Siltanen's position is that the libretto is an independent artwork (which in terms of copyright it is). Therefore Siltanen feels that the librettist should not forfeit any of his box office royalties to the party that is paying for the not inconsiderable costs of having the performance material prepared – unlike the composer, who is contractually obliged to do so. For this reason, he also does not want to sign a publishing agreement with my publisher. *Käärmeen hetki* has been published, but only the music, not the libretto. *Eerik XIV* has not been published at all. Therefore the cost of preparing the performance material for *Eerik XIV* fell to the producer, and there was no one to market the opera to other producers after the premiere.

2.3. MIDI and other formats

The libretto for *Eerik XIV* did not begin to near completion until a few months had already passed from the point where I had timetabled my writing period to begin. Therefore I first wrote an orchestral work entitled *Maestoso* where I was able to work out key themes for the opera and which in abridged form became its Prologue. Working on an opera is much easier if I can work out in advance the 'vocabulary', if you like, that I will be using. The first section of the libretto to be finalised was the opening of Act III, so I began writing that music first. This was not a problem as such, because in many major works I have written certain core sections first and then worked my way up to them from the beginning. If music theatre is the art of mad fantasy, it is equally the art of pragmatic compromises, and I should note that we are not talking about decisions that dilute the original idea but choices that refine it in new ways. Necessity can often become a virtue, as I learned in working with Dance Theatre ERI, a small dance company in Turku.

Today, when nearly all composers use notation software, performers have learned to ask for MIDI versions of new works to familiarise themselves with the music. I have both good and bad experiences of this sort of thing. My librettist and director, for instance, being able to read music, have been able to gain a passable impression of the tensions, timings and characters in the music in this way. Then again, there are performers who imagine that the final product will sound as horrible as the tinny MIDI. In any case, my working process begins with a short score that includes all major instrumental parts on as many staves as I can fit onto a large computer screen. Once the work is completed in short score, I expand it into the full score and reduce it into the vocal score – although my vocal scores contain more parts than traditional vocal scores.

2.4. Character and continuity

The music in an opera must be as distinctly and specifically characteristic as the text, and all musical choices must be justifiable on the basis of the libretto. To be sure, the music can stagnate to underline a single mood, perhaps even for an entire scene, but not beyond that. The need to characterise people, things and events has led me to something quite closely resembling Wagnerian leitmotif technique. But repeating thematic material – which by the way is no taboo for me – lends coherence, a feel of narrative unity. This has been an important point in writing music to Siltanen's librettos, which at least on the surface level are wildly and violently centrifugal and fragmented.

Continuity can be created on several levels in the music. Paradoxically, even sharp contrasts can contribute to continuity, as long as any surprises later come to seem inevitable (combining the surprising with the inevitable on both the micro and the macro level is one of the basic principles of my aesthetic approach). I have often said to musicians performing my chamber music: "Where the texture has continuity, emphasise the discontinuities; and where the texture is discontinuous, emphasise the continuity." This largely describes the relationship of my music to the libretto in my operas, but it is not an inviolable rule. The music may detach itself from the text completely, or it may follow it down to the minutest detail (a technique familiar from the scoring of cartoons and hence known as 'mickeymousing'), or anything between these two extremes. But the music always relates to the text in some way.

2.5. Basic material and allusions

All of my compositions are based on a set of 'basic material', a pitch set construct that somehow governs all the harmonic and melodic structures in the piece. In *Eerik XIV*, for instance, that construct has two elements: a 12-note chord whose pitches are organised according to the overtone series (albeit in equal temperament) and a pentatonic chord corresponding to the pitches of the open strings of a lute. The latter came from the historical fact that Erik was a skilled lute player.

Eerik XIV also contains three significant quotes: a one-off reference to Mahler's *Das Lied von der Erde* (at the point where the libretto quotes the same text); a tune named *Kung Erik* by Hugo Ingelius that is used as a reference to Turku; and Eerik's signature tune, which is the only musical reference to Erik's own era and as such is quite unique: it is the earliest known Swedish example of 16th-century eight-part polyphony in the style of the Low Countries – and it was written by Erik XIV himself. Also, in Eerik's mad scene the orchestral texture contains fleeting references to dozens of national anthems, so brief that I believe they remain just under the threshold of conscious detection for the listener.

My two earlier operas contain no musical quotes, although the folk ballad, Honolulu schlager and stylised choral numbers in *Käärmeen hetki* may sound like it. They are diegetic music, or what in cinema would be called 'source music' – music that exists in the universe of the opera, i.e. is heard by the characters, musical vignettes of a kind. I wrote the most important of these in advance, and the elements contained in them reappear throughout the work.

3. Thesis, antithesis and synthesis

3.1. From drama of fate to drama of character

It may sound like cheap dialectics and oversimplification to state that my three operas represent a thesis, antithesis and synthesis. But this outline allows me to highlight essential dimensions of musical drama in them.

Riddaren och draken, based on a legend, is a drama of fate where the characters are simply objects of events. The force of destiny is represented by the orchestra and organ and partly by the choir, building a long symphonic arc from beginning to end. *Käärmeen hetki*, on the other hand, is a modern drama of character inspired by picaresque novels, psychodrama and thrillers where the characters are subjects (meaning that they can themselves control events). Here, the music reacts more quickly and in more detail to what the characters say, what they think and what their personalities are like.

	Riddaren och draken	*Käärmeen hetki*	*Eerik XIV*
Librettist	poet	dramatist	poet/dramatist
Language	Swedish	Finnish	Swedish, Finnish, English, German
Text type	legend, mystery play	period drama	historical drama in the modern era
Nature of events	simple, fatalistic	pluralist, unpredictable	fatalistic, impulsive
Structure of text	many monologues, short libretto	mainly dialogue, long libretto	as in *Käärmeen hetki*
Characters	archetypes, objects of events	personalities, subjects of events	as in *Käärmeen hetki*
Performance venue	church	theatre	former industrial hall
Acoustics	long reverb → 'broad brush', mainly slow tempos	short reverb → 'filigree work', quick tempos included	electronic amplification, quick tempos included
Overall character of music	(relatively) static, emphasising the space	dynamic, emphasising the process	as in *Käärmeen hetki*
Musical continuity	in surface structures	in deep structures	in both surface and deep structures
Performer hierarchy	choir and orchestra are important	soloists have main focus	soloists and choir
Relationship of music to text	independent, symphonic	follows the text	partly follows the text, partly independent
Genre	church opera, opera-oratorio?	opera, musical drama	opera, 'cinematic opera'

Riddaren och draken is relatively static musically and dramaturgically; it emphasises space and approaches a cyclical concept of time (everything that happens has already happened and will always happen again). *Käärmeen hetki* is dynamic; it emphasises the process and has a clearly linear concept of time. This contrast was naturally highlighted by the fact that the former was written by a Swedish-speaking poet for performance in a church space and the latter was written by a Finnish-speaking dramatist for the theatre. The former became a church opera with oratorio-like elements, the latter became a stage opera or musical drama dominated by dialogue. *Käärmeen hetki* has more and shorter scenes and is almost cinematic in structure. In my third opera, this development was taken even further.

In the first half of *Eerik XIV*, the story is carried by Eerik's disintegrating mind, and fragmented scenes follow each other in rapid succession. In the second half, where the title character has been imprisoned, the story begins to carry Eerik, and the scenes become longer and more symphonic. The work is a drama of fate because of the inevitable cycle of history that the viewer already knows, but it is also a drama of character because of Eerik's monarchical personality, impulsive to the point of madness, and because of Karin's ability to soothe and guide him. We made no attempt to recreate any features of the Renaissance era, although we did include some authentic material such as Erik's diary entries and a scrap of music.

The libretto and score of *Eerik XIV* call for the projection of huge video images, with subjects extending in time to the present day. The feel of the present was further heightened in the performances in Turku by showing the audience not only the events that happened in the 16th century but also a real-time video image of the same, a representation within a representation. However, in the opera the past and the present neither alternate nor run in parallel; they penetrate each other (or, as Bernd Alois Zimmermann beautifully put it: "Time bends itself into a sphere."). The question of anachronisms, with which the text, the music and the production was littered, becomes irrelevant.

3.2. The performance space

Riddaren och draken and *Eerik XIV* differed from *Käärmeen hetki* in that the performance venue had a profound impact on the very concept of the works. *Riddaren och draken* was to be performed in Turku Cathedral, where I knew it would be impossible to hear or see anything, but it is a wonderful interior, a cathedral space unique in Finland. I had ample time to prepare myself to cope with the six-second reverb (!) not only in the texture of my music but in specifying wireless mikes for the soloists (not for amplification but for clarification), measuring the height of the platform needed to enable audience members sitting at floor level to see the stage over the heads of the people sitting in front of them, calculating how much time the trumpet players would need to make their way into the gallery, finding out exactly what the main organ could do, and so on.

Eerik XIV, on the other hand, represented a leap of faith as far as the performance venue was concerned, because the City of Turku did not decide on the renovation of the former engine shed as a performance space until just over a year before the premiere, and it was only just completed before rehearsals began. The only thing we knew in advance was that the space would require electronic amplification and video screens, much like a rock concert. (Notwithstanding this, it was easier for me in terms of composition technique to plan the balance between singers and orchestra as if the work were being performed acoustically.) The video technology enabled us to show not only intimate close-ups of the singers but also 'backstage' shots. The greatest advantage, however, proved to be a communicative one, and as such wholly unexpected: when both sound and image were boosted, the emotional content was amplified too. Not even the most distant audience member could sink into disinterested-observer mood, thinking that "those people are performing something over there, I'm sitting over here, and never the twain shall meet". After this experience, I have found myself increasingly impatiently wishing for better audibility of singers at the Finnish National Opera, even in traditional repertoire. Perhaps contemporary opera works in two distinct ways: amplified in a big space or as intimate chamber music in a small space.

3.3. What role, whose role?

A new opera lives or dies by its casting. The composer must select the voice type for each character appropriately for that character's personality and also ensure that there is a sufficiently diverse lineup of voices in the cast. The director, then (albeit with the composer's assistance), must cast a performer for each role who can pull it off credibly, not only in vocal terms but in terms of stage presence too. No matter how disastrously wrong a casting choice proves to be – because of an error or because of any of a multitude of possible external causes – the audience will always believe that they are hearing and seeing exactly what the creators intended. No matter how convincing the composer's message is, the audience will only be convinced by it if the performer is convincing.

If the singers who will appear in the premiere production are already known when the work on the composition begins (a rare treat for the composer), this is an immense help, as the composer is then better able to imagine the characters on stage. Awareness of the singers also has at least some impact on how the roles are shaped. In *Riddaren och draken*, I wanted to make the angelic Göran a 'trouser role', and Carpelan accordingly revised his lines to make them more androgynous in nature. The role of Göran was performed by Charlotte Hellekant. Later, in planning *Eerik XIV*, at a meeting with the librettist and director I suggested – completely intuitively, out of the blue – that the title role should be sung by Hellekant. It took all of five seconds for them to embrace the idea, and only a few minutes for me to receive a positive reply from her. The outcome was what is probably the most extensive mezzo-soprano role in the history of opera.

It was difficult for me to envision Eerik as a baritone, bass or tenor, because each choice would have made too strong a concrete statement about the sort of man that Erik was supposed to have been. Eerik is such a powerful male role that only a woman can perform it; only a woman can bring out the enormous ambivalences inherent in the character. Erik was Sweden's first true monarch. He was unstable in mind, aesthetic in outlook and educated yet somehow never passed the threshold of adulthood. The contrast with his brother, the testosterone-filled and ultra-pragmatic Johan, was remarkable. By having Eerik played by a woman, we paradoxically avoided making Eerik as effeminate as one might have imagined from his known personality. The same sort of effect must have happened when Sarah Bernhardt played Hamlet or Kyllikki Forsell played Gustav III. The librettist described *Eerik XIV* as a modernised Shakespearean history play, and I consider the 'trouser role' a reference to periods in the history of theatre when gender was irrelevant (men playing women in Shakespearean theatre or women playing men in Restoration theatre).

3.4. More miraculous than meticulous

If an opera turns out not to be good as an artwork, there is no way in the world to make a good performance of it. A good work, on the other hand, can be given a good or a bad performance. If the performance is good, the audience knows that the work is good. If the performance is bad, it may remain unclear (especially in the case of a first performance) whether the problem was with the performance or the work itself.

Whether an opera is good depends (among other things) on how well the personalities and relationships of the characters, the timing and duration of events in the music and on stage, and the dramaturgical arc and high points have been worked out in the libretto and in the music and in the way in which the two work together. There is such a huge number of variables at play here that it is impossible to make sure of everything in advance. You must learn to trust your instinct and luck. The path to true success is more miraculous than meticulous.

This essay is partly based on the article 'Ooppera jatkuu – se on totuus' [Opera goes on – that's the truth] in Pekka Hako & Risto Nieminen (eds.): *Ammatti: säveltäjä* [Profession: composer], 2006.

Opera rage

HEINZ-JUHANI HOFMANN

Confession of love

Concrete stuff, not poetry. And no dream scenes. No distanced, symbolic crap, nothing like that. No ambiguous stuff. When you say something, you mean something. The text would have to be just surface, bare, tangible. That's what the libretto would have to be like, and I'd write it myself, of course.

Maybe at the end of *Ihmissydän* (Human Heart) I somehow got close to that, close to that kind of style. It took a lot of text and a lot of talk, recitative. But before that you had 40 minutes of denser and denser extreme states and hysteria, ending up with child rape, and the end somehow just worked. Jutta made it work. Even though I'd written it for myself. What I mean by that is that I knew exactly how it should be paced and weighted. I could have performed the damn thing myself, and I did so in rehearsal. The point was that it had to be fast enough, leaning forward all the time.

I believe it achieved something of the documentary style that I said in the programme note I was aiming for.

You know, it's hard to create a realistic, natural feeling like that on stage in a monologue when there's no one else there to make it true. When you watch a monologue, you may think: Is she really telling the truth up there on stage? Or is this just a fantasy of hers? Or, heaven forbid, a dream? I'd like to try out this kind of expression in a dialogue. I'd really like that. Rapid-fire stuff where sentences and even words are cut short, people talking and shouting on top of each other. It would be an argument, of course, an extreme state, or about to become one. But that's what opera is, an extreme state.

Sure, I thought *Ihmissydän* would make bigger waves and get more attention, meaning more publicity. I thought it was something that no one else had done in opera in Finland as far as the text and expression goes. I'm embarrassed to admit it now, but I actually thought at the time that it would be to Finnish opera what Sofi Oksanen's *Puhdistus* (Purge) was to Finnish literature. I really did. That every opera ever written after *Ihmissydän* would be compared to it. I thought then, and maybe I still think that the sexual abuse of children has not been addressed in literature like I did in *Ihmissydän*, and definitely not in opera. It's unique.

Well, yes, we did get some publicity: we made the opening spread of *Helsingin Sanomat*, and the 'masterpiece' epithet was flattering. The next week I got a phone call from the Finnish Radio Symphony Orchestra, and they commissioned a piece. Actually, now that I think about it, more things happened after *Ihmissydän* than after *Karjalainen,* even though *Karjalainen* got a lot more publicity and even made the cover of *Opernwelt* magazine. After *Karjalainen*, I was shit-sure that I'd get another opera commission before the autumn. I had been one of the Three Boys in *The Magic Flute* in Savonlinna in 1986, and it would have been such a great story that I fell in love with opera as a kid in Savonlinna and would be thrilled to be going back there. A dream come true. I was so fucking naïve after *Karjalainen*. What was I thinking? That suddenly every man and his dog would want me to write an opera? How pathetic is that? So I sat by the phone, waiting for the call that never came, and in the meantime I fell into this fucking depression that I'm still trying to claw my way back from with pills and therapy. I'm just so damn tired.

I should have just started writing a new opera, commission or no. I should have done what I did with *Ihmissydän*, brought together some people and found the money somewhere. I have so many ideas for operas that one lifetime won't be enough to do it all.

I really, really want to write more operas. That's the only thing I want to write. I could spend the rest of my life writing operas. A new one every two years. That'd be a good pace. I want to bury myself in new stories, cover myself with them. Disappear into them. Do research: read books, watch films, watch documentaries. Saturate myself with them. Find the angle, the approach to take in developing them. Which aspects to focus on. What it is that touches me in this.

I love working with text, writing text. That's where it all starts, with the text. The text comes first, then the music, never the other way around. That would be unnatural.

There's a special moment when you discover the core of the work you are planning, the culmination or end point of the story, and I want to live that moment again many times. In *Ihmissydän,* it was the rape scene, the culmination of the piece. I was lying in bed one night when I realised that that was how the story had to go. Before that, I hadn't even been sure that I would get the opera written at all. I'd written three pieces dealing with sexual violence, and I was afraid that I wouldn't have anything new to say about it. And still...

I thought that once I had finished *Ihmissydän*, its subject – paedophilia – would leave me alone and I'd never have to deal with it again. Bullshit. There was no purge. Those stories, that evil, they're part of me now. Human beings are capable of incredible evil. And I can't exclude myself from that group.

Don't think that you are anything

Now that I'm writing about opera, I'll have to tell you what happened with *Karjalainen*. I've been talking about it for a year and half to anyone who cares to listen. Well, not talking so much as griping, seeking empathy and support for being so badly treated.

Why? Why can't I just let it go? Did it really hurt so much to be humiliated? Is that the only reason I'm now suffering from this fucking depression? I've been incapacitated and unable to work for over a year. I'm in this line of work for the love, and I never had any love from Kokkola, at least not at first.

I'd had plenty of love with my earlier works. Shit, I was the Boy Wonder: the more serious the stuff I wrote, the more love I was showered with. And *Ihmissydän* was the high point. Maybe the piss did go to my head after that. I thought I was God's gift to the art of opera and that no one else could write a libretto that works. There must have been some kind of hubris there.

It was obvious to me as soon as I got the libretto for *Karjalainen* that I would edit it, a lot, especially since the librettist had clearly indicated that I had a free hand to work with the libretto as I pleased. And I did. I have to admit now that I would've gone ahead and rewritten the libretto even if I hadn't had permission. Of course I would! Because it all starts with the text.

Now I look back at autumn 2011 with fond memories. Sure, it wasn't easy, but think about it: being asked to write another opera right after my first one! I thought that this was just how my life was supposed to be. But I had a damn hard time with that libretto. I did tons of research, reading books and watching archive films. I rewrote that libretto, again and again and again. It wasn't until January 2012 that I found what I thought was its core and shaped it like I wanted it. And was I ever pleased with myself! I thought that this would be the greatest fucking opera ever, bitch! I was so full of it. I was so high with the thought that I'd turned a difficult libretto into a drama that actually worked. I was a fucking hero! I really thought so. Sure, I'd done heavy things to it: rewrites, deletions, changes, merged scenes. But I never once imagined that anyone would have a problem with that. I thought they'd be fucking pleased.

I wrote the music for the first scene, 90 pages of it, and sent it to the commissioners. A few days later they replied: this won't do! The libretto had been changed too much, and the opera would never be performed in this form. Everything had to go. You can't change the original libretto. Not a word of it. No deletions, no additions, no repetitions. If I won't set the libretto as it stands, the deal is off.

It was fucking horrible. That feeling. I felt like curling up under the bed. You know the feeling you get as a kid when you know you've done something really bad, something that can't be fixed? When a kid cries and asks if they're going to be put in prison or if they're going to die? You know?

I fell into a panic. I sent my entire libretto to the commissioners for them to read. I was sure that they'd realise what a work of genius it was. But no.

I had a choice: to set the original libretto or not to write the work at all. Thank God I decided to write the opera. I needed the money, of course, and I thought about that a lot. But I also thought that a composer's job is to write music. It's always better to say yes than to say no.

The version of *Karjalainen* that was performed in Kokkola in summer 2012 I wrote in two months. Sure, I'd been humiliated, and I was fucking furious about it, but I can now look back on those months with affection. What a raging determination! I was using my rage and hatred as fuel for my work. But I did it. I set that damned libretto to music. And the opera turned out OK, although I still think my version would've been better.

There's this Icelandic author who said that everyone working in theatre is more or less insane.

I'm done talking about this.

Dominus Krabbe

Pekka Jalkanen

Before my monologue opera *Dominus Krabbe*, I had written two other operas. The first, a children's opera named *Tirlittan*, was written to a commission from the Culture Department of the City of Helsinki for the inauguration of the Stoa Culture Centre (1986). The three-act opera *Seitsemän huivia* (The Seven Veils) was commissioned by the Kokkola Municipal Theatre (1990). *Dominus Krabbe* was written at the request of countertenor Teppo Lampela and decacorde player Mari Mäntylä, although it was formally commissioned by the Dryades music association.

Tirlittan

Tirlittan, based on the children's book of the same name by Oiva Paloheimo, is a two-act children's opera for soloists, girls' choir and chamber orchestra with a duration of 90 minutes. I wrote the libretto myself, based on Paloheimo's book. This was a gratifying task, since the book itself has a straightforward dramatic arc and lots of dialogue that was usable as is. Indeed, the story had been previously adapted for the stage, sometimes with music.

The subject matter of *Tirlittan* is dark, dealing with divorce from the perspective of a child. It all begins when Tirlittan (played by child soprano Suvi Lehto) falls into a canal, gets wet and is lost and finds herself wandering with her ocarina through the strange world of adults. She regularly encounters the figure of her father (bass Marko Putkonen) in various guises: a policeman, a landlord, God ("dear heavenly father") and finally her actual father. Tirlittan lives through the dark side of being a child of divorce. She steals an apple in the market place, seeking attention, and ends up in jail. The jealousy of her father's new, hypocritical wife tears at her heart. She is cast out of all the places she goes, even church. Finally, an immensely rich but friendly lady, Mrs Bonepain encourages her and turns out to be her guardian angel when Tirlittan, having joined a circus as a trapeze artist, the 'golden bird', is startled in the middle of her act by seeing her actual father in the audience and falls. Everything turns out all right in the end. Tirlittan gets better, and both her mother and her father come to see her. Not together, but they both do come.

Tirlittan was directed by Heikki Värtsi and conducted by Luis Ramirez.

Seitsemän huivia

Seitsemän huivia (The Seven Veils) is a three-act opera that lasts about two hours. The libretto was written by director and dramaturge Vesa-Tapio Valo to a commission from the Kokkola Municipal Theatre. By the time I was commissioned, the libretto was already complete. Over a period of about 18 months, I engaged in very pleasant collaboration with both the librettist and director Kimmo Kahra. We met almost on a monthly basis to look at and listen to what I had produced so far, and there were always ideas flying around. The premiere of the opera in autumn 1990 was a grand regional cultural event and was awarded the culture prize of the Province of Vaasa.

The opera is based on the life story of Kreeta Haapasalo, Finland's most famous kantele player of all time, who came from the village of Kaustinen near Kokkola. It is not a biographical or historical opera, however. It is more about exploring the myth of Kreeta Haapasalo and the relationship between art and power. It shows how the Finnish-minded intelligentsia of the late 19th century deliberately transformed the "melancholic, poor and humble" kantele player they had discovered into an icon of the Finnish nation, a "national singer", a "Hellenic Finn". This controversial exercise in image polishing and myth-building proved unsustainable even for those who perpetrated it. The role-play began to seem farcical, and from today's perspective one cannot avoid seeing a parallel between this and the similar efforts by Finnish New Left extremists (*taistolaiset*) in the 1970s to force art into a predefined template. The linguistic pyrotechnics produced by Vesa-Tapio Valo, whose writing style recalled that of poet and playwright Paavo Haavikko, were a joy for a composer to work with.

Seitsemän huivia was directed by Kimmo Kahra, as noted above. The performances were staged at Snellman Hall in Kokkola. The soloists (Helena Salonius, Kristiina Salo, Mia Huhta, Hannu Ilmolahti, Juha Haanperä and others), the Kokkola Youth Choir and the Ostrobothnian Chamber Orchestra were conducted by Pekka Haapasalo. I should mention that a kantele was included in the orchestra along with strings, harpsichord, celesta and toy piano, but there are no folk music or national music elements in the score. On stage, the instrument was heard only once: a scrap of the tune *Kanteleeni* (My kantele) written by Kreeta Haapasalo herself was heard when a saccharine publicity photo was taken of her character.

Dominus Krabbe by P. Mustapää

P. Mustapää was the pen name of Martti Haavio. His father was a vicar at Yläne in South-west Finland in the 1910s. The local parish records contained curious mentions of one Henricus Krabbe, a curate around the time of the Great Hate (the Russian occupation of Finland from 1710 to 1721). He took to drinking, was removed from office and ended up living on the charity of the parish. Haavio took what was known of this ruin of a man and wrote an extensive six-part poem, a 'horror ballad', which he published in his collection *Lauluja vaakalinnusta* (Songs of the great bird, 1927).

The central themes of the poem are guilt and blame. On the wall of the sacristy of the church hangs a portrait of Dominus Krabbe, a long-dead priest. His "eyes icy and brusque" prompt the guilt of sin in everyone who sees the painting. In the night between Midsummer's Eve and Midsummer Day, supernatural things begin to happen. The idyll of the vicarage is broken, and the people are restless and terrified. A string of very strange events unfolds. The vicar's son is feeling bad after having gone out to the Midsummer revels in the village and is afraid of his father's disapproval, imposing guilt by martyr-dom. A light is seen in the chancellery at the vicarage, but it is not his father the vicar waiting for him: it is a horrible little gnome of a man, Dominus Krabbe from the painting in the sacristy. He puts the young man under his spell, making the poor lad feel humili-ated and culpable, but finally reveals the reason for his appearance. Two hundred years after his death, he still cannot find peace before clearing his conscience in one final Mid-summer sermon.

Amanda, the maid at the vicarage, is the next eye witness. She feels lazy and tired. She is supposed to go and milk the cows early in the morning but could not be bothered. Suddenly she feels cold and then frightened: she sees a snorting white horse on whose back there sits a white creature, with "eyes icy and brusque".

In the third part of the poem, Eprami, farm hand at the vicarage, returns from a noc-turnal wooing with rosy thoughts; the birds sing their glittering morning song, and the world is smiling. This bliss is shattered by a "horrible gnome from the churchyard" whose "forehead and nose were of bone".

Optaatus, the church warden, serves two masters, the vicar and the bottle. This wretched man is also superstitious and nearly dies of heart failure when Dominus Krabbe's ghost, still mounted on a horse, appears in the middle of the church.

Midsummer Day is a great day for the young ladies of the vicarage. The multitude of flowers in the church creates an excellent backdrop for appearing in their finest among the fine folk of the manor and others of their class in the congregation. But as the summer hymn is sung, it is not the vicar their father who climbs up into the pulpit; it is a troll of a man, Dominus Krabbe, who launches into a Midsummer sermon. It is about St John the Baptist, whose festival day Midsummer is: about Herod, Herodias and the sinful antics of Salome that lead to the execution of John. Then the ghost breaks off from the text of the day and declares what he has been holding back for two centuries:

"I am like Herod, king of old:
this arm, now bony grown and cold,
did once deal death and slay a man by sword –
that man, like John, a man was of the Lord."

The ghost is speaking of the destruction of a man of the Lord, himself. The congregation falls into a trance: there is speaking in tongues, prophesising and dancing in the aisles. But at the same time, the guilt-inducing brooding presence of the portrait of Dominus Krabbe – i.e. the fundamentalist, rules-driven Church – is dispelled. Alongside Krabbe's sins, the parishioners' ostensibly bloody sins pale by comparison. In the sixth and final part of the poem, all that is left for the old gravedigger to say is that Krabbe has been redeemed and can rest in peace.

Musical idiom: modes, quotes and allusions

I am a minimalist at heart. My music is grounded in diatonicism and an almost archetypal economy of material, repetition and gradual variation – a musical language that has no beginning and no end, it just is. My influences include both American and Estonian minimalists and ethnic music of various kinds. In addition to the *Kalevala* tradition, I have made use of the music of Antiquity, of the Andes, of Romania and of the Roma. Their modal scales and the aesthetics and ethics thereby created speak to me powerfully.

The six sections of *Dominus Krabbe* are each built on a specific pitch set. Each has its own character, mood and expressive value. The core cell is a melancholy three-pitch nucleus, D-E-F. Combined with its transposition up a fifth, it yields the hexachord D-E-F-A-B-C. The first section, the Vicar's Son's Tale, is based on this scale. I might note that director Kimmo Kahra perceived this as having a Japanese flavour and therefore sought inspiration in the simplified world of kabuki theatre: "Glass bells, glass bells in the maple trees." The hexachord might be extended into a Dorian mode – as in the third section, Farm Hand Epraim's Tale – or reduced into a Damon pentatonic mode, E-F-A-B-C – as in Amanda the Maid's Tale. Another reduced version, a Phrygian tetrachord (E-F-G-A) appears in Church Warden Optaatus's Tale and the Vicarage's Young Ladies' Tale. Combining a mode with transposed versions of itself yields chromatic structures when needed. The hexachord of the first section, for instance, yields the entire chromatic scale when combined with its transposition at a tritone.

With a modal approach, both melody and accompaniment – voice and decacorde – are strictly limited to the same material. Only the pitches in the selected pitch set are available for the accompaniment. The motifs and larger units derived from the pitch sets occur consecutively, dovetailed and in parallel, eventually merging into drone-like fields of sound, or soundscapes, as some critics said. Or it may go the other way: a solid entity, whether a scale or a quote, may divide up into fragments 'deconstructively' and recombine into something completely different. What is essential is the emotional content of each particular mode and the static nature of the texture that is typical of minimalism, created through repetition and gradual variation, 'quiet rapture' you might call it. However, these days I seem to be drifting away from classical minimalism and towards post-minimalism. I no longer use repetition quite as much but use constant variation much more, yet my textures are still essentially static, anchored in a fundamental tone.

When each section is based on a specific mode, we might well ask whether a mode is the same as a *leitmotif*. In some sense, certainly. But modes are not tied to specific scenes or moods; they may appear elsewhere, in new situations. My conscious aim in this is to lend coherence to the work, and the way to do this is to use the same material throughout. Is this an instance of Aristotelian *peripeteia*, where the past is always there alongside the present and our linear concept of time, cyclically and unconsciously? This is a question best addressed by someone other than the composer.

In *Dominus Krabbe*, the quotes and allusions I use function more like *leitmotifs* than anything else. I imported three quotes from liturgical music: the medieval chants *Dies irae* and *Kyrie eleison* (*orbis factor*, 9th century) are the terrifying and guilt-inducing emblems of Dominus Krabbe himself, the image of hell as painted by the religious fundamentalists of the 18th century. The *Dies irae* chant yielded a short motif signifying the persistent tolling of the bells of death and the fear of hell. The *Kyrie eleison* chant, with its descending fifth that is almost hard-wired into the Catholic and Protestant psyche as the Sunday-service guilt trip, the 'ritual execution' that begins a church service and enables the manipulation that is labelled pastoral care (Juha Siltala: *Suomalainen ahdistus* [Finnish angst]). In *Dominus Krabbe*, the *Kyrie* motif appears in precisely this function, mostly in a tritone variant. It is used in its original guise, in inversion and in retrograde. The third quote contrasts with the above two: it is the gentle pentatonic *Christe eleison* section from the *Orbis factor* chant.

I used stylised hymns and Baroque textures to give the flavour of a specific time and place: the countertenor part contains soaring melismas, and the decacorde is allowed to indulge in rippling Renaissance and Baroque cadences. It was particularly gratifying for the composer that both the performers, countertenor Teppo Lampela and decacorde player Mari Mäntylä, are Baroque specialists.

Voice registers, sound and texture

The vocal part in *Dominus Krabbe* calls for an extended countertenor voice. What I mean by this is that the singer has to be able to sing not only in the countertenor register but also in the baritone register, being able to shift seamlessly between the two, through a mixed tenor voice where necessary. I had already written for this voice type earlier. I created the dual role of Mrs Bonepain and the Ringmaster in *Tirlittan* by making use of the baritone and falsetto capabilities of Sampo Suihko. The role of the bartender, Carl, in *Seitsemän huivia* was performed by Juha Haanperä using the same sort of macabre morphing. With *Dominus Krabbe*, I had the pleasure of writing for the voice of Teppo Lampela.

Teppo Lampela has a range of three octaves. His light (bass) baritone voice that extends into the tenor register adapts itself wonderfully to a variety of male roles: the vicar's son sounds light and insubstantial, Epraim the farm hand is boisterous and robust, the wretched church warden Optaatus sniffs his nose and breaks his voice every now and again, and the old gravedigger is a bass baritone who has seen it all. Dominus Krabbe himself is a dramatic bass baritone, but only for a short while. The emblem of the terror he engenders in everyone is a chilling falsetto, a disembodied cold and harsh sound of death. Each of the six characters depicted have a separate countertenor idiom that they fall into when Krabbe's ghost appears.

The countertenor is also called upon to do metaphorical cross-dressing, as singing in the alto register is naturally appropriate for depicting the women in the story, Amanda the maid, the young ladies of the vicarage and some voices in the congregation.

Singing for one hour without a break and transitioning smoothly from one voice type and character to another while also acting is an achievement worthy of the Stakhanov Prize.

The accompanist, Mari Mäntylä on the decacorde, is also an enchanting musician, able to go with the flow yet also a perfectionist. I have previously written solo and chamber music works for her, including the double concerto *Aeterna* (2009) for chamber orchestra and her bandoneon/decacorde duo, Duo Dryades. Mäntylä's decacorde is like an orchestra in miniature. It is nuanced, rich in colour and incredibly flexible in the hands of a skilled performer. The decacorde part is not easy by any means. With a duration of one hour, it must be one of the world's longest compositions for guitar. The highly diverse musical texture calls for Baroque and contemporary techniques and also for a knowledge of certain styles of ethnic music. Required techniques include the frequent hemiolas characteristic of the Spanish Baroque and the expressive four-finger arpeggios played on the fingernails. The decacorde part is mostly independent of the voice, as much a solo part as an accompaniment. The excellent ensemble work by the two musicians in working with this rhythmically complex texture deserves special praise.

Dramaturgy

The poem *Dominus Krabbe* contains a huge number of contrasts and characters, such as masculine vs. feminine or coarse vs. tender. At the top level, the guiding dramaturgical principle is that of a static situation repeatedly shattered by a catastrophe. Every section in the poem begins with an idyll, whether the garden of the vicarage at night or a Midsummer meadow in bloom. Each time, the image is violently interrupted by the appearance of the ghost of Dominus Krabbe, prompting feelings of guilt and horror in everyone. In the music, this appears as the juxtaposition of diatonic and chromatic writing. The idyll is represented by a minimalist texture with diatonic motifs and non-conflicting modes, while each catastrophe brings in harsh chromatic harmonies with a crash. There is often a transition, an extensive and expressive scale passage, bridging the change. Sometimes, especially in the falsetto sections, it functions like a Baroque ritornello. The melodies of the dead priest are ragged and extremely anguished. Instead of the stepwise material in the more tranquil passages, his music features wide leaps interspersed with chromatic stepwise passages. At its most extreme, when Krabbe's ghost humiliates the vicar's son with the line "Take it – sit – there's a chair", the voice part leaps up more than two octaves from the bass baritone range for two notes! The rhythmic profiles follow the same pattern: the idyll has a steady pulse, while the catastrophes proceed in a recitative that disrupts the rhythm of the poetry. It is not until the fifth section, Krabbe's sermon, that the situation is resolved. At the moment when Krabbe makes his confession, the unruly recitative of Herod, Herodias and Salome melts into a diatonic melody over a freely pulsing tolling echoing the *Dies irae* in the decacorde and finally ends up in the liberating pentatonic material of the *Christe eleison*. It is at this point that we discover what the real reason for the clergyman's self-destruction was: "Each and every one of us has killed himself for Salome's sake." Director Kimmo Kahra considered that at this point the disgraced priest becomes a redeemer, Christ, who absolves both himself and his parishioners from the burden that they have endured for two centuries.

Here, P. Mustapää introduced a *peripeteia* – a dramatic twist that changes everything. There are several such moments in the poem, and in the music I have provided more. For instance, the initial reaction to Krabbe's sermon is not an instant outburst of ecstasy but a moment of flageolets on the decacorde, a moment of celestial emotion.

67

At two points in the poem, P. Mustapää wrote a line in italics: in the first section, "Glass bells, glass bells in the maple trees"; and in the third section, related to the rosy-red of Epraim the farm hand, "My darling is gone". At these points, I decided to turn the vocal part over to the decacorde player. This presented no problem, as Mari Mäntylä had studied voice as her second instrument in Basel. For the sake of symmetry, I also gave her the line "And a lovely girl in the transept danced like Salome" in the fifth section. These slight deviations from the established norm increased the energy and gave the impression of there being an outside party observing the events. Looking back, these moments are also musically motivated. The first instance is a single-note melody with a minor-second deviation. The second instance is a canon sung with Epraim, based on a minor second and a major third, a reduced version of the Damon pentatonic mode. The third instance divides the third into seconds, creating a Phrygian tetrachord – the same motif that Krabbe reaches in his confession "for Salome's sake". An independent motif for Salome thus emerged of its own accord. After the final 'outside line', the decacorde begins its own Salome dance, a virtuoso arpeggio texture based on the aforementioned tetrachord. Once the congregation has calmed down, it is time for redemption: the decacorde plays a seemingly unending gradually descending five-minute scale passage that ends up on the instrument's lowest note, A1. This turns into the motif of the old grave-digger, who represents Kharon the ferryman, and with this the troubled priest finally goes to his rest.

Dominus Krabbe has been very well received. It was premièred at the Helsinki Festival, in the German Church in Helsinki, in August 2012 and has since been performed at the Turku Chamber Opera Festival, the Naantali Music Festival, at Törmälä in Rautalampi, at the Tampere Biennale and at the Lohja Tenor Festival. Currently, future performances have been booked up to 2016.

Grand emotions of a tiny human being

About the potential of opera to depict the ordinary and the political

OLLI KORTEKANGAS

My opera *Isän tyttö* (Daddy's Girl) was performed in Savonlinna in 2007. After the final performance, an opera lover came up to me and thanked me, saying that she had enjoyed the performance. Then she went on: "But you know, it isn't really right to use everyday language in an opera, is it?" Prepared as I was for critical comments, this came completely out of the blue. I was so amazed that words failed me.

This illustrates common expectations that people have about opera. Opera is supposed to be something noble and uplifting that transports the listener away from everyday life, beginning with its choice of words. I have nothing against transcendence as such, and there is certainly a time and a place for nobility and upliftingness. But opera today is many other things and much more than 'escapist entertainment for the elite', a slogan from decades past sneering at the traditional function of opera that my aforementioned critic was advocating, albeit unconsciously.

I probably took offence needlessly at the above comment. Perhaps the lady was just trying to tell me that opera should remain within the bounds of a certain tried and true tradition. But on the other hand: if it had always done that, how would opera as an art form ever have been able to revitalise itself?

Richest of all art forms

For me, opera is the richest genre of music there is (no offence to symphonic composers!) and also the richest art form of any kind. This is not a qualitative claim nor even a particularly adventurous one. I am merely restating a cliché: opera is the marriage of all art forms. And yet opera is above all music, drama in (and of) music. All of its other elements are subordinate to the music, even if at any given moment an opera may be an exercise in ballet, spoken drama, lighting, performance art, circus, or what have you.

I like to compare opera with cinema, these two art forms having much in common. Paradoxically, while cinema is regarded as a modern art form simply because of its technological nature, opera is persistently regarded as old-fashioned. Even today, you can hear people saying that operas are dusty things of the past, aesthetically incomprehensible and dramaturgically either banal or opaque; it's all about singers standing around in cardboard scenery, and you can't make out the words. But opera today is nothing like that. Statements like this beg the question of where those people have actually seen and heard opera, if at all.

"Extreme multimedia work"

So what is opera today like? While writing this essay, I happened to read an article by Vesa Sirén, a journalist with *Helsingin Sanomat*, about the opera scene in New York (5 Nov 2013). He quotes Ben Spierman, the director of the Bronx Opera, who said: "Opera is an extreme multimedia work. It has always been that and is even more so now, with video and the Internet incorporated into productions. Opera can satisfy all your cultural needs, whether they have to do with music, visual art, video, drama or social interaction."

Contemporary opera and theatre took electronic multimedia on board with astonishing rapidity and enthusiasm. As with all things new, there is a danger of overplaying the novelty. My critical remarks in this respect are derived from my experiences as a viewer and listener, not so much as an author. Visual input can have enormous power, and moving images in particular tend to dominate the stage. Using video can easily lead to the aesthetic experience falling flat – in some strange way, video is both overwhelming and shallow – and productions can end up resembling one another. Using close-ups to intensify the stage action usually draws attention to itself for its own sake. If a moving image includes sound, it is necessarily amplified and often processed in some way. This begs the question of whether amplification should not be used across the board to create a coherent sound world for the production. I will return to the question of amplification below.

Ultimately, what should govern the use of video, the Internet and all other new technologies is the same principle as for any other means: tools are tools, and what is essential is how you use them. It is not so much about the stuff you have as the stuff you do with it, about imagination, skill and good taste (or deliberately overstepping the bounds of good taste, as the case may be). My experience is that the presence of a live performer on stage still cannot be surpassed by any kind of technology. And that goes for live fire too!

Words and expression

It is true that it is often difficult to make out the words in an opera. This may be due to any number of factors: the composer's incompetence, poor acoustics, the loudness of the orchestra, careless diction by the singers, and so on. It is a good thing that opera houses these days have surtitling. That is a much better option than amplification, which I feel has no place in the conventional idiom of operatic expression – and I should note that I consider that major contemporary operas continue to belong to this category – and does not support classical voice technique well. Besides: you do not really have to be able to make out every word in an opera performance. All competent librettists know and accept this.

Opera, like cinema, has a grammar, vocabulary and idiom all its own. Granted, these are not something that an uninitiated person can easily comprehend, but they are worth the trouble of getting to know them. By 'idiom', I do not of course mean things like whether an opera libretto should use formal or everyday language but a deeper and broader construct made up of things like the subtly dynamic relationship between a vocal melody and an orchestral backing or the capability of music to carry the story even without words.

Opera remains a viable art form, and like its sister, cinema, it has the capacity to make a powerful impact on the contemporary viewer and listener. It can address any topic between heaven and earth just as it always has, anything that we can see and experience around us – including the political and the ordinary.

Politics and theatre

Creating an artwork on a political topic is always a challenge, and authors of opera like all other artists have been fascinated with this challenge for centuries; consider *Un ballo in maschera* or *Nixon in China*. Politics is often described as theatre, and certainly it is a fitting subject for drama. Of course, focusing on the politics of the day unequivocally dates an artwork; but opera, thanks to its diversity, lends itself well to depicting great events in history. It is also especially well suited to allegory, and this provides librettists and composers with an avenue for criticising the powers that be (and, on the other hand, for sucking up to them, of course).

I feel that *Yhden yön juttu* (One Night Stand), my latest opera at the time of this writing, is very much a political opera. Its point is to look at the strangely twisted merging of globalisation and privatisation in our era and particularly the downsizing of the welfare state in the face of economic pressures. This is illustrated in concrete terms in two scenes set at a health centre. The first is a chaotic gallery of archetypes of contemporary people damaged in several ways, with ariosos and ensembles. In the second, five years later, the health centre is closed and its ruins are home to the central character of the previous scene, the Nurse, now a substance abuser, who sings an appropriately macabre aria.

From the particular to the general

Opera can best depict everyday life through an individual. This is one of the definite strengths of opera, and for me perhaps the most important. Opera is at its best when it highlights the "grand emotions of a tiny human being", giving the viewer/listener someone to identify with and telling the story of an individual and the people close to him or her. This allows the narrative to credibly illustrate the era in which the action is set and the social phenomena in that context, progressing from the particular to the general. Other art forms can do this too, but what makes opera special is that everything is sung, and singing is "heart speaking to heart", as has often been said.

Let us return to *Isän tyttö*. In Act I, scene 4 we are in a dressmaker's workshop in a Finnish city in the year 1968. The setting and the work being done is explicitly stated in the libretto: "Sewing, sewing, warm clothes for a cold world." While this line is concrete and understandable, it also carries a deeper philosophical meaning: diligence at work while dreaming of a better world. The music whirrs like a sewing machine, spinning a single mechanical idea around and around. The women in the workshop are a collective whose opponent is Siiri, the industrious and authoritarian manager. Siiri does deals on the phone, and the details of her one-sided conversation, including words like "spasibo" ('thank you' in Russian), indicate that we are in the heyday of Finland's Soviet trade. The hierarchy in the workshop is very clear: the boss is the boss and the workers are workers.

Soon another group enters, a gaggle of girls. "Do you remember me?" the children's choir sings, and it soon becomes apparent that the two levels of reality do not in fact inhabit the same time and space. The girls are not the seamstresses' daughters; they are the seamstresses themselves several decades earlier, with bruises and scabby knees, with dreams and disillusionments.

This scene has proved to be one of the best-received in the entire opera, and I believe this is because it is at once 'ordinary' and 'unique': two levels of ordinary life intersect and form a third, extraordinary level. This is surprising and touching, a potentially meaningful experience. This is the sort of thing that can happen in opera, and this is where the art form finds its strength. This is also how opera manages to uplift its viewer and to transcend everyday life – whether through an ennobling experience or through emotional impact, it both perpetuates and continuously revitalises its rich tradition.

Enchanted by chamber opera

Juha T. Koskinen

The programme book of the Savonlinna Opera Festival in 1992 contains an article on the history of the festival that includes a photo from a rehearsal for Verdi's *Don Carlo* in summer 1979. Behind the director's desk we see Martti Talvela, pensive with his arms and legs crossed, and a few rows behind him on the right a small boy wrapped in a hoodie and a blanket, deep in concentration. I realised that that was me, aged six. It was in Savonlinna that I developed an interest in opera, being allowed to watch rehearsals and performances as my father played violin with the Opera Festival Orchestra. When I decided to become a composer at the age of 15, I almost immediately began to map out stories that would make a good opera. Combining music and drama seemed like the most natural thing in the world. At the age of twenty-something, my sketchbooks and diaries filled up with notes for opera scenes. Text seemed to be coming out faster than I could write it down. Opera became an enchanted garden for my dreams and my nightmares, a garden where I could hide from the everyday world.

I find that my opera scores involve a certain paradox: in order to be sure that the opera works on stage, I have to write it dissociated from the stage, without giving any thought as to how it might be executed visually. My composition process is such that my operas end up as a series of continua and transitions in time and space, and I would claim that there is no essential difference between my works for the stage and my works not for the stage. But further to the paradox, my operas are of course specifically intended to be staged. Perhaps the staging is after all included in the score, even if there are no stage directions. I believe that my skill in taking the needs and limitations of the stage into account when working on the score has improved with experience and that this development is apparent if we compare the scores of my first opera, *Velhosiskot* (The Witch Company, 1996), and my principal work to date, *Madame de Sade* (2010). *Velhosiskot* is extremely dense and packed. The score seems to allow for no reality beyond itself; it is almost bursting with its expressive desire. *Madame de Sade* is more flexible in accommodating the physical reality of the stage. The electronic interludes provide distance from the score and create new levels of time alongside the linear narrative.

The following is a brief description of each of my operas, with a quote from the libretto and freely associated comments.

Velhosiskot (The Witch Company, 1996)

Red Woman (Adagio cantabile e misterioso): *"Even now, less often but it does happen, one can see an angel coming down to earth. Not a product of a great machine left running, for such wonderful beauty can only be God's newest artwork. But what a waste it is to send angels down here, for the ignorant to destroy and to overwhelm the aware with their burden of grief. But perhaps angels have no other place to live..."*

The musical scarlet thread of my first opera is a chorale that I wrote myself. It is a chromatic tune whose lyrical high point comes in scene 3 of the opera, where the Red Woman sings a 'dream song' to the main character, the Girl. The chorale is softly harmonised for strings at the line "But perhaps angels have no other place to live...", the viola doubling the melody in the upper register. At the same time, a bass voice recites the requiem mass in Latin. This scene is a snapshot of what was then my intuitive conception of opera: at its best, opera can capture the listener in a hypnotic, dream-like state. Opera can juxtapose various levels of reality and move effortlessly between the conscious and the unconscious. The production of *Velhosiskot* directed by Janne Lehmusvuo ended with the Girl stepping through a door, out into the unknown. This matched my journey of having to abandon the Romantic conception of opera that I had had in my childhood and youth. It was time to come to grips with a more venal reality.

Eukko, pidättekö vainajista (The Old Woman – Are You Fond of Dead People?, 1999)

Myself: *How do you feel about dead people?*
Sakerdon Mikhailovich: *Very negatively. I fear them.*
Myself: *Quite. I can't stand them myself, and if I ever saw one, I'd be sure to kick it.*
SM: *You shouldn't kick the dead.*

Myself: *I'd kick it in the face with my boot. I can't stand dead people or children.*
SM: *Yes. Children are just shit.*

The libretto based on the short novel by Daniil Kharms is set in Leningrad in the 1930s, and at its core is of course a vodka-drinking scene that explosively charges the mood. Before the music comes to its climax, the main character, the author referred to as 'Myself' asks his friend Sakerdon Mikhailovich: "Do you believe in God?" and he replies laconically: "To ask someone whether they believe in God – that is a tactless and obscene thing to do." Harms's logically crystal-clear but bewildering narrative inspired me to write an incredibly complex score skirting the bounds of what is technically possible. In the event, the music was not quite as dangerous as the raked stage built in Almi Hall at the Finnish National Opera for the production, which almost caused a disaster at the premiere. The bass soloist accidentally knocked over a table, which skidded downstage at great speed and fell into the orchestra pit. Luckily, it did not hit any of the musicians. Seppo Ruohonen as the main character struggled to cope with the rhythmic tangles of the score but made an incredibly accomplished job of it, committing himself fully to the role. The entire project was somehow all about working with your heart in your throat, struggling against time and doubt. I wrote the score under considerable pressure, while on a computer music course at Ircam, in Vincennes near Paris, at a semi-circular table in a cramped, funnel-like flat.

Brunelda – Amerikan sydän (Brunelda – The Heart of America, 2002)
Brunelda: *Delamarche, come here and do my hair! Ah, oh! You're so rough! Ah, go ahead then! (Where's my angel costume?)*
Robinson: *That must be a stage costume that Brunelda has saved; after all, she's a singer.*
Brunelda: *Oh, I don't sing any more. Not any more. Eek! You're so rough, go away! You pull my hair so hard, my scalp must be bleeding! Oh! Robinson, come here and help me! Have you no heart... mm, omm, ow! Yes, that's what you can do! Suck up, suck up, after doing the job badly!*

Brunelda, the grotesque SM domina in the novel fragments entitled *Amerika* by Franz Kafka, is dressed up as an angel in the 'opera ritual' that I created with Karla Loppi. Brunelda's mercurial moods follow a cycle that is randomly purposeful, just like her music. Her singing sounds at times like stumbling vocal exercises, at times like Wagnerian pathos. Sometimes she viciously parodies poor Delamarche, who is obliged to perform a demanding vocal part even though he has not been trained as an opera singer.

When Brunelda insinuates to Delamarche, who is looking for a towel: "Are you trying to get into the tub with me?", the pianist noodles away in the style of Robert Schumann. In preparing to leave for the outdoor circus in Oklahoma (with Brunelda dressed as an angel), well before the corny 'Brunelda Rag' that concludes the opera, the clarinet pipes out a cheerful motif in thirds that may recall Magnus Lindberg's orchestral fanfares of the 1990s.

Scrabble vs. Komet (2004)

Scrabble [in German]: *Komet is Scrabble's redeemer! DESTROYER! DEFILER! DISPERSER! DEFORMER! DECOMPOSER! DESCRABBLER!*

The opportunity to write the brief opening scene for the 'opera saga' *Kommander Kobayashi* created by the Novoflot opera company in Berlin gave me an insight into a completely different way of making opera than what I had become accustomed to in Finland. After the libretto was completed, I had about one month to write an opera scene 15 minutes long. Because I was working remotely, I had no chance to hear the singers until at the rehearsals, and I had absolutely no idea what kind of music the other composers in the project were writing. Even more challenging was that the libretto was in German. I could have chosen English instead, but I was attracted by the expressive potential of the German language. In the libretto by Tobias Dusche, a strange 'Puzzletierchen' named Scrabble works itself up into an erotic frenzy in expectation of total destruction. When the comet finally hits the spaceship, the outcome is not quite as unambiguous as in the final disaster in Lars von Trier's film *Melancholia.* After all, this was only the introduction to an extensive series, so we could not put all our cards on the table yet...

Madame de Sade (1998/2010)

Renée: *The Marquis de Sade and I were one, we were God's bloody miscarried bastard who will not be himself until he escapes himself.*
Madame de Montreuil (Renée's mother): *Divorce him. Your husband isn't even a human being.*

Having seen the play by Yukio Mishima at the Finnish National Theatre during my studies in the early 1990s, I found myself constantly troubled by its poetically overheated idiom. Later, I realised intuitively that the boiling cauldron of emotions underlying the seemingly calm surface was an excellent catalyst for music. Mishima's characters had to resort to extensive monologues to explain their complex and contradictory psychology to the audience. This is where music has the unique potential of expressing inexpressible emotional turmoil. A typical musically delicious situation is one where a character both adores and despises another. In Baroque opera, affects were kept strictly separate, but we post-Wagnerian composers enjoy plumbing the dark depths of the human psyche. A new opera may at its best be a cataclysmic research project that gives voice and expression to something that had hitherto been missing from the domain of our experience.

While working on *Madame*, I wrote down these notes (December 2009):

The music of the opera is based on three initial characters/elements:

1) fidelity – vice (water)
2) happiness – unhappiness (earth)
3) tenderness – cruelty (fire)

The first is associated with Renée, the wife of the Marquis de Sade, the main character of the opera. Renée's personality is shaped in the course of the opera, the insecure questioner of the introduction growing into the ecstatic visionary of Act III.

The second is associated with Madame de Montreuil, Renée's power-hungry mother, who has had the Marquis imprisoned. It is not until the end of Act II that Renée finds the courage to challenge her powerful and implacable mother in open conflict. And finally, in Act III, when the Revolution has turned social roles upside down, Montreuil's confidence begins to waver.

The third is associated with Renée's younger sister Anne, who wistfully recalls her Romantic escapade with the Marquis in Venice.

Towards the end of the opera, Renée describes her memories as unspeakably horrible insects trapped in amber. Anne's memories of Venice are just shadows on the water as far as she is concerned.

Although the Marquis de Sade is never physically present, he exerts an influence throughout the narrative. As the women's illusions of life and the social order collapse concurrently, the only sustainable vision comes from the Marquis's pen as he languishes in prison. The women join in a chorus: "The world in which we live is a world created by the Marquis de Sade."

The stylistic ideal for the opera could be described as decadent Rococo, with an added layer of non-linear structure as I imagined Noh theatre might include. The music is basically smooth on the surface but pierced by brutal cracks of the whip. The 'sacred light' of the epilogue breaks through the cracks and crevices in the texture.

Lusia Rusintytär (2015)

Here I am, O Lord Almighty,
with thy lightning bolts now smite me,
send thy fire from heaven's vault.
Whether I do wrong or rightly,
or embrace the cross so tightly,
for a witch they shall me fault.

The genesis of the monologue opera *Lusia Rusintytär*, commissioned by the Oulunsalo Soi Festival, differed in many ways from my earlier experiences in the genre. All of my previous operas, except for *Scrabble vs. Komet*, were based on a subject I had come up with myself, and I had mostly adapted the librettos myself too. With *Lusia Rusintytär*, the process was quite different. Mezzo-soprano Virpi Räisänen discovered the tragic tale of Lusia Rusintytär Korhonen, who was accused of witchcraft at the Oulu assizes in the 17th century, and presented it to me as a possible subject for an opera. I liked the idea and wrote a piece named *Lamento di Lusia* (2012) to explore the musical ground for this potential opera project. The team was joined by visual artist and author Hannu Väisänen, who contributed a multiple-monologue libretto that included stylised folk spells and parodies of archaic judicial and ecclesiastical parlance. Väisänen is skilled at writing musical variations of *Kalevala* metre, but for me the project gave considerable difficulty in discovering an appropriate musical idiom. The reason for this was quite simply that this was the first time that I was writing a work for the stage that touched on the Finnish folk singing tradition. But with six operas under my belt, I more than welcome new challenges!

My first and my last opera

ILKKA KUUSISTO

I The Moomins make an opera

Overture

Opera had a hard time taking root in Finland. There is a centuries-long history of opposition to the genre here, and there are constant calls to shut down our only professional opera institution. My idea of writing an opera for children emerged from the naïve hope of educating a new generation for whom the existence of opera would be self-evident.

I had become acquainted with opera since the late 1930s, as my father was the chorus master of the Finnish Opera (later the Finnish National Opera) at the time. I was allowed to watch a great many performances; my favourites included *The Desert Song, Il barbiere di Siviglia* and *Parsifal.* When I was myself asked to become chorus master at the Finnish National Opera in the 1960s, I was more than happy to leave the bureaucratic duties that I had ended up in. At that time, the Finnish National Opera was grievously understaffed, and as a result I found myself doing all sorts of things. I was a répétiteur, accompanied rehearsals on the piano and eventually also conducted performances. I was allowed to stand in for George de Godzinsky as conductor in performances of the operetta *Victoria and Her Hussar* and the opera *Porgy and Bess.* I managed to get good reviews, and Sakari Puurunen, the manager of the Helsinki City Theatre, began to recruit me as conductor for his theatre. The new building of the City Theatre was nearing completion, and its facilities were excellent compared with the old Opera House (now the Alexander Theatre). Puurunen's sweet-talking had its effect. He also promised me that we could produce operas at the City Theatre. We did, but only once: Purcell's fine opera *Dido and Aeneas* was performed in a co-production with the Sibelius Academy directed by Kalle Holmberg. I was conductor at the Helsinki City Theatre for seven years and had the opportunity to conduct some wonderful musicals and to write incidental music for plays. The notion of writing an opera came to me while watching the play *Vihkiäiset* (The Marriage) by Witold Gombrowicz. I discussed the idea with Puurunen, who directed the play on the small stage of the City Theatre. He was interested enough to contact the publisher, only to find out that some German composer had already written an opera based on the play. I lost interest, and instead of an opera I wrote a children's musical named *Kiri kiri* (Spurt!) to a libretto by Roope Alfthan. It was a moderate success and has been performed at several theatres.

I came back to the idea of an opera for children. I had enjoyed the Moomin books of Tove Jansson and found myself thinking what the Moomins would sound like if they were singing. The casting came naturally: Moominmamma is a contralto, Moominpappa a bass, Moomintroll a tenor, the Snork Maiden a soprano, Little My an angry screamer, Mrs Fillyjonk a dramatic soprano, her maid Miska a lovely lyrical soprano, Emma a busy mezzo, and Snufkin never sings but instead plays his harmonica. The ghost arranges surprises for everyone, and so on. It was a nice and colourful ensemble, especially since the Moomin characters were based on real people whom I somehow knew.

I decided to take the idea to the Director of the Finnish National Opera, who at the time was the conductor Leif Segerstam. The finances of the Finnish National Opera were in their usual perilous state, and so Leif said: "The Finnish National Opera won't commission the *Moomin Opera*, but if you write it, we'll perform it." That was good enough for me.

Act I

I wrote a letter to Tove Jansson, saying that I would phone her after she had had a chance to think about my intention to write a *Moomin Opera*. When I eventually phoned her about a week later, she was very kind but would not commit herself either way. Instead, she invited me to her home to talk about it. We agreed on a time, and on the day I entered her studio I was feeling a bit tense. The place was full of artworks, mostly her own paintings. We sat down to a tableful of vodka and gherkins. It was an auspicious beginning for a project to write a children's opera. Very promising!

Tove thought that the idea was a good one but said that she had never written a libretto before, and although her Finnish was flawless (her native language was Swedish), she said that she would not write a libretto in any language. What she could do would be to write a story in Swedish that an experienced writer could then adapt into a libretto. I suggested that we approach Esko Elstelä, and Tove agreed. Skål! There goes another gherkin!

A series of very pleasant meetings followed, and the ball started rolling. Sometimes we were joined by Tuulikki Pietilä from next door or went along Tove's secret corridor in the attic to Tuulikki's studio to marvel at her graphic art.

Act II

The Finnish National Opera began to look for a suitable production team, the principal question being who should direct. The assignment was joyfully accepted by the dancer and choreographer Heikki Värtsi. There is not much actual dancing in the *Moomin Opera*, but the movement element is very important. The Moomin costumes do not allow for facial expressions or mouth movements, so the characters would have to communicate through their movements to indicate to the audience who is singing at any given time. Värtsi's imagination generated an unusual movement language that injected humour into the production. Set designer Thomas Gripenberg executed the designs sketched out by Tove Jansson. At her suggestion, the Swedish designer Hans Kling was engaged to create the Moomin costumes; he had made some fine Moomin dolls. His work was exquisite, but the costumes were too hot for the singers. Moominmamma and Moominpappa in particular nearly fainted with heat exhaustion in the performances. Some of the costumes were remade at the Finnish National Opera to make them lighter and better ventilated. Tove Jansson followed the project closely and commented on it. She said that the Snork Maiden should have a gold earring. The Finnish National Opera did not have one big enough, so Tove went to her jewellery case and brought in a solid gold bracelet that the Snork Maiden then wore on her ear. Everything was going well. The only thing missing was the actual music.

The summer of 1974 was exciting. I had bought a sailboat and brought it to the Saimaa lake system. The boat had been built on Åland and was called *Rock*. I had spent quite a lot of time on the water; at one point, I had even wanted to go to sea and train to be a ship's captain. But this was the first sailboat I had ever had, so I needed to practice handling it. My earlier boats had been motorboats, apart from the galleass *Ilmatar*. After a couple of weeks, I felt confident enough to take my wife and our six-month-old son Jaakko out on the lakes. The weather begged to disagree. We set off from Taipalsaari towards Lappeenranta and then to the open expanse of Suur-Saimaa in the middle of Saimaa lake. I had been in sailboats with friends on the open sea, enjoying a constant wind. In the lakeland, things are very different: the wind constantly changes its direction as it eddies and swirls around the islands, and you have to fiddle with the sails all the time. As the wind rose further, we began to look for an anchorage. We found a sheltered sound out of the wind, cast anchor, struck the sails and prepared to have a bite to eat and go to bed. Then a motorboat approached, and its driver politely informed us that we were anchored slap in the middle of a busy boating lane. He kindly offered to tow us to a better location. Off we went with a terrible banging and clunking, as our helper had failed to realise that a sailboat has a large keel and towed us straight into the rocks.

The night was relatively calm, however, and in the morning we were ready to set off again. But the anchor had become wedged between the rocks on the bottom during the night, and try as I might I could not dislodge it. The boat had a tiny outboard motor, a Seagull, and I tried reversing the boat in the hope that the anchor would come loose. Not a hope. With a heavy heart, I took out a knife and cut the anchor line. The wind was strong again and growing stronger, and before noon we were already looking for a place to stop. We came up to an island named Sikosalo, with a promising jetty. We sailed there and moored without asking anyone's permission. The wind was already so wild that my wife's stylish cap blew off into the lake and was never seen again. We spent a safe couple of days moored at Sikosalo. A kind man came to see us and gave us permission to wait out the high winds.

After the winds died down, we decided to return to Taipalsaari. When we reached Riuttasaari island and dropped anchor, we heard the first rumble of thunder. We had to take emergency measures as a storm was rising. We still had one anchor, but it was smaller than the one we had had to leave behind. I was worried: if the wind blew really hard, we could be dragged along despite the anchor. I thought about tying copper wire to the stays to make lightning conductors. The night was rough, with lightning illuminating the landscape at frequent intervals, and the rumble of thunder was reinforced by the high cliffs of the island. Tove Jansson would have described it as a "fateful night". No wonder that this adventure recalled the exploits of the Moomins in the opera ship, an opera stage set afloat and cast adrift by an underwater volcano eruption, earthquake and resulting tsunami. The courage of the stage manager, Emma, inspired the Moomins to take action to save the opera ship. Tove Jansson said that children love the threat of danger. With hindsight, our ordeal on Saimaa was a healthy and useful source of inspiration for this particular story.

Act III

It was already August, and I realised that the *Moomin Opera* had to be delivered to the Finnish National Opera in a couple of months. The libretto was finished: Esko Elstelä had done a fine job in not only translating the manuscript but dramatising it as well. I had talked to Elstelä about insinuating opera lore into the work in order to educate children about the art form. It had to include a scene where a couple of instrumentalists would wander onto the stage. There also had to be some classic opera props, like the rose from *Rosenkavalier* or the swan from *Lohengrin*. Moominpappa is a Baroque bass, while Moominmamma, the Snork Maiden and Moomintroll are Romantic in style. Mrs Fillyjonk is a Wagnerian, while her maid Miska is excessively lyrical and classical. Emma is a dramatic mezzo, and the ghost was cast as the Phantom of the Opera, who gets upset if the singing is bad.

I completed the piano score by the end of August. The Finnish Music Information Centre had promised to make the copies needed by the Finnish National Opera. On the agreed date, I went to collect the copies. I was very surprised when Jarmo Sermilä, the then director of FIMIC (Finnish Music Information Centre, nowadays Music Finland), said that they had had something more important to do and pointed to the copier, which was churning out a work by Joonas Kokkonen. Sermilä had not realised that it was not me that needed the music, it was the Finnish National Opera, where rehearsals were scheduled to begin the next day. I phoned Juhani Raiskinen, the Director of the Finnish National Opera, and he reacted exactly as I would have, sitting in his chair years later: "Goddamnit, you bastard, you haven't finished it!" My honour was wounded, and we Ostrobothnians do not take that sort of thing lying down. I promised that the music would be there by the next day. I was employed as a producer at Finnlevy, the record label arm of the Fazer music company, at the time, and I asked for and received permission to use the company's industrial-strength copier. I spent my night in the copying room making a dozen vocal scores. I made the covers out of a scrap of stylish green textile wallpaper left over from the renovation of my study at home. I used adhesive binding and could really have done with a purpose-made press, but squeezing the copies between the hinges of a door worked just as well.

I completed the full score at Martin Wegelius's villa at Pohja a month later. The premiere was on 7 December 1974. My son Jaakko later came to see the opera. I was conducting that night, and when the opera began, opening with the sound of the earthquake, a bass drum roll, I could clearly hear Jaakko exclaiming in the audience: "I want to go home!"

II The Aino Ackté opera and Aarre Merikanto's revenge

In spring 2008, rumour had led me to believe that the Finnish National Opera would commission an opera from me for the centenary of the Finnish National Opera in 2012. The idea of writing an opera about the opera singer Aino Ackté probably came from Pentti Savolainen. Before this, the Ilmajoki Music Festival had asked me to write an opera to a libretto by Panu Rajala. I had held off from giving an answer because, as I said to them too, the Finnish National Opera was planning to commission me. The spring passed, then the summer, and no word from the Finnish National Opera. Instead, the director of the Ilmajoki Music Festival, Sari Mäkinen, remained keen to sign an agreement. In pragmatic Finnish fashion, I thought that a bird in the hand..., and I promised to write an opera for Ilmajoki. The agreement was signed on 3 April 2008. I read Rajala's libretto and considered it very feasible. It was entitled *Taipaleenjoki* (Taipale River) and focused on the battles at that river in the Winter War (1939–1940). The libretto was mainly based on actual events and included delicious extracts from the poem collection *Kiirastuli* (Purgatory) of Yrjö Jylhä, who was there himself. I was well under way with this project when the Finnish National Opera announced that they would be commissioning me for a centenary opera featuring Aino Ackté. I paused for thought and looked at the timetables and decided that writing two operas within the time given was within the realm of possibility. I said yes to the Finnish National Opera, and that agreement was signed on 25 November 2008. Thus I found myself trapped between operas. *Taipaleenjoki* was proceeding as planned, while *Aino Ackté* was still very much on the drawing board, even as far as the libretto was concerned.

The librettists of the *Aino* opera, Pentti Savolainen and Juha Kandolin, lived in Spain and travelled to Helsinki from time to time to show me what they had done. Pentti Savolainen is thoroughly familiar with Ackté and has written a lot of authoritative stuff about her. Juha Kandolin was in charge of the shape and dramaturgy, and the project was proceeding promisingly. *Taipaleenjoki* was completed on schedule, but the libretto for the Ackté opera seemed to be suffering from an embarrassment of riches, as is common for librettos. The amount of text you need for an opera is only about one third of what you need for a stage play of the same length. Therefore the text had to be edited, and this had to be done skilfully to preserve the coherence of the narrative.

The opera opens with the strict instruction of Aino's mother Emmy. She had had ambitions for an international career that never came true. Aino is thus harnessed to fulfil her mother's dream. Aino is driven to desperation by her mother's incessant chiding. Aino protests vigorously and finds her voice in the process; Emmy finds that her teaching has borne fruit.

Pentti Savolainen had chosen to write the libretto in the slightly archaic language of the early 20th century. This was a justifiable choice, and I continued to work on the music. The following scenes worked well in this style. As Aino departs for Paris with Emmy, the composer Oskar Merikanto encourages Aino with cordial and patriotic sentiments. Yrjö Weijola once wrote a poem entitled *Suomesta lähtiessä* (Departing from Finland) that Oskar Merikanto is known to have set to music. The poem survives, but Merikanto's music has been lost. I wrote a song to the text as I imagined Merikanto would have written it. But somewhat later I discovered that the style of the text was having an undue impact on the music. I did not want to write an entire opera consisting of pastiche, and I began to grow uneasy with the project. I tried to think of a way to escape from the old-fashioned niceties of the text. It was then that I came up with the idea of a libretto in multiple languages. This would mean that the language would be setting the scene for the various sections of the narrative just like the set design does.

The principal languages would be Finnish, Swedish, French and English. The departure from Finland would also be spiced by a scrap of Russian from the gendarme at the harbour. I was pleased with this notion and started to think about who could translate the libretto. French was my first concern, as in my scheme it would account for the largest portion of the libretto, about 30%. The person I hoped to engage for this task was Martina Roos. She is a diploma-holding singer, an actor and a director, and I had worked with her previously on the play *Fjäriln vingad* (Butterfly flying) by Erik Söderblom, for which I had written the music. Martina is a consummate professional in several fields, and her native language is French.

Martina agreed to translate the scenes that took place in Paris. A Swedish translation was provided by Lena von Bonsdorff with Martina, and an English translation was provided by Leslie Jauhiainen, whom I knew from the Chorus of the Finnish National Opera. Martina is a multilingual person and was thus able to lay down guidelines for the translation work as a whole. Setting a French text to music involves a great many nuances and variations. If you do not know the language, you cannot possibly know when you can truncate a word or add an unstressed vowel to the end. As work progressed in this fashion, I noticed the original libretto gaining in sharpness and the lines acquiring character that made writing the music that much simpler. Martina is not only a professional singer but also a lecturer in drama at the Sibelius Academy. She was tireless in correcting my music to better fit the vowel durations and word stresses of French. I was making progress, and Martina's singing demonstrated to me that I was going in the right direction.

Martina also had an instinct for finding places where the drama could be enhanced in operatic fashion. As an example, I might mention Emmy's violent reaction when Aino, having won the opera competition in Paris, announces that she might now marry Heikki Renwall:

Emmy's aria
I have sacrificed my entire life to your happiness, to your art. If you marry, you will be a shapeless matron in no time, just look at me! Do you imagine you would ever get to the Met with children at your feet? Nobody will hire a young soprano who is married and who could

thus become pregnant at any minute, and then her career would be OVER! You, who could become a world-famous star. You, who have a better voice than Melba. I knew you wouldn't have the character to do it. Go on, get married, then I can concentrate on your sister Irma, she has a better talent for this than you do, anyway.

In the original libretto, this scene lacks an edge. The situation ends with painter Albert Edelfelt attending the competition and handing Aino a letter. This does prompt the viewer's curiosity: what is in the letter? The scene ends with Aino opening the letter and reading it to herself and then saying: "Oh, mother! You won't believe what Edelfelt writes! He wants to paint me! The great master! Oh mother, can you imagine that this is happening?"

I believe that every composer would agree with me that Martina's version, given above in italics, is the one that an opera composer needs.

In the competition scene, Aino sings Gounod's 'Jewel Song' in its original form with orchestral accompaniment, which is what actually happened at the competition. The comments of the jury are drawn from real life. I was the chairman of the jury at the Lappeenranta Singing Competition on several occasions, and I made notes of some of the things my fellow jury members said; I then ascribed these to the Parisian judges in this opera. The libretto thus includes comments (translated into French) that originated with Aulikki Rautawaara, Birgit Nilsson and Juhani Raiskinen.

Those are not the only quotes I used. I made an arrangement of the light-hearted *Il Bacio* by Luigi Arditi, which Aino Ackté is said to have included in her recital repertoire. She also performed it at the exhibition opening at Edelfelt's studio. In the opera, this is recreated as a ballet scene where the exhibition guests spray varnish on the recently completed portrait of Louis Pasteur (in a literal parody of the Swedish term for the opening of an exhibition, *vernissage* or 'varnishing') and comment on other works by Edelfelt hanging on the walls.

There is a Finnish quote too. When Aino was Director of the Domestic Opera (the precursor of the Finnish National Opera), she and conductor Leo Funtek had an argument. The archives of Fazer Artists Management yielded a letter from Elsa Salminen, manager of the agency, to Antonietta Toini, relating an opera rehearsal where Aino gave Funtek a piece of her mind: "The conductor is there only to beat time! I decide the tempi and everything else!" For historical reasons, I replaced Funtek with Oskar Merikanto, who in my version is quite as offended as his younger colleague Funtek was in real life.

Finnish attitudes to opera are also typified by the notorious statement of javelin gold medallist Seppo Räty: "Opera, fuck no!" I wrote a song on this text as light relief for the opera, since it does embody something essential about Finnish sentiments regarding the art of opera. This number is included in the context of the Savonlinna Opera Festival, which Aino Ackté founded. Local resistance to the festival was initially widespread until it dawned on the good citizens that opera was a gold mine.

Aino Ackté's career culminated with performances of Richard Strauss' *Salome* at Covent Garden in London. Celebrating Aino's success, I wrote a farewell choral number in old English madrigal style. The lyrics were modified from those written by Thomas Hood and begin "I saw thee, lovely Aino". The song is followed by a speech given by Thomas Beecham, who conducted the *Salome* performances. At its end, he presents Aino with a silver platter, explaining that it is not the same platter on which the head of John the Baptist was presented but one specially commissioned from a silversmith. Beecham gives his speech in true vaudeville style.

Act II opens with a grand party at Aino Ackté's villa on Tuurholma. There is dancing fuelled by a Finnish polska, spiced with scraps of Swedish-language drinking songs from the choir. After a debate on language policy and Edelfelt's admiration of Runeberg, Aino and Albert say farewell. The rest of the action has to do with founding an opera company.

Now this tale becomes the story of the opera that was shelved. With all probability, Aino Ackté was the person responsible for Aarre Merikanto's opera *Juha* not being produced at the Opera when it was completed in 1922; the opera had to wait 45 years for its premiere.

This story invites speculation. It is generally acknowledged that the orchestra pit at the old Opera House was not large enough for the orchestra required. It has been speculated that the vocal parts in the opera were simply too difficult. I have my doubts about this, because the soloist ensemble that the Opera had in the 1930s was of a very high calibre. Notwithstanding the above, my personal feeling is that Aino Ackté, who had very competently written the libretto for the opera, would have wanted to create the role of Marja herself. This would have been quite possible in 1922. However, in looking at the score Ackté would have noticed to her chagrin that the 27-year-old composer had cast Marja as a mezzo-soprano. She must therefore have felt that Aarre Merikanto had written the wrong music.

The Aino opera is axed

According to the agreement signed on 1 November 2008, the Finnish National Opera was to receive the vocal score and full score by 1 January 2011. I had submitted the vocal score and the final version of the libretto to the Finnish National Opera well ahead of time, in August 2009. On 7 September 2009, I was informed by the opera that the libretto would not be accepted by 1 January 2010, the deadline for completion of the libretto in the agreement. We were therefore back to square one with the libretto.

A meeting followed where I tried to find out the reasons behind this decision and brought up some names of people who I thought might help in editing the libretto. I also asked the artistic director Mikko Franck whether the scene at the Paris Opera where Aino storms out would not make a good dramatic opera scene. He replied: "Well, look, I don't speak French." This, I assume, was an adequate explanation as far as he was concerned.

I nevertheless gave the names of my emergency rescue team for the libretto: for linguistic richness, go to Ilpo Tiihonen; for psychological depth for the character of Aino, go to Markus Nummi; for dramaturgical enhancement, go to Keijo Kupiainen. The Finnish National Opera never got back to me.

In January 2011, I was in Oulu on a gig when Mikko Franck phoned me at the hotel and said that *Aino* had been removed from the programme and replaced with Aarre Merikanto's *Juha.*

The spirits had spoken! Aino Ackté had steamrollered *Juha* in her day, and now Aarre Merikanto used *Juha* to sidetrack *Aino.* It was an almost perfect revenge, but Aino fought back just enough to make the performance of *Juha* not so much a celebration as just another day at the office for the Finnish National Opera. The brilliant Camilla Nylund was miscast in the mezzo role of Marja and was scarcely able to make any use of the scintillating qualities of her voice. What was worse was that the director had not understood Merikanto's work at all.

I will admit I was seriously ticked off. But when something goes disastrously wrong, something else may come together beautifully. *Taipaleenjoki* at the Ilmajoki Music Festival proved to be a delight. It was performed to full houses in three summers, conducted by Mikk Murdvee and directed by Tuomas Parkkinen. Therefore I can accept without rancour that opera directors decide what they decide and that's that. Mikko Franck is one of the greatest talents in Finnish music, and I have great admiration for his artistic work. This admiration dates back to my tenure as Director of the Finnish National Opera when he was first engaged to perform there.

Bottom line: Have written 18 operas with a total of 43 productions, three of them abroad; one opera unperformed.

PS. In its current multilingual form, the libretto for *Aino Ackté* works like a charm and is multi-faceted, great fun and profoundly moving.

The composer as a conduit for cosmic vibrations

TIMO-JUHANI KYLLÖNEN

What do opera, composing and the arts mean for me?

Opera is the art form that is closest to my heart. It combines all branches of the arts: instrumental, orchestral and vocal music; drama; dance; choreography; poetry; and set design. I have been interested in and enamoured of the arts ever since adolescence. I was living in Sweden at the time, and in upper comprehensive school and upper secondary school I participated in amateur drama groups doing productions for instance of Ancient Greek drama (*Lysistrates* by Aristophanes, *King Oedipus* by Sophocles, etc.). In addition to playing the accordion and the clarinet, I also painted in oils between the ages of 12 and 16 under the tuition of an artist. I wrote my first composition, *Kevätaamu* (Spring morning), at the age of 12, having heard a bird sing its inimitable melody on my way home from school. I later spent a lot of time in the woods on my own and learned how to imitate birds with a whistling technique I developed myself. Perhaps because of this, melody, emotion and the natural environment have always been important to me in my work as a composer.

My pursuits in the various branches of the arts have also influenced my composing. If I need to name influences, I would not limit myself to music. In addition to the great composers (Johann Sebastian Bach, Ludwig van Beethoven, Wolfgang Amadeus Mozart, Johannes Brahms, Giuseppe Verdi, Giacomo Puccini, Richard Wagner, Franz Schubert, Robert Schumann, Sergei Prokofiev, Arnold Schönberg, Alban Berg, Dmitri Shostakovich, Olivier Messiaen, Jean Sibelius, etc.), I would name great figures in world history and great painters (Paul Rubens, Anton van Dyck, Vincent van Gogh, Michaelangelo, Leonardo da Vinci), and also philosophers, authors and poets (Aristotle, Socrates, Ludwig

Feuerbach, Johann Wolfgang von Goethe, William Shakespeare, Gabriel García Márquez, Paulo Coelho, etc.).

I write music for my fellow human beings. I wish to convey a higher cosmic energy to them where humanity, friendliness, compassion but also the struggle between good and evil are reflected, from the greatest depths of the universe. Composing, like creativity in any branch of the arts, stems from the compelling need of an artist's sensitive soul to communicate. I have the eternal fire of creativity in my heart. If I do not write music regularly, I do not feel well. In my compositions, I reflect the world around me: people, society, feelings, nature, etc. The natural environment and the warm, cosmic sense of harmony it yields is an inexhaustible source of inspiration for me. And music, for me, is a reflection of the harmony of the universe.

My inspiration also comes from literature, poetry, cinema and my own life experiences, of course. I feel that without a colourful and powerful life experience, no composer can write music that touches his fellow human beings. I wish to communicate the vibrations of my psyche to the people around me, above all their positive energy. I believe that goodness is what keeps the world going. I write music that I myself, as its first listener, honestly and sincerely like. It is an euphoric sensation for a music creator to find that the performers performing the music and the audience listening to it are on the same frequency and receive the music warmly.

My five operas

Having said all that, the subjects for my operas come from the very concrete real world. At the time of writing, I have written five operas and am working on a sixth one, about Ernest Hemingway, and my seventh opera *Metsän henki* (The Spirit of the Forest), op. 94.

My first opera was *Roope, poika, joka ei uskaltanut pelätä* (Roope, the boy who did not have the courage to be afraid, op. 76, 2007). It was commissioned by the Suzuki Opera Studio in Vantaa. The libretto for *Roope* was written by Leena Laulajainen. It is an opera for the whole family with a social message, the story involving communication problems between parents and their children. I have a diploma in orchestra conducting completed in Moscow, and so I conducted the premiere myself with the Amici Music chamber orchestra at Martinus Hall in Vantaa. The opera was performed nine times in all, and the positive feedback we received from schoolchildren for instance in the form of drawings and writings was encouraging. The communication was successful: the opera had spoken to both children and adults.

My second opera, *El Libro de los Reyes* (Kuninkaiden kirja/The Book of Kings, op. 30), came about in much the same way. The libretto, in Spanish, was written by Maritza Núñez. The process was a complicated one, and it took several years to receive its brilliant premiere at the Gran Teatro Falla in Cádiz in Spain in spring 2009. The theatre orchestra was conducted by Spanish conductor José Luis Aranda. On that occasion, I was appointed composer-in-residence of the orchestra and chorus of the Gran Teatro Falla for five years. The opera was performed in Finland by the singers of the Kapsäkki music theatre company (with baritone Juha Kotilainen as the King and soprano Reetta Risti-mäki as the Queen) and two Spanish singers of the world premiere (among others tenor Miguel Durán as Minister of Trade), together with the Hyvinkää Orchestra, conducted by Aranda, at Sello Hall in Espoo. This opera too has a social message, dealing with corruption and kidnapping and criticising the monarchy and the Catholic Church.

My third opera, again to a libretto by Maritza Núñez, was a dramatic monologue entitled *Tango solo* (op. 82, 2010). It tells the story of people who disappeared during the military dictatorship in Argentina through the story of one survivor, a socially excluded Argentinean woman. Soprano Riikka Hakola and the Uusinta chamber orchestra premièred the work with great success under Nils Schweckendiek at Sello Hall in Espoo in January 2011.

My fourth opera emerged in the middle of writing my fifth... which is why I will first write about the fifth.

My fifth opera was *Norppaooppera* (The Seal, op. 86), an opera for the whole family commissioned by the Savonlinna Opera Festival. This commission came to me through an open round of applications held by the festival. It was almost like winning first prize in a competition! Like my earlier operas, this one has a social dimension. The festival had organised a story competition in autumn 2011 in which 80 schools participated. The European School in Helsinki won the competition with the story *Snow and climate change*. This was adapted by author Iida Hämeen-Anttila into a libretto that was completed in June 2012. The story tells of the threatened freshwater seal species (norppa) in the Saimaa lake system, their pups and the negative impact of climate change on their habitat. Winters that are too warm do not have enough snow for the seals to build lairs. The festival also held the world's first ever opera music video competition. In autumn 2012, I visited Savonlinna to conduct my *Norppalaulu* (Seal song, op. 86a) for a recording, which was then distributed along with the sheet music to all schools in Finland over the Internet. The video competition was won by Nepenmäki School in Joensuu. *Norppa-ooppera* was the first family opera to be performed at Olavinlinna Castle. The premiere was on 20 July 2013, and I was pleased with the cordial feedback from children, adults and the press alike.

My fourth opera, *Miksi juuri minä?* (Érase que era, una niña/Why me?, op. 85) was commissioned by the Teatro Británico in Lima. I began work on this opera on a two-month grant from the Kone Foundation in January 2012. This opera too had a libretto in

Spanish by Maritza Núñez. Because I knew that the libretto for *Norppaooppera* by Iida Hämeen-Anttila would not be completed until June, I decided to write this opera about bullying in schools in the intervening six months, despite the fact that because of the video competition I would have to write the *Norppalaulu* extract from scene 1 of the opera in May 2012. *Miksi juuri minä?* was premièred at the Teatro Británico in Lima, Peru on 6 October 2012. Because the final, eighth performance was sold out, a further six performances were given. The Finnish premiere and seven subsequent performances were given equally successfully by the Juvenalia opera studio at Sello Hall in Espoo on 17 January 2014. Here, too, I received a great deal of positive, sincere comments and drawings from schoolchildren.

Pragmatism and collaboration

I do not write my own librettos, choosing instead to trust the professional skill of an author to write a good libretto. This has proved to be a good choice, particularly with author Maritza Núñez. She has written librettos for other composers too, for instance for the opera *Frida y Diego* by Kalevi Aho. I begin work on a composition at the piano, sketching out a sort of vocal scarlet thread with pencil and paper. This is much like I would begin an oil painting, with a dim outline of the image. Only then do I 'colour in' the outlines with harmony and orchestration and type out a fair copy on the computer.

With *Norppaooppera*, I read through the libretto several times and thought about where the musical high points might be. I also considered the casting before talking to the librettist about the actual number of characters that would be needed and their voice parts, i.e. soprano, mezzo, bass, baritone or tenor. The artistic director then selected the soloists, and the stage director had something to say about the casting at this point. In the early days of my writing the music, in autumn 2012, I also met the set designer, choreographer and costume designer. It was obvious from the first that the frightening King Wind would be a bass (Johan Tilli), the main character Lumi Seal would be a soprano (Minna-Liisa Värelä), the Old Roach would be a baritone (Juha Kotilainen), and so on. I first wrote a vocal score so that the soloists and chorus could begin learning their parts in good time, six months before the premiere. Only then did I score the 90-minute work for a large symphony orchestra, in time for the first full rehearsal with soloists, chorus and orchestra.

As soon as I had completed the vocal score of *Norppaooppera*, I invited the soloists to my home for feedback, for instance to report if a particular part was not suitable for their voice. I studied voice for a year while studying in Moscow and enjoy performing as a singer myself, as for instance in the Russian Gypsy romances on the first CD recorded by the Kirkkonummi Female Choir, which I conducted for 15 years. When I write an opera, I sing through all the solo and chorus parts myself to ensure that everything is singable. I edited *Norppaooppera* in this way before the vocal score even went to press. I also contacted the chorus master and talked about changes to the chorus parts. I have always aimed to customise my music for its performers, whether instrumentalists, singers or orchestras, so that it will sound as natural as possible.

This is what I did with the concerto for organ, strings and percussion commissioned by the Organ Night and Aria festival in Espoo (op. 89). Its inspiration was the poem *Jumala on kaikkialla* (God is everywhere) by Edith Södergran. The concerto was premièred by the Orchestra of the Finnish National Opera conducted by Marco Ozbiç and with Ville Urponen at the organ at Espoo Cathedral on 7 August 2014. I worked closely with the soloist to finalise the music before the orchestral score was published.

Because Atso Almila, who was to conduct *Norppaooppera*, could not make the first piano rehearsal at the Sibelius Academy in early June 2013, I conducted the rehearsal. Once again I could draw on my conducting experience, and my singing lessons too, as I sang the parts of the soloists who were not present.

Folk poetry and Finnishness

I have an intimate relationship with the *Kalevala* and other Finnish national themes. I believe that growing up as an immigrant in Sweden strengthened my sense of Finnishness. I even had a Finnish dance band in Sweden. My sense of Finnishness was further strengthened when I went to Moscow for a total of about ten years to study the accordion, orchestra conducting and composition. I wrote my first solo song to a text from the *Kalevala* while studying in Moscow, *Vaka vanha Väinämöinen* (Old and steadfast Väinämöinen, 1978) for piano and baritone. Later, I wrote *Kaksi Kalevala-laulua* (Two Kalevala songs, op. 41, 2002) for female choir and piano to a commission from the Joensuu Female Choir in Finland. Later still, I arranged this work for soprano and piano, and at the request of the choir for choir and orchestra. The latter version may be heard on the CD *Se virtaa siellä edelleen* (Flowing still) of the Joensuu Female Choir. Kantele player Ritva Koistinen commissioned *Two Kalevala-Nocturnos* from me and premièred them at my 50th-birthday composition concert organised by the soloist department of the Sibelius Academy in 2005.

I have plans to write a full-length opera based on the *Kalevala*. The pieces I have written on this theme so far were inspired by the dramaturgical structure of the text, or in the case of the kantele work an old melody from the folk tradition.

The refining effect of opera on other compositions

Operas – along with working with texts in various languages in my vocal and choral works – have definitely had an impact on my other compositions. They have taught me awareness of dramaturgical arcs and extensive musical forms. So far, I have set librettos in Spanish and English. I have also used other languages such as Russian, Norwegian and Swedish in my vocal and choral works. I speak seven languages myself, which has served me well for instance in attending the two dozen composition concerts that I have had around the world. Each language, like folk poetry, has its own tonal world that influences the related music and melodic thinking. Each language has a melody and rhythm all its own, and through composition I can go deep into the structure of the language and explore these properties. I love writing operas, because it is a chance for a composer to use all the soul, colour and talent that he has and to go with the vast, refreshing flow of the art of opera.

The status of the composer and of contemporary opera

It is gratifying for us composers that in Finland public funding and grants from various foundations enable the writing of much contemporary music, including opera. Without this support, much less music would be written. Composing music is very time-consuming, and without grants and commissions not many of us composers could work as fulltime freelance composers, which is what I have done for 30 years now. All of the operas I have written so far were commissioned. It is hugely motivating to know when beginning a long process that there is a producer and a production infrastructure ready to perform the work. The premiere of my next opera, a rock opera, is scheduled for the Teatro Británico in Peru in April 2015. My chamber opera *Metsän henki* (The Spirit of the Forest, op. 94), based on a libretto by Maritza Núñez, to be written with the support of Arts Promotion Centre Finland, is scheduled to be premièred by the Kapsäkki music theatre company in 2016, and my chamber opera *Ernest Hemingway* will be premièred at Sello Hall in 2017. The premiere of my eighth opera *The Blue Moon* (op. 95), libretto by Maritza Núñez, is scheduled to take place in Peru in April 2017.

I believe with all my heart that opera has a future. The experiences gained through performances of my four family operas have convinced me that new generations must and can be brought up to appreciate classical music and opera. It is important to write operas intended for children and adolescents. Both they and contemporary operas for adult audiences constitute a viable alternative to the American-driven global entertainment industry that would otherwise overwhelm the already marginalised genre of classical music.

Opera – an impossible art form

Or an unexplored renewable source of fascinating possibilities?

Jukka Linkola

My relationship to opera stems from my childhood. I have always loved the mysterious coexistence of music and theatre. Opera is the apex of the pyramid in this curious union.

But what exactly is opera?
Opera is generally understood to be a story told through singing, acting and instrumental music, and of course by visualisation with all possible means.

It involves the transposing of a concept of time and units of time to the universal language of music. I say 'language', although it is not possible in any way to 'understand' this language in the sense that one can understand spoken language, let alone the logic of science. It is not possible to draw exact parallels between elements of music and elements of language. Every person experiences the language of music in their own way.

Music can only ever be felt, and thus it occupies a level different from spoken language. The language of music is encoded in the human genome in some deeply mysterious way that may be forever beyond the reach of scientific study.

There are many kinds of opera, in many musical styles. However, musical style should be no obstacle to an opera engaging in a working relationship with people today. A performance of a Baroque opera today provides an intriguing additional element in that the music works as a Brechtian distancing factor, adding a special spice to the narrative.

As a child, I was fascinated by the plurality of opera, and this can happen even now, though rarely: sometimes everything just comes together on stage with such synchronicity that the fullness of the art just overwhelms you in the audience.

Is this overwhelming sensation what Wagner had in mind? Wagner's notion of a comprehensive artwork (*Gesamtkunstwerk*) was a brilliant concept. Today, this concept can leverage the vast technological potential at our disposal, and a visual fantasy world that can be created with modern means is a veritably inexhaustible treasure trove.

Can opera be art for everyone?

I think so, and this is what we should strive for if productions are funded with public money. Bodies relying only on private funding can of course do whatever they please.

It is of vital importance that contemporary operas be written on subjects that are relevant. The story must work dramaturgically for the people of today's world; we cannot live in a museum. The story should not be too labyrinthine. If the plot is too obscure, viewers will be left unmoved. I believe that there are unwritten laws of drama to which, say, the dramas of Shakespeare or folk tales shaped over centuries conform.

The goal of every artist should be to attain the emotional level in art. If music does not touch listeners, they will not want to hear it ever again. Good music always conveys both an emotional enjoyment and a deeper, intellectual enjoyment and fulfilment, connecting with the soul over a broad spectrum. It is lovingly tender on the ear and on the brain.

A constructive and self-sufficiently complex score may bewilder and alienate an opera audience, but if the production and the performers manage to captivate them anyway, then the opera can be deemed a success and a worthwhile experiment. What is interesting here is to note that an opera can work even if its music is incredibly dense and 'difficult'. There are no rules or laws on how to write an opera.

The feeling of 'here and now' should be the goal even in productions set in the past. After all, in architecture and interior design one may find a 17th-century cabinet in perfect harmony with an otherwise modern décor. Composers in the 21st century have a staggeringly broad range of means at their disposal compared even with their Romantic predecessors. Because of this, opera can never be killed off – opera is immortal.

As a child, I would write imaginary operas, many of which later turned into musicals, or *Singspiels*, to use the German term applied to stage works with both sung numbers and spoken dialogue. The idea or inspiration for these usually came out of a sort of rapture, a 'blessed state' if you will, where the laws of improvisation govern the making of music almost compulsively. When you realise you have written some music that you think is really good, the resulting physical sensation is almost like an orgasm. I can never explain afterwards exactly why I wrote what I wrote. Intuition dominates, and I feel a composer must trust his intuition implicitly. Inspiration may come or not, it cannot be commanded, although the celebrated Finnish author Paavo Haavikko once said jokingly that "the best inspiration is a well-paid commission".

I have always been drawn to subjects with dramatic strength and high tensions. In order to pick a story to work with, the subject and the mood of the text must have a powerful effect on me. For instance, ever since my youth I have felt that the folk poem known as the *Ballad of Elina's death* was an opera waiting to happen. The national dimension and identity may be important for some people, but I believe that good music can emerge without any such underpinnings.

Dramaturgy

In an opera, the dramaturgy of the music must be subtly insinuated into the dramaturgy of the text and the narrative. I believe that the libretto must be completely finished and polished before the composing proper begins. After all, sentence structures and sentence lengths govern the phrasing of the music to a large extent. A critical 'parlando' reading of the text before a single note has been written down is useful for eliminating unnecessary words. Explaining things and events from many different angles is all very well in a novel but may stretch out an opera to unnatural lengths. The history of music shows that operas tend to get cut and restructured while the work is in progress. Deviations are also traditionally allowed for instance at high notes in arias, if only for reasons of occupational hygiene. I feel that simplifications are always justified if thereby we can avoid making the listener feel uncomfortable.

Too much text is always a problem. We may roughly say that in an opera libretto 15 pages of text translates to about 60 minutes of music. Many librettists seem pathologically unable to grasp this fact. The sad truth is if that a new opera today lasts for more than three and a half hours, it is too long. We need only look at how challenging Wagner's operas are to stage. I have seen a number of amusing video recordings of Wagner operas where the shots of the audience reveal the listeners to be dazed, or indeed fast asleep. Opera festival audiences may take the opportunity at performances to catch up on sleep, as opera tourism with all its evening activities is really quite tiring.

At the risk of sounding snippy, my view is that many contemporary operas commit the sin of boredom with musical meandering, endlessly spinning out things and lacking even the most basic dramaturgical rhythm. To be sure, some such works have received international awards – kudos to their creators for that!

Work

Surprising though it may seem, I continue to use nothing more than pencil and paper along with my brain to write music. After trying out several notation software packages, I have been unable to orient myself to using the computer even just as a music typewriter. I usually sketch out ideas at the piano, which I find a pleasant way of working. I first write out a piano score or short score where features such as pedal tones can be tipped in. These first versions are usually full of orchestral ideas, key harmonic elements and, most importantly, tonal pick-up points. Singers always have to be helped. Only a small percentage of singers have perfect pitch. I always write out the final full score without an instrument; I can hear the orchestra in my head exactly as it should sound and can write what I hear. Many composers prefer to listen to the crappy output of a computer or a sequencer. My feeling is that machines lie so heavily that the disadvantages outweigh the benefits. Your experience may differ, of course. I always collaborate with the singers if at all possible, even after the premiere. In *Robin Hood*, for example, I wrote several alternatives in places. Sometimes one finds that a particular passage is uncomfortable for a certain voice type. I believe that any composer who is not yet dead and buried has the right and indeed the responsibility to step in and make the rough places plain.

Finland

I see Finland as one of the world's most important and most highly developed opera countries, which is nothing short of miraculous considering our population!

There are many reasons for this. Our culture enjoys public financial support, and education and training are of high quality and affordable. Every opera ticket is heavily subsidised by society. Many Finnish composers have been commissioned to write operas, for Finland or for abroad. I myself have written ten operas to commission. As each such project takes up between 5 and 18 months, I have spent ten years of my life writing operas. Since my composing career has lasted 40 years, opera accounts for 25% of my work, although in recent years (2000–2013) the figure has been as high as 80%.

I have been privileged to work with opera abroad, as there is interest in my works beyond the borders of Finland. Many of my works have also been recorded, *Robin Hood* and *Hui kauhistus* (One Spooky Night) on DVD and *Matka* (The Journey) on CD.

Outlook

My operas have had a decisive influence on all my output. The timelines of opera projects have taught me to play the long game. An opera is like a marathon, a long and arduous journey. But on the very next day, once the fatigue has dissipated, you want to do it all over again. After each opera, climbing this mountain and writing this seemingly impossible amount of music has seemed easier. A composer should not be afraid of work, because that fear inhibits the freshness of the creative process and complicates things. Anyone writing extensive works (symphonies, operas, concertos) must stick with it, lonely as it is. You must love what you do. And this is something that you cannot do on the side; it requires full-time commitment.

I am thankful to the Finnish government for allowing me to focus fully on doing what I consider important: in 2012, I was appointed an Artist Professor for a ten-year period.

Future

Mozart is still going strong,
Verdi is still going strong,
Puccini is still going strong...

Why shouldn't there be contemporary opera? Some works always sink without a trace, that is a simple historical truth. But there are always gems that will remain and survive unto the next generation. Someone in the future will always be looking for such gems. As do we when we are young.

What price an experience?

ULJAS PULKKIS

The art of opera

For me, opera is one of the greatest achievements of Western art. No other art form moves me as profoundly as opera does. It is a comprehensive experience that at its best completely immerses the viewer, to such an extent that you wish that the performance would never end. Many operas work equally well if listened to on disc. Simply knowing that you are listening to an opera makes the imagination race and prompts images of staging in your head. But if we took the music out of an opera production and converted it into a stage play, everything would suddenly seem stilted and artificial. Contrariwise, even many of the very best stage plays almost cry out for musical support, and music is often used to enliven them.

In our day, the art of opera in its most impressive form is in danger of withering. This is understandable in some way, as no other art form is nearly as expensive to produce, especially if we calculate the costs per viewer. As recently as 100 years ago, opera performances were grand and spectacular occasions on which both public and private money were cheerfully spent. In its heyday in the mid-19th century, opera was a great business. Today, what used to be the function of opera is performed by Hollywood films. The cost of producing a major Hollywood film easily outstrips the government budget of a small country, yet they still make a profit. And the reasons why they are profitable, why people go to see them, are the same as they were for opera once upon a time: films move people, and seeing a film in a cinema is very much a comprehensive experience, with music and all. I believe that Hollywood owes more to opera than it does to drama or literature.

From the composer's perspective, we might deduce that everything was fine until the middle of the 20th century, after which it has been downhill all the way. However, the art form has been not so much declining as reshaping itself, just like every other art form has always done throughout the history of humanity. It is up to the composer to consider to what extent and how he or she should contribute to such change. Opera is a gratifying art form in that a single work may have an unusually wide impact on all branches of the arts. Opera in its most impressive form – a grand, full-length work for orchestra, choir and soloists, performed for an audience of thousands – is a rare beast; new works appear much more rarely than, say, new orchestral works. Therefore every new opera is a statement and an element in the definition of what contemporary opera is. You can say of an orchestral work that it is not what today's orchestral works are like, but you could never say that of an opera. New operas are rare, and every new opera is exactly what opera is today.

Four works

I have written two operas and two opera-oratorios. Here is a brief description of each:

1. *Neito* (The Maiden) is a 75-minute work for symphony orchestra, male choir and two women soloists. It is a setting of the tale of the Maiden of Pohja from the *Kalevala*, with a libretto I wrote myself. *Neito* was premièred at a season ticket concert of the Finnish Radio Symphony Orchestra.

2. *Syrsor och myror* (Crickets and ants) was written for the 125th anniversary of the Society of Swedish Literature in Finland (SLS). It is a 40-minute work for symphony orchestra, mixed choir and male and female soloists. The text is based on the old fable of the grasshopper and the ant, the libretto being written by Bengt Ahlfors. The work was premièred on the main stage of the Finnish National Opera and was dramatised. The production also included dance, with choreography by Kenneth Greve.

3. My first proper opera was *Viisi naista kappelissa* (Five women in a chapel), a 65-minute work for a sinfonietta orchestra and five female soloists. The libretto is based on a play by Arto Seppälä about a dead man mourned by five women and was written by Erik Söderblom. The work was premièred at the Helsinki Festival.

4. My second opera is on a wholly different scale: the full-length opera *Kekkonen*, which clocks in at 2 hours 10 minutes. It is scored for symphony orchestra, 12 soloists, mixed choir and children's choir. The opera features the most memorable moments in the life of the late President Urho Kekkonen. The libretto was written by Lasse Lehtinen, and the work was premièred at the Ilmajoki Music Festival.

Is an opera just Chinese whispers...

An opera is a collaborative effort. It is not the sole responsibility of the composer, nor indeed to the composer's exclusive credit. A modern opera works on several levels that may be followed simultaneously or separately. Creating an opera is an intriguing process that sometimes resembles a game of Chinese whispers: first the librettist alone or with the composer finds a story, book or play suitable for converting into an opera. The librettist writes his or her interpretation of that source into a libretto. At this point, the librettist probably certainly has ideas about where the music could be slower and aria-like and where intermezzos should go, whether the music should be fast or slow, where the voices could be superimposed, and so on. The librettist produces 10 to 30 pages of text.

Once the composer gets his or her hands on the libretto, it very rarely survives the process intact. The intermezzos will not go where they should, and sometimes music completely contrasting with the text is required for dramatic effect. Arias commonly require less or more text than the librettist imagined, and entire scenes may be deleted or added as the process goes on. The finished composition is the composer's interpretation of the libretto, perhaps 300 to 700 pages of full score.

When this falls into the hands of the director, the director finds himself or herself either following or contradicting the stage directions included in the libretto while taking into account the dramatic requirements of the music. The director has considerable power in shaping the mood of the piece: for instance, having Salome sing her famous kissing scene to a banana would scupper both the libretto and the music. Today, a director's interpretation of a score rarely matches what the composer or the librettist would have wanted. The score submitted by the composer can make the director's job very easy or incredibly difficult: an oratorio-like score full of through-composed text gives much less for the director to play with than a score with staging awareness.

The set and costume designers work in parallel with the director. Their artworks are subordinate to the staging, even if they are designed before the director begins his or her actual work. Yet a striking set can prompt a gasp in the audience when the curtain goes up, before a single note of music has been played or a single person appeared on stage. With today's technology, lighting is becoming as important as sets.

Once the director is finished, it is up to the conductor to interpret the work. The director rarely has any influence concerning tempo relationships or dramatic buildups. The vocal soloists also each provide their own interpretation, and the conductor principally listens to the soloists' wishes regarding tempo and intensity.

...or a joint artwork?

Considering all the work the results of which are visible on stage in a performance, it is entirely possible to watch a production several times and find new things each time, perhaps focusing in turn on the story, the directing and the music. For me, contemporary opera is at its best when instead of Chinese whispers we have genuine interaction among the creative artists involved. A costume designer may say something about a costume intended for a particular soloist while the music is still being written, and the composer may then take this visual cue and run with it. The librettist and composer must obviously collaborate, but the director may also work with the librettist to avoid clashes of interpretation.

Every opera composer must be familiar with the feeling of jealousy that erupts when you see a director's interpretation of an opera that you have written. There are historical reasons for this, but it is also due to the disparity in the amount of time spent by each person in the chain. The librettist works for maybe a month, the soloists for about two months, the director for two to three months, but the composer takes about two years to write a full-length opera. During those two years, the composer becomes immersed in the subject and acts out the action of the opera in his head time and time again; he may even come to believe that the events in the opera actually happened to him. A completed score is the composer's baby, which the composer wants to guard from all harm. In writing an opera, a composer must constantly remind himself: This work is not only mine. The very word 'opera' is the plural of the Latin word 'opus' (work), indicating that an opera is a collection of works performed simultaneously.

About the libretto

An opera libretto is subject to much the same rules as the music. The librettist must absolutely have an awareness of how music works and of the history of opera. A ten-page opera libretto cannot hold as much information as a ten-page short story. The librettist's most important job is to dish out new information in appropriate doses. Music works much like language, and in setting text it is a good idea to have the music follow the language. The opposite approach would be a special effect, not something you could use as the default. What this means in practice is that if every sentence in the libretto contains new information that is relevant for the plot, then for every sentence the music must also contain something new. Text with a dense information content almost begs not to be set to music, because there seems to be no room for it. This can be deduced from librettos written by composers themselves: Wagner for instance narrates the same events over and over again. Composers like librettos where the story progresses slowly and the focus is on emotions, not action. I think that a composer cannot write his own libretto. Opera is by definition a joint artwork, and an important component is missing if the text is completely subservient to the music, which is what happens when a composer writes lyrics to his own music.

Librettists have had a considerable amount of influence on the development of opera. The dichotomy of serious and comic opera, which was strictly observed for a century, was largely determined by Metastasio, a librettist who separated *opera seria*, or elevated art, from the comic *opera buffa.* This distinction helped audiences understand operas better, as it was clear to everyone from the start what any new opera was about, what kind of characters there would be and whether the story would end happily or sadly. In 18th-century opera, librettists were also directors and stage managers. It is illustrative that the poster for the premiere of *The Magic Flute* states in large type *"The Magic Flute*, a grand opera in two acts by Emanuel Schikaneder", followed by the names of the singers and actors – and at the very bottom, in small type: "The music is by Mr Wolfgang Amadé Mozart." There has been some movement back in this direction in modern times, and with good reason. When a new opera is premièred, it is usually credited equally to composer and librettist. It would still be very unusual to see the librettist get higher billing than the composer, though.

About opera in our time
Resources
Opera is a curious art form in that it did not evolve – it was invented. At the turn of the 17th century, a consensus emerged to revive ancient Greek drama. It was decided that all the dialogue should be sung and accompanied by an orchestra. The era was open to innovation, and the new art form was welcomed with enthusiasm. Opera was born out of a merger of old and new in suitable proportions: there was much that was new in it, but also much that was old and familiar. And, of course, people were ready to invest huge sums of money in artistic development back then.

The next giant leap in the development of opera came in the 19th century when entire cultures competed in who had the most advanced arts. Up until the 18th century, Italy had effortlessly dominated the arts, but with the advent of Bach, Mozart and Beethoven it was clear that Germany had risen to the top of the field in orchestral music. Italy had to invest in something to keep up with the Joneses, and that something was opera. Indeed, in 19th-century Italy opera became a matter of pride for society at large, from the nobility right down to the peasants in the fields. But the rest of Europe was not content to stay still either. The German cultural sphere, having gained the upper hand in orchestral music, developed a need to dominate the world of opera too. The reform of German opera began with Meyerbeer but came to be identified with Wagner. Richard Wagner was the Steve Jobs of opera: he gave the public not what they wanted but what they did not yet even know they wanted.

The struggle for primacy in opera caused opera to develop at a rapid pace, because plenty of resources were thrown at it in Italy, France and Germany. Indeed, in Italy writing operas was such a lucrative business that any given opera house might have more premieres of new operas than old productions in their repertoire in the course of a season. Italian composers of that era – Rossini, Donizetti, Bellini and somewhat later Verdi – were national heroes and died rich. Opera houses fought each other for premieres of operas by the most prominent composers, and even two new works by the same composer might be premièred at the same opera house in the same year. Composing operas was quick and prolific in those days. Today, there is no such healthy competition between national cultures, at least not in the area of opera. Finns do not take pride in Finland producing better contemporary operas than Sweden, and Canadians are not hellbent on closing the gap with the superior opera productions of the USA. All new Western operas are shared property: successes are enjoyed together, and everyone is satisfied. Is this perhaps a bit dangerous?

By the middle of the 20th century, the era of the great opera composers was over. Puccini died in 1924 and Richard Strauss died in 1949, but a number of composers continued on the path laid out by them. However, there were already too many works in the grand style to allow for any more to be performed. The repertoire of opera houses was – and indeed is to this day – dominated by Wagner, Puccini, Verdi and Mozart. If venturing beyond that, the next names on the list would be Rossini, Donizetti, Richard Strauss and Bizet. There is a long list of brilliant opera composers, and after that come new contemporary operas, at the bottom of the list back then as they are today.

The closer we came to the millennium, the less people thought of opera as the most effective art form of all. No one whistles opera tunes at work any more, as in 19th-century Italy, and opera composers are no longer the most famous people in the world, an epithet that the *New York Times* bestowed on Puccini at the turn of the 20th century. As opera gradually lost its influence, works began to emerge that could be construed as a cry for help on behalf of the art form as a whole – works that sought to stimulate all the senses so aggressively that the result is quite terrifying. A case in point is the opera *Die Soldaten* by Zimmermann.

Scarcely any operas written after 1950 have entered the core repertoire of opera houses to rub shoulders with the classics. Exceptions may be found in young musical cultures such as in the USA and Finland, where performing domestic operas written after the 1950s forms a component of national cultural identity.

Opera needs volume in order to develop; every opera house should commission and perform at least four operas per year, not one every four years. Worries about audiences staying away in droves are unfounded, because as history has shown, audiences do not necessarily know what they like. Car manufacturer Henry Ford said that if he had conducted a consumer survey as to what kind of transport people wanted, the finding would have been that they want a faster horse. A shortage of premieres denies new operas a vital opportunity: the opportunity to fail. New and innovative art does not necessarily immediately catch on, and as history has shown (again), a composer's first opera is rarely his or her best. Who today can even remember who wrote such utterly forgettable operas as *Der Kampf mit dem Drachen* (R. Strauss), *Oberto* (Verdi) or *Männerlist größer als Frauenlist* (Wagner)?

Shortage of resources has contributed to the revival of a genre popular in small circles in the 19th century: chamber opera. The majority of new operas, or works billed as operas, written after 2000 are chamber operas with one or two soloists and an ensemble of only a few musicians. In such productions, the music becomes less important while the importance of the libretto and the director remains unchanged. The production is thus more democratic, but the composer is deprived of the opportunity to create the unique wash of sound enabled by a large orchestra and chorus, which can be devastating in and of itself. In the absence of this power, effectiveness must be sought by more subtle means, and often this means that the composer must collaborate with the librettist and the director more closely while writing the music. Today not only composers but also opera directors earn their stripes in small-scale productions, where director and composer are on a more equal footing. Together with new productions of the classics, this trend has served to raise the status of stage directors in opera. A century ago it would have been inconceivable for a director to be acclaimed for an excellent production.

About reform

One of the most significant reforms in the history of opera as far as composers are concerned happened in the mid-19th century, at which point conductors increasingly began to assume overall responsibility for opera productions, including both coaching the singers and rehearsing the orchestra. This trend emerged in both the Italian and German language areas. The conductor taking responsibility allowed composers to write more complex music, and this had far-reaching consequences. The most significant difference was that it was no longer possible to speed-write an opera in two weeks; a new standard had been set. It became commonplace for composing an opera to be an extensive project that might take anything up to several years.

It has always been the duty of the composer to take the art of opera forward, but this should happen by feasible increments. Many ground-breaking works involved a single innovation: Mozart's *Don Giovanni* was apparently a comic opera yet did not have a happy ending; *La traviata* invited the audience to identify and sympathise with a golddigger courtesan; *Tristan* deprived listeners of the security of an identifiable key; and in *Salome*, a scene where the title character kisses a severed head is set to the loveliest music imaginable. These are small steps and do not even attempt to reform all of the parameters of opera at once. There are plenty of parameters in opera, after all.

Modern orchestral instruments were designed to play tonal music, modern opera singers have been trained to sing Wagner and *bel canto*, and modern audiences have grown up on a diet of historical classics, not world premieres. These are points that should be taken into account when writing music for these forces and these audiences, but that does not mean that the composer needs to surrender to them. If an opera written today is musically atonal and deliberately difficult to sing and sets a libretto that contains no traditional drama at all, it forms a powerful statement against everything that the art of opera conventionally stands for. If an opera libretto contains no conventional sentences or identifiable plot, or perhaps no words that are actual words in any language, it may by analogy be construed as a statement against opera librettos.

About opera in the future

In considering a new opera, it is obvious that the topic is of paramount importance. Wagner was quite uncompromisingly anchored in his German mythology, but Verdi received reams of libretto summaries to consider. Puccini, by contrast, spent a lot of time searching for dramatic topics or plays on which to base his operas. When we consider what a huge amount of work goes into creating and producing an opera, the story that forms its foundation must be absolutely solid before we can even think of erecting such a massive edifice on top of it. While the characters in operas have changed considerably over the centuries, the conventional laws of drama that go back to Aristotle's *Poetics* still apply. If there is no culmination in a drama, it is difficult to sustain. Drama requires conflict, and the audience must be given space for understanding things on their own. All this requires an exquisitely sensitive understanding of the process and the objective. It would make no sense to put hundreds of people to work for months on a whim just to try out whether an idea would work or not.

For the future, I would like to see opera being developed specifically as a joint artwork, drawing on the latest innovations like always through history. Opera productions should involve more visual artists: specialist in computer graphics, 3D modelling and sound synthesis. Cinema and opera should approach one another on an equal basis, not just by using film as a stage backdrop. A libretto could be written by a team of screen-writers, and the librettists, director and visual designers should have right of refusal concerning the music. All this should be executed in a top opera house in a large city and as performances running right through a normal season, not at a specialised festival. Opera houses should dare step away at least for a moment from their Classical-Romantic repertoire and focus on art that is creating something new, at the risk of failure.

What is the cost of music?

In writing operas, I have come to appreciate the human voice differently. In my first vocal works, I imagined the voice as a lucid melody, akin to an expressive instrumental sound. My image was that of a vocal soloist as a superhuman star soaring over an orchestra. Consequently, the music I wrote was like the never-ending high point of an aria. I thought I was respecting the human voice, although the result was quite the opposite.

It was not until writing the opera *Kekkonen* that I came to understand the nature of the human voice. It is not like an instrument, it is like breathing: it cannot be fast all the time or slow all the time. I used a simple method: I sang the parts myself before asking anyone else to do so. Naturally, I do not have an opera singer's technique, but I reckoned that if my voice and my body were excessively strained by a particular vocal line, then the soloist would probably be strained too. This is not just a question of range, tessitura or orchestration. Whether a vocal line is straining or not depends on the style of the music, the shape of the phrases and the vowels to be sung. It's the economy, stupid: in a high range, it costs more to produce an [ø] than an [i], and chromatic lines cost more than diatonic ones. So it came down to a cost-benefit analysis: if I was writing a 'more costly' structure, I asked myself whether the desired effect was worth paying the price.

I extend this notion to writing for instruments. Brass instruments operate on the overtone series; they can naturally produce the notes of a dominant seventh chord, which is then transposed down using valves as necessary. The keywork on woodwind instruments is designed so that a diatonic scale is the easiest to play, and chromatic pitches require the use of additional keys. On string instruments, the strings are tuned so that it is possible to play diatonic music with the left hand moving as little as possible.

By analogy, consider a water glass. If a water glass were alive and it had a personality, it would be contented when full and sad when empty. The purpose of existence of a water glass is to contain water. The purpose of existence of orchestral instruments is to play tonal music, because that is what they were developed for. If these instruments had personalities, they would be contented when playing tonal music and stressed when playing chromatic music. Continuing the above economic thinking, as a composer I reckon that the more atonal the music, the costlier it is for both performers and listeners.

This is why the aesthetics of composition that took hold for some time after the middle of the 20th century, derailing the train of development fuelled by Puccini and Richard Strauss, were too costly to survive. Music must be allowed to evolve in interaction between composers, performers and audiences. None of them must be allowed to dictate to the process. Audiences cannot be allowed to demand to hear nothing but beautiful music, and composers cannot be allowed to demand to write nothing but noise. Throughout history, the ranks of composers have included traditionalists, cautious reformers and extreme radicals. Traditionalists sink into the mainstream without a trace, and extremists are dismissed as buffoons. Gesualdo wrote twelve-tone music in the late 16th century, and Wysnegradsky was experimenting with microtonal music at the turn of the 20th century. Both of these approaches were too abruptly radical to gain a following. What music in general and opera in particular needs is cautious reformers who have the skills to take music towards new paths while remaining firmly rooted in our musical legacy. In the 2000s, new opera has fortunately returned to the fork in the road where we went astray on a path of thorns after Richard Strauss and Puccini.

Conclusion

After the four major opera projects that I described above, my ambition is to be able to plan my next projects with more care. I dream of creating a production as part of a team including the librettist, director, soloists, lighting designer and composer. Everyone would have the opportunity to guide the production from the perspective of his or her strengths. Everyone would share in the responsibility but also take credit for the end results. This would result in a true joint artwork, and one that I believe would be more rewarding for the audience too.

"Let me speak!"

The history of the opera *Anna Liisa*

VELI-MATTI PUUMALA

In August 2008, after the final performance of the premiere week of my opera *Anna Liisa*, the production team and I sat in a bar somewhere in Kallio in Helsinki, and I could not stop myself crying. I had a strong feeling that our unique and smoothly running team would now irrevocably break up and that the perhaps most important phase of my composing career was coming to an end. For a few months, I had been privileged to be part of a group that supported me and pulled together to make something remarkable come to life. Writing an opera was one of the greatest and also most difficult things I had ever done as a composer. The difficulties were not so much musical, although there were plenty of musical issues to solve in the long process. The principal problems came from understanding the complexities of an opera production and from having to accept changes by force of circumstance. I will return to this below.

I discovered the play *Anna-Liisa* by Minna Canth soon after my début concert as a composer in 1993. In 1994, I made my first margin notes in my copy of the play concerning the key moments in the drama. To this day I do not know why exactly I selected this play in particular for my first opera. I knew I wanted to set a text with concrete people, action, tensions and compelling emotions. I believe I was looking above all for a play that works through the experiences of the individuals depicted. The pressures bearing on Anna Liisa stemming from the dilemma between the dark secret she is harbouring and her virtuous appearance appealed to me strongly. Anna Liisa is an individual, and she is also profoundly alone, and this tension eventually tears her apart. In the strongly Christian agrarian society of late 19th-century Finland, the only escape from such a dilemma was suicide or throwing oneself on the mercy of God to seek forgiveness.

Anna Liisa attempts both of these, and the scene where she connects with her God had a powerful effect on me. However, the way in which Canth had written the scene did not give me the tools I needed to handle it. Yet this was one of the first scenes for which I began to sketch music, although those early sketches never made it into the finished opera. I was looking for a lucid and clear harmonic colour that would match the mood I had found in the text. A lucid harmony in the upper middle register (an upper pentatonic cell softly fractured by a lower pentatonic cell) created an exposed, pure sonority that matched my impression of this encounter between a human being and God. Although I ended up discarding this particular sonority, the discovery of this sound was an important moment in the composition process: the work had begun. Another impressive moment was the scene where Anna Liisa's secret is finally revealed to her parents. Canth's version of the scene is somewhat heavy and slow-paced, but its inevitability and the horrified realisation of the parents made it a devastating moment. I was obliged to condense and intensify the scene in terms of its text and particularly its music, but I already knew that this would be an intense scene. I could already see Jorma Hynninen brandishing an axe and shouting "You serpent, I'll kill you!" At the time, I of course had no idea that Hynninen would ever perform the role, but from the very beginning I saw Kortesuo as played by Hynninen. It was extremely fortunate that Jorma eventually created that role, after several twists and turns.

I began the opera project in the late 1990s by starting to plan a libretto. Pekka Hako saw how advanced my ideas for adapting a libretto from the play were and suggested that I write the libretto myself. My initial idea was to retain Minna Canth's language and only resort to cuts and cautious editing of the most archaic phrases. This idea actually hindered my development of the libretto, because it was not until much later that I realised that while retaining the original language is a value in itself, the libretto nevertheless required text that was not found in the original play and did not even have to be by Canth herself. First, I had to decide what this opera would be about. You cannot make an opera libretto out of a stage play by just cutting and condensing. You must know what it is you are about to create, what the topic and themes of the opera will be; what forces the main characters represent, what their aims are and what their functions are in the drama.

I had been working on the libretto by myself for quite some time before I dared show it to director Atro Kahiluoto, a family friend. With him I had my first serious discussions about the themes in *Anna Liisa*. Atro introduced me to Erik Söderblom, and this meeting was a milestone in the history of the work. Erik had adapted and directed a production of *Anna Liisa* himself as a young man, so he was well acquainted with the play. Erik's excruciatingly probing questions, analysis of the meaning of the characters, consideration of the dramaturgy and empathetic reading of the text helped me move forward with the libretto, sometimes making quite substantial changes to the characters. Erik's questions also made me think about the ultimate reasons why I had chosen this story in particular. Some questions I was able to answer, but I will probably never be able to explain my true motives. And perhaps I would not want to even if I could. Our discussions extended over several years and helped me sort out the basic framework of *Anna Liisa*. I made some quite radical changes for instance to the characters of Mikko and Johannes. I learned to understand the profound loneliness of Anna Liisa and her desire to please her community. I also learned to see her as a modern individual who boldly makes her own decisions notwithstanding the pressures of society at large, even if those decisions resulted in a painful separation from her nearest and dearest and their worldview. I learned to see her as an artist.

Writing the libretto also proved to be a process not unlike composition. Details changed, and a lot of material fell by the wayside even while I was writing the music. Some of the libretto was already being set to music while the rest was still not finalised. The end of Act III had not been resolved in the libretto by the time that much of Act I already existed in short score. For some scenes in Act III, such as the octet, the libretto and short score were completed almost in parallel. This was a very stressful way to work, but at least in this case it was the only option: while writing the music, I was able to tweak and fine-tune the text according to the musical needs of each scene.

My wife, Tiina Käkelä-Puumala, was intimately involved in the writing of the libretto. She patiently read and commented the various versions of the libretto that I imposed on her. Over several years, we had innumerable discussions at our kitchen table about the libretto and about the characters in *Anna Liisa*. Without her support, I would never have finished the libretto. I also asked her to write to bits of text to flesh out Canth's scenes. At some point in the planning, I realised that I needed a framework, a prologue, for the action. I wanted a scene set in the future from the actual action of the opera (and the original play): Anna Liisa is in prison and ponders her relationship with people close to her. I wanted an impressionistic and fragmented text quite unlike Minna Canth's style, and that is exactly the kind of text that Tiina wrote for me. Also, because I had envisioned the role of Husso as being performed by the folk singer Sanna Kurki-Suonio, I wanted to have something of her own for her to sing in the opera. There was a place for a set piece in the hearing scene in Act III, and so I asked Tiina to write a mock ballad that would somehow comment on the action of the opera. Tiina has a sensitive ear

115

for pastiche, and what she eventually produced could easily be passed off as a genuine folk ballad.

By a fortunate coincidence, I received a commission to write the opera. In the mid-1990s, the then director of the Finnish Music Information Centre (now Music Finland), Pekka Hako, was conducting composer interviews that he then compiled into a TV series named *Maestro* for Mainostelevisio (now MTV). After one recording session, he asked me about my future plans. I told him about my opera project based on the play *Anna-Liisa* by Minna Canth. He saw the project as having potential for the Savonlina Opera Festival and took the idea to the artistic committee, of which he was a member at the time. The Savonlinna festival was looking for new chamber operas to be performed in the concert hall excavated into the rock at Retretti Art Centre. Einojuhani Rautavaara's opera *Aleksis Kivi* (1997) was the first opera produced there. *Anna Liisa* was meant to be the next. I was elated and honoured that the artistic committee warmed to the idea and decided to commission an opera from a composer with no prior opera experience who had profiled himself as a composer of challenging instrumental music. The commission was hammered out with Paavo Suokko, the administrative director of the festival, and I signed the agreement in summer 2001. The premiere was to take place in 2003, but instead of Retretti it was to be produced at Savonlinna Hall, which was scheduled to be completed in summer 2002. I believe that Jorma Hynninen played a major part in Savonlinna taking an interest. Because of the Minna Canth connection, the City of Kuopio – her home city – was brought on board as a co-commissioner. The idea must have been to transfer the production to Kuopio at some point. So now I had a commission from the distinguished Savonlinna Opera Festival, and I felt really good about the project.

One of the major challenges in writing *Anna Liisa* was to find a comfortable and feasible approach to Canth's language and to 19th-century people from the perspective of my 21st-century musical idiom. Soon after my début concert in 1993, I found that I was yearning to go beyond the musical style that I had developed up until then. One of the attempts to broach wider horizons was the *Chain* tetralogy (1995–1998), where pseudo folk music and quasi-modal melodies and harmonies played a vital role. The radiophonic work *Rajamailla* (Borderlands, 1998–2001) attempted to assimilate as many musical idioms as possible. In *Anna Liisa*, I was able to continue these developments, or at least to use the experiences to imagine what the musical world of *Anna Liisa* would be like and how to resolve the insoluble conflict between the world (values) of the past and the world (values) of the time of my composing.

The music in *Anna Liisa* is in one of my current idioms, which is atonal and dense and based on serialist principles. But there are other elements added to this basic texture, such as the pseudo folk music melodies and harmonies referred to above. Also, the twelve-tone row governing the basic texture yields extracts and combinations that border on diatonic. There are thus 'alien elements' both as inserts (e.g. the lullaby at the end of Act I or the hymn sung by Riikka and Anna Liisa in Act III) and as developments of my own idiom (as in the scene between Pirkko and Anna Liisa in Act I). What made the composing even more complicated was that while I was working on *Anna Liisa*, my musical interests were already drifting in other directions, away from melodic and harmonic textures and towards noise and sonority. I already knew when writing *Anna Liisa* that the idiom I was using would not be the idiom in which I would write my next works or even my next opera. Somehow the not-quite-of-this-time nature of *Anna Liisa* made me distance myself from my own musical idiom. The works that I wrote in parallel with *Anna Liisa,* such as the piano concerto *Seeds of Time* (2004) and the minor string quartet piece *Credenza* (2005), seem to represent a musical and expressive language quite different from the more traditional *Anna Liisa*.

I began the composition work proper in June 2001 and completed it in autumn 2007. The orchestration was finished by spring 2008. If I recall correctly, I began with Act I scene 2 on a sweltering hot summer day. Much of Act I was written that summer, and I continued to work intensely on the opera for the following year. I eventually had music written for various scenes throughout the opera, though mostly for Acts I and II. The twelve-tone material I had developed for the opera proved very flexible, allowing the extraction of both expressive melodies with wide intervals and innocent diatonic fragments. The twelve-tone row was not the only musical source I used; as the work went on, I added large amounts of other musical material. Analysing all the things that went into the score would require an essay of its own. Perhaps the most important borrowed material came from the collection of folk songs from southern Ostrobothnia collected by Toivo Kuula. I went through these thoroughly and used fragments of them for instance to construct an expansive set of variations for Act III. Rhythmic changes and the merging of melodic cells rendered this much more than just a folk song arrangement – it was more like a modern paraphrase of folk melodies, although with Kuula's spirit still discernible. A similar alienating effect was given to a traditional lullaby used at the end of Act I. Of course, I applied the same merging principle to many of my own musical materials. I did not rigorously apply twelve-tone technique but simply used it as a tool for developing melodic ideas and as a framework from which certain harmonic ideas were derived.

I initially planned to write an overture and sketched it at some length. However, the addition of a prologue led to the abandoning of the overture. I used the core motif of that sketch at the end of the prologue and later at the very end of the opera. The interval material in the overture sketch also yielded a sequence of three chords (quasi-dominant – tonic – subdominant) that I used extensively in the course of the opera. This sequence is not tonal, of course; it is a framework where chords made up of different intervals and hence having different colours create specific effects in the texture.

Writing the opera was an unusually extensive process, although in the context of the history of music it is scarcely unique. It was ultimately a good thing for the end result that the opera actually died at one point. At the time, I of course could see nothing good in this premature death. It felt like the saddest moment of my career: I was losing the most important commission of my life. The management of the Savonlinna Opera Festival had changed, and I had felt for some time that the project was going nowhere. The commission was there, but there was no information on the production, soloists or timetables for a long time. I was left completely alone with my opera project. Then one day I received a phone call from Jan Hultin, the new administrative director at the festival. He said that for financial reasons they would be unable to produce the opera in the summer for which it had been planned.

Composing is a complex psychological process. There are times when the composer finds it impossible to be in contact with other people, because the work at hand has a great many sensitive, vulnerable and uncertain points that are impossible to describe to any other person who does not have an understanding of the nature of the work or a capacity for identifying with the composer's periods of doubt. Such a person would have to have perhaps more faith in the project than the composer himself. By contrast, there are projects where progress requires outside impulses and even some pressure to speed the composing process along. With hindsight, I could have done with some of that when writing *Anna Liisa*, especially at the beginning. Once I found the support, the project came back to life.

Notwithstanding this new development, I aimed to finish the opera by the end of 2003 if at all possible. The premiere of my piano concerto *Seeds of Time* had been agreed to be held in Helsingborg in 2004, and I had to start writing that in good time. I was still working on *Anna Liisa* in March 2004 when I realised that it was nowhere near being completed and that I would have to shelve it for the time being. It was high time to get on with writing the piano concerto, because that was a commission I did not want to lose. When I gathered up all my sketches, short scores and piano score printouts and put them in a folder that I then shelved, quite literally, I felt not at all certain that I would ever return to the project. Some years went by, and the answers I gave to questions about the opera became increasingly vague and anguished. The aborted and apparently failed opera project undermined my self-confidence. At some point, I wondered aloud to my friend, the conductor Susanna Mälkki whether I should abandon the project altogether and declare it a failure. It was becoming a block on my imagination, a bugbear from which I could not escape.

But in the meantime, things were happening offstage, so to speak. At some point, Pekka Hako and I went to the Finnish National Opera to talk to General Director Erkki Korhonen about the project, but this came to nothing. One of the most promising ideas was to produce the opera at Louhos in Nilsiä, an open-air stage in an old quarry where the Cava opera foundation produced operas in the 2000s. The idea of producing my first opera outdoors seemed quite impossible, but the fact that anyone showed any interest at all gave me some motivation. Besides, the outdoor setting with pond and all was really quite inspiring.

In the mid-2000s, a sequence of events was set in motion that eventually resulted in *Anna Liisa* being staged. Pekka Hako and Jorma Hynninen were key players, once again. Hynninen had a close relationship with the Kapsäkki opera company, a tiny outfit whose director Reetta Ristimäki decided after some discussion to take a huge plunge and undertake a project of unprecedented size for them. It was a considerable bonus that the Tapiola Sinfonietta had retained an interest in performing the opera despite the years of delay and a manager replacement. The orchestra decided to incorporate the opera production in its regular programme. Without the artistic and financial contribution of the Tapiola Sinfonietta, the opera could scarcely have been produced at the level of quality that was finally attained. Kapsäkki managed to raise funding for the project, and it all began to look quite realistic. The Helsinki Festival eventually also came on board, providing a venue but not playing more than a nominal role in the production itself. The performances were staged at the Alexander Theatre, which was after all the best possible place for them. After all her varied travels, *Anna Liisa* had found a home.

So now the opera had a production team, performers and timetables, and a venue that would prove to be just right. Now all I had to do was to finish the thing. I had been appointed Professor of Composition at the Sibelius Academy from autumn 2005. During that first autumn term I had scarcely any time at all to write music, and during that academic year I did not complete a single work. In 2006, I wrote one solo song. It was not the best situation to attempt to finish a major work, especially as it had been out of sight and out of mind for so long and I seemed to have lost touch with my day-to-day composition routines. Once the production was in place, I revived *Anna Liisa.* It took me a long time to come to grips with the project again. In January 2006, I wrote the first new music in my sketchbook, beginning with Anna Liisa's song in the Prologue. The work was intermittent, as there were many new things to take care of in my new position, and that took up a lot of my energy. However, as the casting and other practical elements began to fall into place, the project took on a more concrete form. Helena Juntunen agreed in 2006 to take the title role. Erik Söderblom was to direct, and Jan Söderblom was to conduct. During 2007, I wrote as much as I possibly could, and increasingly anywhere I possibly could. I recall writing orchestrations in the back seat of a car on trips to Ostrobothnia, on commuter trains on my way to teach and in airport lounges. Anywhere, in fact, where I could open my laptop and spread out my short scores so that I could punch in a few notes.

The title role of *Anna Liisa* was originally written with the voice of Mari Palo in mind. I had written my first song cycle for her in the early 2000s as a sort of sketch or study for *Anna Liisa*. Reetta Ristimäki then suggested Helena Juntunen, posing me a difficult yet agreeable problem in that I now had two best options to consider for the role. I would have liked to see Mari Palo as Anna Liisa, but I was just as excited to have Helena Juntunen play her.

It is difficult to say how much the replacement of the lead singer affected the shaping of the role. When I began the project, Mari Palo was in my mind for instance when writing the first duet between Anna Liisa and Husso in Act I. By contrast, I was definitely thinking of Helena's expressive voice when writing the duet between Mikko and Anna Liisa in Act III scene 3. A greater change occurred in the role of Mikko, whom I envisioned as a bass baritone almost to the very last. At the auditions, however, it became apparent that no suitable bass baritone was available. Jorma Hynninen and myself had thought of Ville Rusanen as suitable for Johannes, and at the auditions Ville gave a very impressive performance both vocally and in terms of presence. At the suggestion of Erik Söderblom, Ville was cast as Mikko and Juha Hostikka as Johannes. For myself, this change resulted in a huge amount of work, as Ville's voice was higher than the role of Mikko, which I had almost finished at that point. Ultimately, however, the changes amounted to relatively little, even though I had to get rid of all the low-register stuff. As far as the overall sound goes, the change was probably for the better. Not only had I thought of Mikko as a bass baritone; my view of the character had been very close to Canth's Mikko. However, in the writing of the opera Mikko had changed a lot, acquiring more nuances, more conflicts and more human qualities. It was therefore easier and more feasible to bring the soprano and baritone together musically for instance in Act II scene 3. The original soprano–bass-baritone combination would have emphasised the difference between them more. Also, Helena and Ville have voices that match perfectly, and this was perhaps the most important reason for me to decide to re-score the part of Mikko.

Anu Hostikka and Jyri Lahtinen, veterans of several Kapsäkki productions, were cast as Pirkko and the Vicar. The auditioned chorus consisted of voice students and professional singers. In the final stretch, Tanja Kauppinen-Savijoki was brought on board to bring a compelling touch to the important role of Anna Liisa's mother. Jan Söderblom was the conductor, as noted above. I had been working with him since 1994 and could trust him to understand my music, as he was familiar with my idiom. Ville Matvejeff made an invaluable contribution in coaching the soloists and chorus. He also accompanied the stage rehearsals in July and August before the orchestra came in. Without his acute hearing and positive attitude, the rehearsal process would have been much more laborious and perhaps impossible.

With all its preparations and ups and downs, the opera occupied nearly all of the noughties, 15 years of my life if we include the work on the libretto. After this process, I was a different composer. Creating an opera helped to think in large arcs and long time spans, but it also helped me believe that details and nuances play just as large a role in largescale forms as they do in small-scale ones. The opera also taught me mental and physical endurance. It allowed me to form part of a larger creative team. That was perhaps the psychologically greatest difference from anything else I have done. The support and pressure from the team at various stages in the project had a crucial impact on how the opera turned out. And it was a wonderful feeling to eventually turn the product over to the singers, conductor and director for them to do their thing.

I am grateful to the many people who believed in the project at its various stages and dared take a chance on it. Initially, Hako, Hynninen and the then management of the Savonlinna festival for believing in it. Later, Kapsäkki for taking a financial risk on it. The singers for giving up months of their lives and declining safer performance opportunities, especially the wonderful Helena Juntunen in the title role. The Tapiola Sinfonietta for putting a huge number of hours into my opera. And Erik, Janne and Ville for believing in the opera through and through.

This is how an opera should be born. Someone has a story that he believes in. He commits all his expertise to it, taking a risk. But this is not enough: he has to find other people believing in the same goal and also willing to take a risk. A team with a common goal. If this happens, then we can reach both the minds and the hearts of the audience. I continue to believe firmly that the most compelling artistic experiences come from an artist having something to say, an experience of life that he conveys through his art. Entertainment is about anticipating what the audience would like. Art is about presenting well-articulated views. Art loses something of its essence if it aims to please everyone. Audiences are convinced if they are touched. We need individuals who come together to present a well-articulated view of our world, a view that the audience can then assess. Opera is a valuable art form, and therefore there is no point in producing an opera without taking a risk.

How my operas came to be

Einojuhani Rautavaara

I have said that my compositions always begin with an 'atmosphere', a powerful mood or feeling. Such an atmosphere may be found in a very specific situation that may in turn symbolise larger current issues. This was the case with my first opera, *Kaivos* (The Mine). I was in Zurich when by chance I met some Hungarians who had fled their country after the uprising of 1956 had been crushed by Soviet tanks. Their stories gave me the basic idea and setting for the opera.

The setting is often of crucial importance in opera, as witness the primeval Germanic forest with Wagner or the sea in Britten's *Peter Grimes*. But things can work the other way around too: the setting and political background of *Kaivos* proved fatal. I entered it in an opera composition competition at the very moment when Finland's political relations with the Soviet Union cooled (in a period referred to as the 'night frosts') and made it impossible to award the opera a prize or to stage it.

Wagner and Britten had a profound impact on me as I explored the world of opera. I still have a score of *Die Walküre* in my bookshelf in which I wrote a detailed analysis during my studies in New York. But when I include works such as *Pelléas et Mélisande* by Debussy and *Wozzeck* by Alban Berg among my influences, it is clear that these very different works were not 'models' in the usual sense. My appreciation of them was admiration, not imitation.

Auringon talo (The House of the Sun) was also inspired by real life. On one cold winter's morning I read in the newspaper that two elderly Russian emigrant ladies had apparently frozen to death in their house, Solgården (Swedish for 'House of the Sun') at

Littoinen near Turku. The newspaper report of the tragedy and the background of the ladies was enough to inspire the libretto for my next opera.

But at least two of my operas were due to my friend Jorma Hynninen, the lead singer in many of my operas. He persistently asked me to write an opera about Vincent van Gogh, being a keen amateur painter himself. I was doubtful because of van Gogh's celebrity: there were already many books and plays about him, even films. How could I find an approach of my own? But I eventually did, and so far *Vincent* has been staged in four productions in Germany and Austria.

Another topic persistently proposed by Hynninen was Finland's national author Aleksis Kivi. After similar doubts and procrastination, I tackled the subject, and Jorma's voice was of course in my head while writing the title role. *Aleksis Kivi* has been produced not only in Finland but also in Mulhouse and Strasbourg in France and in Cosenza in Italy. In 1990, an English-language version was performed in Minneapolis (although the director opined that the final number, *Sydämeni laulu* (Song of my heart), could only be performed in Finnish). The production at the Finnish National Opera between 2009 and 2011 demonstrated that it was possible to find new approaches to our national author.

Matti Salminen is another singer whom I had in mind when writing a specific role, namely the title role in *Rasputin*. I dearly hoped that he would consent to take the role, going so far as to sit down at the piano in the office of the General Director of the Finnish National Opera and sing Rasputin's evocation of Siberia from Act I to make my point. (The General Director, Erkki Korhonen, remarked: "Well, not the best singing I've ever heard...")

In a new production, the problem often seems to be that the director wants to find an original and different approach. In many cases, the action is set in a different era, which can result in quite bizarre conflicts – after all, it is impossible to transfer music into a completely alien stylistic environment.

I feel it is clear that a composer's operas should not differ stylistically from his other works. This may create an issue if the result is that the vocal texture is exceedingly difficult, with singers required to leap hither and yon in sevenths and ninths (which for the listener is little short of torture). *Kaivos* is largely built on twelve-tone rows, but I developed a technique where the instrumental parts, the 'accompaniment' if you will, is dodecaphonically constructed but the voice parts are simply derived from the harmonies thus generated, selecting pitches so as to maximise expressiveness and vocal quality.

It is fascinating to plan the libretto and music for an opera simultaneously. I have found that not only do the text and action in the libretto inspire the music; sometimes a libretto might lack a final scene but the music written thus far clearly indicated what had to happen at the end and what should be sung there. The music in *Vincent* becomes clearer and brighter towards the end. It would be impossible to end the opera in suicide, although that is what happened to Vincent in real life. A gunshot, whether on stage or offstage, would be banal and anticlimactic. Therefore the opera ends with an apotheosis of life, as we see it in the artist's paintings. Accordingly, the orchestral work adapted from the final scene is named *Apotheosis.*

While writing the final act of *Auringon talo*, it was still not clear to me how the opera should end. The many characters in the libretto and their various problems had to be neatly tied together and resolved somehow. I pondered over the matter in discussion with my wife Sini, and she suddenly said: "Make it a dance!" I do not know what it is exactly that she meant, but eventually I wrote a solemn polonaise in which all the characters, living and dead, join in. Finally, the dance master announces: "Les jeux son faits!" (The revels are ended!)

Modernism typically takes its subjects from the here and now or from the very distant past, distant enough to allow freedom of interpretation. I wrote *Marjatta matala neiti* (Marjatta, Lowly Maiden) for the Tapiola Choir and *Sammon ryöstö* (The Myth of Sampo) for the Helsinki University Chorus (now the YL Male Voice Choir). I could not in all honesty call these operas in the conventional sense, so I decided to call them 'choral operas'.

But the third work in this early-historical trilogy is a proper opera, *Thomas.* It is set in the transition from the era of myths and legends to the historical era. The subject is a gratifying one to write about, because although Bishop Thomas was an actual historical person, extremely little is known about him. This is intriguing when we consider what an important politician and lord of the Church he was for the emerging nation of Finland. An opera librettist thus has very free hands to fill in the gaps in his biography. Even the two historical pieces of information that I used in the libretto – that Thomas had killed a man and forged a letter from the Pope – are from the letter of resignation submitted by Thomas Anglicus and seem purposefully chosen, as they are offences that by canonic law allow resignation from a bishopric.

The central character in this opera is not Thomas but 'the Girl', a mysterious figure who never speaks and only sings in vocalise (perhaps comparable to Ira in *Kaivos*). This character represents a wondrous apparition in my life at the time, my wife Sini, for whom I also wrote the part.

My later title characters Vincent van Gogh, Aleksis Kivi and Grigory Rasputin have such a huge volume of research behind them that there is no room for imagination on part of the librettist. Besides, reality tends to be much stranger than fiction.

It is vital for me to write the libretto myself. I find teamwork difficult, and in the past it has led to failure. The only opera I have ever written to someone else's text was *Apollo contra Marsyas* (1970). Although the sad fate of *Kaivos* had sapped my self-confidence, I was still interested in the art form. I asked Bengt Wall, a Swedish author of my acquaintance, to write a libretto.

What he sent me was a comedy symbolising the modern era, specifically issues of musical style, but set among the gods of Antiquity, *Apollo contra Marsyas*. It seemed like a good idea initially, even if the subject matter was rather alien, and I went to work with gusto. Around that time, the Finnish National Opera announced a composition competition. According to the rules, candidates were required to submit a completed Act I and a full libretto, which I duly did. But the work began to feel increasingly laborious, and having thoroughly read the libretto I found myself losing faith in it. I was prepared to abandon the project and accept that I would probably only be able to set a libretto if I wrote it myself. But then disaster struck: *Apollo* won the composition competition! I would have to finish the damn thing...

I bit the bullet and completed *Apollo contra Marsyas*. It was handsomely staged and quite well received, since the popular-ish, jazz-ish and rock-ish music I had written for Marsyas went over gratifyingly. But I took an important lesson away from this: no more teamwork for me. Besides, there is a huge advantage in using your own text: you can add, delete, change and adapt at will – no need to ask permission or explain or negotiate.

Anyone performing an artwork should remember that the performers are subordinate to the work. An artwork must never be changed for ideological (i.e. political or religious) reasons. When *Rasputin* was revived after a year, cuts were made and the production had been changed. The cuts removed the imagery of the title character being a groping sexual abuser, and the staging eliminated the minor but amusing reference to Rasputin's knack for identifying religious ecstasy with sexual debauchery. The portrait was thus flawed and unsatisfactory.

Tietäjien lahja (The Gift of the Magi) is one of the stories that has travelled with me for decades. I read the original short story by O. Henry in New York in 1955 and decided immediately that I would set it to music when the time was right. The time was not right until 1993, and at that point I specifically wanted to write an opera for TV. It includes a duet where one of the singers is walking on the street and the other is sitting at home. Of course, it is entirely possible to perform *Tietäjien lahja* on stage; the TV version is not canonic. The opera has been performed in concert in Canberra, Australia.

An opera composer would be well advised to write for a small ensemble. An opera scored for chorus, large orchestra and two dozen soloists represents a huge financial risk for any opera house. A small-scale chamber opera always has a better chance of survival. Of course, the four productions of *Vincent* in German-speaking countries that I referred to above would seem to prove the opposite, as the score is quite elaborate, but the popularity of the title character is probably the explanation. *Rasputin*, written for similar forces, was only produced at the Lübeck Opera in 2006 after its premiere production, which was also given as a guest performance in St Petersburg.

Generally, Finnish operas are exported as guest performances by Finnish forces, which are easier to achieve than productions abroad. CD recordings, or preferably DVDs, are essential for the wider marketing of operas. Such recordings have been crucial for achieving productions abroad for many of my operas.

Writing an opera is such an extensive project, taking many years to complete, that it is only natural that operas are mostly written to commission: *Marjatta* was commissioned by the City of Espoo, *Thomas* by the City of Joensuu, *Vincent* and *Aleksis Kivi* by the Savonlinna Opera Festival. *Tietäjien lahja* was commissioned by Finland's TV1, and *Auringon talo* and *Rasputin* by the Finnish National Opera.

An opera is always a marriage of literature and music. In *Vincent*, one might say that visual arts, or at least colour, are added to this mix. After all, the opera is about the life and personality of a famous painter. I wanted to write orchestral works on three van Gogh paintings: *The Starry Night, Wheatfield with Crows* and *The Church at Auvers.* I used three twelve-tone scales with widely differing interval structures as 'pigments': one consisting mostly of minor and major seconds, the other of minor and major thirds, and the last of fourths.

Many musicologists have noted that my output as a whole seems to be a sort of 'work in progress', with the same ideas and textures appearing many different works, in similar guise or slightly modified. (Actually, this method is a venerable one and can be found in the output of many past maestros.) An opera often breeds entire families of works. *Vincent* is a case in point: its music generated my Sixth Symphony, *Vincentiana*, and the finale of that was later published in adapted form as a separate work entitled *Apotheosis.*

Auringon talo later generated the orchestral work *Autumn Gardens*. When I was writing Act I of *Aleksis Kivi*, conductor Markus Lehtinen asked me to write a piece for a foreign tour of the orchestra of the Espoo Music Institute. He was to conduct the premiere of *Aleksis Kivi* as well, and he suggested that I write an orchestral piece based on the material I was working with. The resulting work is called *Lintukoto*, or *Isle of Bliss*, after a poem by Kivi.

In the choral opera *Sammon ryöstö* (The Myth of Sampo, 1974/1982), there is a melody sung by the Mistress of Pohjola, the mysterious call of the North. This vocalise reappears almost note for note in the final opera of the 'Kalevala trilogy', *Thomas*, sung by the Girl. There must be some personal magic in this archaic melody, as it made a further appearance in an orchestral variation in *Näkyjen kirja* or *Book of Visions* (2003–2005).

I do not believe that anyone familiar with my music would accuse me of a lack of imagination. My apparent repeating of myself simply represents the 'work in progress' developing a theme in new environments and new instrumentations. Musicologist Wojciech Stępień writes: "His [Rautavaara's] self-quotes are a spiritual mantra reminding people of the lost paradise that Western art should strive to find."

An opera may yield a song that can be arranged for choir. I adapted an entire choral cycle from *Aleksis Kivi*, *Halavan himmeän alla* (In the Shade of the Willow) for both mixed and male choir, and it became quite popular. From *Rasputin*, I extracted *Neljä romanssia* (Four Romances) for male choir.

Some historians have claimed that the whole idea of opera was the result of a misunderstanding. In Renaissance Italy, Greek descriptions of certain stage performances in Antiquity were understood to have been sung and accompanied – and because there was a drive to revive the idealised culture of Antiquity, this strange art form was duly 'reconstructed' in Florence. But it has survived, through many twists and turns.

Opera has been 'reformed' time and time again, every time with the aim of stressing the importance of drama, of words, of staging – the feeling being that music was overshadowing everything else. This was what happened with Gluck in the 18th century and Wagner in the 19th. In the 20th century, the situation became even more complicated. Anton Webern wrote: "When we abandoned tonality, we lost our principal tool for building works of extended duration."

Opera is a tradition capable of renewing itself. T.S. Eliot wrote: "Individual talents reorder tradition." Talent in itself is not enough to reorder tradition; we need individual talent. And then there is the strange word 'reorder'. Eliot uses the same words as we all do, but in a highly individual way.

Jorma Hynninen, an opera singer with a long and distinguished career, once said: "I have noted that only those operas endure where the dominant element is melody, in a way that touches you and is memorable."

Fat ladies singing in Latin

HERMAN RECHBERGER

When children in a music lesson at a school in East London were asked what opera is, an awkward silence fell until one dared put up a hand and answer, after some encouragement from the teacher. In an abashed whisper, the boy said: "Fat ladies singing in Latin."

Actually, he was not so very wrong – and considering the traditions of the genre, he was spot on. Firstly, what an ordinary consumer not familiar with the world of opera remembers from an opera performance is usually the well-fed ladies (or indeed gentlemen) who favour the crowd with the immortal melodies of opera composers and are rewarded with applause, sometimes even before the music stops. Secondly, regardless of what language is actually being sung, the text is usually not nearly fully comprehensible.

Seriously, though, opera is a serious matter, with the possible exception of comic opera. Opera is about intrigue, kissing, rape, murder and death, all while singing – the last usually at some length. The demise of the art form has often been predicted precisely because it is so absurd. But survive it does, indeed thriving more than ever. In the year 2000 alone, 17 new Finnish operas were premièred.

The demands an opera places on its composer are not so very different from the demands placed by other art forms on their respective creators. It is often said that writing an opera requires a strong sense of drama. My feeling is that if a composer lacks this basic skill, he should not even attempt to write a piano sonata or indeed any other kind of music.

Before discussing my ideas about writing an opera, I would like to present a brief list of my stage works, with commentary.

Part I

Zin Kibaru

An opera for children based on an African tale, written in 1977 to be performed by children or adolescents. The score is partly graphic and calls for a guitar, recorders, violin, traditional percussion, sound backgrounds and instruments made by the children themselves; also soloists, a girls' choir, dancers and two soloists. The libretto consists entirely of gestures; the 'text' is vocalise only. The tale tells of a river spirit that destroys the crops but is vanquished by the singing of one brave villager. *Zin Kibaru* was commissioned by the Kajaanin Tyttölyseo secondary school and was performed several times under the direction of Gudrun Viergutz and recorded by TV2. A puppet theatre version is planned.

Laurentius

The first opera in music history that is completely sung in Latin. (And despite the quip about fat ladies earlier, this is no joke.) I wrote the libretto myself on the basis of sources in the Italian National Library, execution protocols from the Roman Empire and chronicles. It is the story of St Lawrence, a martyr whom the Romans burned to death on a gridiron. The work was commissioned by the Church of St Lawrence in Vantaa for the Millennium Jubilee Year. Another special feature in this opera is that it has no orchestra but instead four synthesisers that create two fantastic sound worlds (they are not used to imitate real instruments). The first of these sound worlds represents archaic early Christianity, while the other represents the military might of the Romans, with a pulsating rhythm akin to rock music. There are sixteen male soloists and a chamber choir.

Aika ja uni (The Age of Dreams)

For the Millennium, the Savonlinna Opera Festival came up with the idea of commissioning an opera jointly from three composers. The commission was awarded to me along with Olli Kortekangas and Kalevi Aho. The format was an opera trilogy, to be linked by orchestral intermezzi written by Kalevi Aho. My contribution was entitled *...nunc et semper...*, a 30-minute cross-section of the history of humanity in Europe. The chorus, unseen by the audience, leads in the action by striking stones against each other (in the beginning there was the stone). Consisting of 12 mini-tableaux, this first part of the trilogy is a sort of 'via dolorosa' of humankind and leads into the second part, an independent mini-opera by Olli Kortekangas about a love story in a totalitarian society. This, in turn, leads seamlessly into the concluding part by Kalevi Aho, which concerns a trial against a 'religious fanatic'. The trilogy was performed 12 times in all across two summer festivals, in 2000–2001. The idea for the libretto came from the author Paavo Rintala, but each composer fashioned his own final libretto. My contribution was scored for large orchestra, mixed choir and some small solo roles. It revels in a plurality of language, drawing on my love for Greek and Latin, touching on my Catholic upbringing and making reference to the Austrian 'saints of music'; but it also highlights the darkest moments of the 20th century that overshadowed my youth. The music moves freely between church, market and circus.

School opera *Noitasapatti* (Black Sabbath)

The Finnish National Opera, the librettist Ilpo Tiihonen and myself developed the concept of a music drama whose roles and chorus parts could be rehearsed independently in a school music class. The Finnish National Opera would contribute one musician (keyboard), two principal soloists – the Judge (baritone) and the Accused (soprano) – a director and props and costumes for each production. As an option, the extra instruments specified by the composer (almost all of the percussion instruments) were to be made by the pupils in crafts class. The project would also include discussions of the ethical implications of diversity in religious education classes and of historical facts about witch hunts in history classes. The libretto is based on an actual event in Vaasa in the 16th century. At the end of the opera, the audience gets to decide whether the prisoner accused of witchcraft is to be condemned to death or acquitted. (So far, she has always been acquitted.)

La piedra de Don

Don Quixote by Miguel Cervantes de Saavedra is the second most read book in world literature. What is it about 'The Knight of the Woeful Countenance' that fascinates us? Perhaps there is a little Don Quixote in all of us, a lone wanderer fondly remembering the good old days, a fighter against windmills of whatever description. Are we not involved every day with Sancho Panza, who does not understand our dreams? Don Quixote is an archetype found everywhere, a fool in his lifetime whom we wish to pardon after his death. *La piedra de Don* is a mini-opera featuring three women who meet around an imagined gravestone to honour a knight who, mad with love, is plunged from one adventure to another. *La piedra de Don,* instead of following the novel, looks at the 'Knight of the Woeful Countenance' through the eyes of his horse Rocinante and the horse of El Cid, Babieca. His importance is emphasised with quotes from the music of señor Luis Milán and señor Diego Ortiz and from the poetry of Federico García Lorca, Nazim Hikmet and Cira Andrés, but also from the poetry of Miguel Cervantes de Saavedra and traditional *canto jondo.* The work is scored for two sopranos, mezzo-soprano, four recorders (piccolo, soprano, alto and tenor), classical guitar, Baroque guitar, flamenco guitar, harp, treble viol and bass viol. All three vocal soloists also play small percussion instruments. *La piedra de Don* was commissioned by the HI!BAROQUE ensemble.

Euridice

Euridice is a reconstruction of the first fully preserved opera written by Jacopo Peri in 1600. The original manuscript only contains the vocal parts and thorough bass numbering. *Euridice* was premièred in concert by the Finnish Radio Chamber Choir, members of the Viva Brass ensemble and soloists from the Sonores Antiqui ensemble of the Finnish National Opera.

The following is a list of my works for the stage that have not been performed yet:

Die Nonnen

My first opera, heavily influenced by medieval music. The libretto is by me. A wandering singer requests accommodation for the night at a convent and through the power of his singing makes the nuns reveal their history before entering the convent. Their stories vary from the agony of love to the murder of a lover. The nuns come from different countries and sing in their native languages. The role of the Singer is to be sung in the language of the country where the work is performed. At the end of the opera, it is revealed that the Singer is none other than the Devil himself. Once they realise this, the nuns return to their devotions, and the Evil One disappears. The melodic material is derived from *Piae Cantiones*, combined with cabaret style and modern composition techniques. Space is allowed for free improvisation. The score was originally (1988) written for Renaissance instruments and voices; the revised score (1990) includes optional parts for modern instruments.

Der Wunschpunsch (The Notion Potion)

This is an opera for the whole family, based on *Der satanarchäolügenialcohöllische Wunschpunsch* (The Satanarchaeolidealcohellish Notion Potion), a children's book and play by Michael Ende. The libretto was written by myself. The story tells of a magic potion that turns all wishes into their opposites. The sorcerer Beelzebub Irrwitzer receives a visit from Maledictus Made, an auditor from Hell, reminding the sorcerer that he has only partly fulfilled his contract with the Prince of Darkness. Irrwitzer has not poisoned enough rivers, destroyed enough forests, manipulated the climate effectively enough, flooded enough rivers, and so on. He has until midnight to 'fix' things. The world is close to destruction by toxins and environmental pollution, but eventually everything turns out all right, and evil receives its just reward. Jakob Krakel the raven and Maurizio the cat save the world from the destructive intentions of Beelzebub Irrwitzer and his aunt Tyrannija Vampyrella. This opera is for six soloists, children's choir and chamber orchestra and involves audience participation.

Das Opernschiff (The Opera Ship)

An opera based on the children's book *Am Südpol, denkt man, ist es heiß* (People think that it's hot at the South Pole). Penguins dressed in white tie and tails await the annual visit of an opera ship from Vienna (!), with an ensemble that will perform an opera for them. The ensemble performs *La traviata*, but in their confusion they forget parts of the text, and the singers improvise a new version of the opera. There is a secondary plot involving generational conflict: penguin uncle Otto, who plays the violin and loves opera music above all, and penguin Leo manage to persuade Lotti, who prefers pop music, to listen to an opera at least once in her life. I used the verse libretto by Elke Heidenreich, which is also available in a Swedish-language version, as it stood. The score includes a small chorus consisting of the minor soloists and a chamber orchestra. The work won 2nd prize in a composition competition for children's operas in Cologne.

Die abenteuerliche Schwalbenreise (The Adventurous Journey of the Swallows)

This opera was commissioned by the OPERA + MORE company in 2006. The premiere was to have taken place at the Theater Spielraum in Vienna on 9 May 2008. The opera was completed as agreed, but the fee was never paid. Funding for the rehearsals, which had already begun, suddenly disappeared. The alleged funding providers for the commissioner and proposed director Reinhard Deutsch had left him in the lurch, and the premiere was cancelled. The verse libretto is by the well-known Austrian author Irmgard Klell. It is a children's opera and tells of the adventures of swallows while migrating to Africa. Some of the vocal parts are written for children, and the opera is accompanied by a small chamber orchestra. The music uses the style of musicals, and there are influences from ethnic music styles (Italy, Greece, Egypt, Africa).

Helike Athanatos (Immortal Helike)

A grand opera in Classical Greek, based on an idea by Andreas Drekis and a libretto by the Munich philologist Franz Knappik. The opera features the earthquake and tsunami that destroyed the city of Helike in the northern Peloponnese and the attempts to excavate the buried temple of Poseidon. The love story of Diotima and Kleanthes forms a secondary plot. Residents of the city at the time of its destruction, they live again in the present day as the city is excavated. The opera is scored for symphony orchestra with the addition of a santouri, a Cretan lute and a synthesiser, a large chorus and eight soloists. The musical material incorporates musical modes from Ancient Greece. The international jury of the Andreas Drekis composition competition, including the Austrian composer Werner Schulze, the Greek composer Spiros Mazis and the German conductor Alois Springer, awarded the opera 1st prize in 2010. So far, only parts of the opera have been performed by German and Finnish orchestras.

Part II

On stage

Ever since the age of six, I have made a habit of being on stage: first in school plays (I even played Juliet once), later as a rock musician, then during my music studies and later playing a number of instruments in two Finnish ensembles (Sonores Antiqui and Köyhät Ritarit). My stage experience has helped me understand how the stage works and how to deal with it as a composer. Sometimes this is more of a disadvantage, as I tend to encroach on the director's territory.

My own libretto

As the descriptions above indicate, I prefer to write my own librettos as adaptations of original texts. Only in isolated cases (such as Ilpo Tiihonen's *Noitasapatti* or Irmgard Klell's *Abenteuerliche Schwalbenreise*, or particularly with verse librettos such as Elke Heidenreich's *Am Südpol, denkt man, ist es heiß*) have I left the writing to the author and used the libretto as it was delivered to me. I feel that intense handling and shaping of the text allow the principal components of the opera – text and music – to interact intimately. The rhythm and colour of each language is very important to me. I analyse text by its rhythm and create a linear map of the text before I set it to music.

Chain of misunderstandings

Nothing is more irritating than a word or sentence with misplaced stress. It can lead to all sorts of misunderstandings. Speaking of misunderstandings... It was a misunderstanding that led to the birth of opera in the first place. People wanted to revive Greek tragedy and imagined that the text should be sung. The result was an art form that became one of the most respected genres of the fine arts in the modern era. Nothing challenged it until modernism – and that too was the result of a misunderstanding. What composers then regarded as the apotheosis of the art form (depicting reality faithfully and illuminating it critically) was considered by audiences to be too demanding.

Neglected operas

There have always been neglected operas. Many works have been overshadowed by their more famous siblings, such as Tchaikovsky's *Mazeppa,* Weber's *Euryanthe*, Strauss's *Danae* and the operas of Smetana and Rimsky-Korsakov; and there are many more which are available on recordings but which are unknown to the public at large. The first operas ever composed, such as Monteverdi's *Orfeo* or Caccini and Peri's *Euridice* or *Dafne*, are rarely performed by opera houses in their standard repertoire. Schubert's one-act operas *Der vierjährige Posten, Die Zwillingsbrüder,* etc., are not standard repertoire. The line of forgotten works includes not just minor works by major composers such as Verdi but also most operas by composers such as Dvořák, Massenet, Schmidt or Zemlinsky.

How I write an opera

There is of course no longer any such thing as a patent formula for writing an opera. Rossini must have been the last composer to write to a formula, and it is telling that he later became a celebrated chef. A composer writing an opera must be far more than a beginner. He must know how the stage works and have an instinct for how much time must be allowed for an event on stage to be effective. This requires both insight and experience. Writing an opera begins with finding a topic. The composer may read novels with a view to whether they could work on stage. The composer may read plays, in which case he must ask himself: what would music add to this drama? If a play works well as it is, why set it to music? How does one resolve the question of whether a particular drama requires music? Or whether a particular novel lends itself to dramatization? For myself, I have to get the feeling that a particular text would make an exciting night at the theatre; then the right music will come to me. I always try to hear the voices of the characters first. I also try to envision the basic mood evoked by the music, the atmosphere. I think about all this before writing a single note. I do not begin at measure 1 and continue to the end; I plan out an entire act beforehand, because I must feel the tension spanning the act. Then and only then can I think out the musical idea of the act. Every act must have a single musical idea that sustains it. Such an idea can be anything: a motif, a rhythmic cell, a play of tonal colour. Having identified such a key idea, I develop it together with the text. I sketch out formal plans and schedules and develop the act layer by layer. Each act is developed like this until the entire work is finished.

Singing someone into the bog

In mythology, music is a gift from the gods that has huge power over human beings. Early cultures in particular believed in the magical power of music. From Ancient China to Ancient Egypt, from the Indus culture to Ancient Greece, the belief in the power of music to influence the human mind and to broaden its horizons was ubiquitous. The Finnish national epic, the *Kalevala*, speaks about music more evocatively than any other national epic. The kantele, the instrument that serves as the symbol of music in the *Kalevala*, was created as the product of a number of recycled natural resources: the sounding board from a pike's skull and the strings from a woman's long hair. The Finnish proverb "music is made of sorrows" should not be understood as a description of the melancholy character of Finnish music but as a symbol of a woman's harsh life. Väinämöinen, the principal character in the *Kalevala*, is a shaman and singer and imbued with a musical gift similar to that of Orpheus, who could make the forest animals and the shades of Hades weep with his song. Väinämöinen was more brutal than that: he sang his opponent into the bog.

But whatever the myth, there is always a story describing the power of music. Examples include the singing of the Sirens, attempting to lure Ulysses and his crew to their doom, and the aforementioned Orpheus putting the watchdog of the Underworld, Cerberus, to sleep with his singing.

Where do the ideas come from?
When I begin to write an opera, my sources of inspiration are much the same as for any other kind of music. Or perhaps somewhat different, as opera is a genre that combines various branches of the arts. Asking a composer about his inspiration is much like asking him to define his creative ability. My answer would be: from the religious perspective, it is an emulation of God's creation; from a more neutral perspective, it is a vital process of renewal. After all, that which does not renew itself does not stay the same but withers and dies...

And what are the tools?
I write music using traditional means and then enter the result into a computer that automates various processes for me. A composer can now be his own music typesetter, much like the invention of the typewriter made the work of authors much easier. We should recall what an enormous amount of work it was to copy out vocal, choral and orchestral parts by hand. Not everything was published immediately back then.

"Play it, Sam"
In recent years, many operas have been commissioned and produced in Finland. Yet most productions are given only a few performances and then the operas vanish without a trace. This applies largely to orchestral works too; audiences always want new things. Our music institutions have fallen into a pattern of demanding new premieres all the

time, and that is after all what we composers are working for. The entire system seems geared towards putting out world premieres rather than creating and performing music. But even as we composers rack our brains to come up with the next new thing, we should remember that all music is new whenever it is performed. Bruno Walter once said: "The worst thing that can happen to music is remembering what you have heard before." Sir Simon Rattle added: "Looking at each other and sighing and saying: 'Oh, that was really wonderful five years ago.' That is the beginning of routine."

Yet it would be so very important to record the unique and rare performances of today's contemporary works, at least once, for future generations.

8,000 hours of opera

Large music encyclopaedias generally contain about 800 articles on composers (alive or dead) who have written at least one opera. To call such a list incomplete would be a massive understatement. What is more, the actual list is growing every day. If we assume five operas per composer (many have written far more) and an average duration of 120 minutes for each, then the result is something like 8,000 hours of opera music. No wonder that opera houses have to engage in a process of picking and choosing.

The halo

I have never retreated into the corner reserved for contemporary music specialists. All of my works, and especially those for the stage, are aimed at finding approval with the public at large. A sensual sound, a dramaturgy that is never boring and the visual impact of the staging must combine to produce a barely discernible halo that surrounds the listener.

Favourites

As a composer of our time, I naturally have a number of historical influences whom I respect but do not admire so much as to want to copy them. I love Baroque opera in general because of its vocal virtuoso brilliance and its scope for improvisation. My favourite opera without question is Mozart's *Don Giovanni,* where the brilliance of drama and music go hand in hand. Other historical works on my list of favourites are the operas of Verdi, which are so obviously Italian in their melodic writing and which contain a dramatic power that still captivates listeners today. And what about today's music? asks a slightly offended reader. Well, I have a long list, from John Adams to Bernd Alois Zimmermann, but one 20th-century opera stands a head above the rest: Korngold's *Die tote Stadt.*

Why do I write music?

Or, more specifically, why do people write massively laborious operas in this day and age, indeed more than ever before, even though the costs of a single performing season at an opera house could feed many composers? If I knew that, my life would probably be in danger, since I would then have to explain it to my colleagues, to much confusion. Perhaps I can sidestep this with a Zen Buddhist maxim: the journey is more important than the destination. And to quote a pessimistic statement from the Austrian composer Olga Neuwirth: "Today the question of why one would choose such a profession scarcely makes sense any more, as composing has become increasingly absurd. I ask myself why I would spend hours on end seated at a desk: the question is no longer for whom I write music but why I continue to write music at all. That is the real question. Ours is an old craft that has become wholly anachronistic and has no place in the world. A composer puts dots on paper."

Craftsmanship is needed

For me, the outlook is not so bleak. A shoemaker or a carpenter also makes things and sells them to make a living. He will not give up his trade even if he has unsold products in his shop. He is a shoemaker or a carpenter in body and soul, just like I am a composer in body and soul. Music will always be needed, and so will good craftsmen. Technology has made composing easier. But good music (also a concept that begs a definition) cannot be made just by reading through the operating instructions for a synthesiser.

The future of opera

A wise person once observed that theatre exists because theatre is for the people who have hidden their childhood away in their pocket so that they can continue to play all their lives without anyone else noticing. The same could apply to opera. Once cannot imagine human life without audiovisual experiences. We live with them every day. Sometimes they are annoying, sometimes irritating, sometimes inspiring and sometimes boring. We all live in a big theatre and play roles in our own lives. I firmly believe that the music drama (including operetta and musical) will remain popular. The future of opera is secure.

Epilogue

Let us imagine an elderly lady asks me what I do and I answer that I am a composer. She may respond: "A composer? I thought they all died ages ago." But no, madam. May composers live and prosper. Long live music; long live opera and theatre; and above all let us raise three cheers to the (well-fed) ladies and gentlemen who perform our creations with enthusiasm and passion to audiences perpetually hungry for drama.

An opera in five acts

Kaija Saariaho

Act I
Memories

Asmall, cramped and hot auditorium, singers downstage firmly rooted on the spot, unintended comedy. Sometimes great voices, sometimes wonderful music, but above all a lack of oxygen.

The ballet performances were more inspiring. I particularly remember *Swan Lake* and *Sleeping Beauty* in the 1960s. Tchaikovsky's music was fantastic, the dancers were beautiful, and I believe I had my first crush on the Prince in *Sleeping Beauty*. Liisa Tuomi in the title role of *Annie Get Your Gun* at the Helsinki Folk Theatre: I admired how freely she moved on the stage, compared with the stiff demeanour of opera singers. The film of Leonard Bernstein's *West Side Story* came to Finnish cinemas soon after it was released in the early 1960s, and its soundtrack was one of the first LP albums that I was given as a birthday present.

Then there was the Saturday afternoon in my childhood home that I spent listening to *Tristan und Isolde* with the score for the first time. It would be decades before I saw that opera live on stage, but the passion, pain and expectation buried in the music and the score remained so sharply with me since that listening experience that none of the productions I have seen have diluted the feeling. It was such an overwhelming merger of love and music. For several decades, I had a photocopy of a page from Act II Scene 2 on my wall: "Isolde! Geliebte! Tristan! Geliebter!"

And then there was the Savonlinna Opera Festival in summer 1975 with Aulis Sallinen's *Ratsumies* (The Horseman), and in the autumn Joonas Kokkonen's *Viimeiset kiusaukset* (The Last Temptations) at the Finnish National Opera. Both were a far cry from the musical language in which I was interested at the time, at the beginning of my composition studies, but both impressed me with their sincerity and depth. The wonderful text by Paavo Haavikko in *Ratsumies* was striking, and the song cycle *Neljä laulua unesta* (Four Dream Songs) related to the opera is in my mind one of the finest Finnish song cycles of all time.

Maa

In 1991, I entered the Finnish National Opera as an employee for the very first time, having been engaged to write the music for *Maa* (Earth), a ballet by choreographer Carolyn Carlson. The seven-movement work was not only the most extensive work I had written to date but also the first I had ever written for the stage. It was the first time I had the opportunity to watch at first hand how a stage production is created with all its elements, above all the lighting. The experience remained with me, and I began to conceive a work for lights and human voices, a sort of spin-off of one of my earliest pieces, *Study for Life*, for soprano, tape and lights. I was thinking of an abstract work that would not have a linear narrative but just voices, lights and possibly a stage reflecting colours and surfaces. I admired the new digital lighting systems that I saw in rock concerts on TV. I imagined a sensitive and precise polyphony of lights following the music. I had read the poetry of Jacques Roubaud and used some of his texts in *Maa* and in *Nuits, adieux* for vocal quartet (both 1991). For the new stage work I was envisioning, I had in mind Roubaud's book *Échanges de la lumière*. Its sections are fictitious documents of evenings where a group of people from different walks of life gather to discuss light, each from their own viewpoint. I had already used extracts from this book in *Nuits, adieux*.

I also reviewed in my mind the various opera experiences I had had after moving to Paris, and even before that while studying in Germany. I began to realise that opera could be defined as a meeting place for the arts, where other branches of the arts deepen and strengthen music.

It was seeing Peter Sellars's production of *Don Giovanni* in 1989 that finally blew up my conception of opera as an expensive and cobwebbed pursuit. On the contrary, to my amazement I found that going to the opera can be a powerful, topical and profound artistic experience that feeds our senses and can even challenge us to think about our own lives more than any other art form can.

Act II

L'amour de loin

My abstract plan gradually receded into the background. I developed an interest in creating human characters in music, realising how important identification is in opera; and identification can only happen through a story. I started looking for a story that would be like a fairy tale but a clear narrative that my musical idiom could fit. Yet I had doubts about starting to write an opera, because my music was so non-dramatic in nature. While leafing through Jacques Roubaud's output once again, I came across a book called *La fleur inverse*, in which, among other things, he referred to the life story of an early troubadour named Jaufré Rudel. The relevant passage was no more than a few lines long:

"Jaufré Rudel de Blaye was of very high birth, the Prince of Blaye. He fell in love with the Countess of Tripoli sight unseen, purely on the basis of what pilgrims to Antioch had told him. He wrote many songs about the Countess, lovely of melody but with few words. Out of a desire to see her, he equipped himself for a Crusade and went to sea. During the voyage, the troubadour fell ill, and he was carried to the convent at Tripoli and left there for dead. When the Countess was told about this, she went to see the troubadour; and encountering her he woke up, regained his hearing and his sense of smell and praised God for giving him strength enough to see the Countess. Then he died in her arms. The Countess arranged a funeral for him and on the same day withdrew into the convent, grief-stricken by the man's death."

The life of Jaufré stuck in my mind, and in discussions that I had about opera I showed the passage to others, asking them whether it might be a subject for an opera. The feedback was largely negative, however, as no one could see the story as containing the sort of drama required for an opera.

There were also several technical issues to be resolved. I had only ever set texts that already existed, carefully selected – or, as I often say, texts that 'select me'. Only few texts speak to me, and I could not imagine carrying the story in any other way than through a narrator. In my mind, I replaced Mozartesque recitatives with spoken texts and had the singers only sing poetic texts, aria-like. I took Mozart as my model in other respects too, and in thinking about the casting I imagined two couples, the troubadour and his lady on the one hand and a more earthy, perhaps humorous couple (friends, servants, etc.) on the other. I heard the narrator as a bass voice, perhaps a pilgrim.

The story expanded into images, colours and scents in my mind. I always seek out contrasting pairs when creating music, and here I was building contrasts outside the music too: the green coast of France and the cool stone castle versus the hot, exotic, heady Tripoli, and so on.

My formal notion was combining a mirror with a closed circle. At this point I contacted Jacques Roubaud to invite him to write the libretto for the opera, and initially he was interested. We worked on the story together. Jaufré's death became the chronological centre point of the tale, from which the narrative continued partly in the realm of death until it returned, dream-like, to its beginning.

I felt I was making good progress with the opera project, and I began to prepare for it by writing music around the subject: a piece called *Lonh* for soprano and electronics in the Occitan language. Jacques Roubaud and myself recorded Jaufré Rudel's song *Lanquand li jorn*, whose text I had found in the French National Library when searching for Rudel's manuscripts. I used this as the foundation for *Lonh*. The piece was written for Dawn Upshaw, with whose voice and interpretations I had been enchanted since the late 1980s. She premièred *Lonh* in Vienna in autumn 1996.

Before that, in August 1996, she had premièred my song cycle *Château de l'âme*, my first work for voice and orchestra, with the Philharmonia Orchestra conducted by Esa-Pekka Salonen at the Salzburg Festival.

The song cycle premiere went well, and I was encouraged to contact Gerard Mortier, the then director of the festival, to offer him my opera project. He was enthusiastic about the idea, but in the meantime Jacques Roubaud had pulled out, and I no longer had a librettist. I returned to Rudel's biography and its dimensions. I thought about compiling a libretto from various sources describing Rudel's life (Heine and Rostand, for instance, had used Rudel's life story in their writings). At times, I envisioned a multi-lingual text operating on several levels. In my vocal music until then, I had often used collages of text fragments, and I had also used this technique for parts of *Château de l'âme* and *Lonh*.

However, Gerard Mortier – probably fortunately for me – would not hear of me writing my own libretto, and so we began searching for a librettist while also searching for a director.

Over the past years, I had become very fond of Peter Sellars's productions, many of which directly influenced my operatic thinking. The aforementioned *Don Giovanni* was a starting point, and then I had seen Stravinsky's *The Rake's Progress* (with Dawn Upshaw as Anne Truelove) and Messiaen's *Saint François d'Assise* in productions directed by Sellars and conducted by Esa-Pekka Salonen in Salzburg. The Messiaen production impressed me hugely and gave me the final push, the self-confidence that I needed – and this was due to the fact that this production was so enormously different from the one that I had seen earlier in Paris.

In discussion with Peter Sellars, Amin Maalouf had emerged as a possible librettist. Gerard Mortier contacted him, and he expressed an interest but wished to finish the novel he was working on first.

Peter Sellars had a crucial influence on the libretto: once when the three of us (Amin, Peter and myself) were talking about the opera, Peter said that I had never once when telling the story mentioned more than three people: Jaufré the troubadour, Clémence and the Pilgrim. I realised that I had never had proper musical ideas for more than these three characters, and Amin was immediately on board with the idea of having a cast of three. The material written for the two characters who were cut ended up in the choral parts.

Working with Amin proved easy. I had feared that the text would not, for some reason, 'fit' my music. But this is not what happened, quite the opposite. Amin's libretto solved the issue of the narrator: no narrator would be needed, as the dialogue carried the story quite naturally.

Years of preparation (including the writing of *Oltra mar* for choir and orchestra while I was waiting for the libretto, material from which I recycled into the opera) meant that actually writing the opera was a relatively short but extremely intense process lasting about 18 months.

The musical material in the opera is divided into three different types of material that behave in different ways, each associated with one of the main characters. I created three harmonic environments, three orchestrations and three modes for the vocal parts. The key dramatic moments are accentuated with the 'Fate' chord, which combines the harmonies of Jaufré and Clémence.

As the work progresses, the harmonies of Jaufré and Clémence evolve from alternation to superimposition. Finally, Jaufré's music merges completely with Clémence's music just before he dies.

In terms of vocal writing, the musical identity of the Pilgrim shifts constantly between the music of Jaufré and that of Clémence. Otherwise, the Pilgrim's orchestration is very clear: his entrances are always preceded by a microtonal string field and a descending flute motif.

L'amour de loin also includes an electronic element, which I executed with Gilbert Nouno at Ircam. Each character in the opera and their music is surrounded by a sound world that forms part of the orchestration.

While writing the opera, I finally understood at least in part why exactly I had chosen this particular subject; something that I had often been asked and could not answer. All the three characters in the opera represented a part of myself: troubadour Jaufré was the musician, Clémence was the expatriate woman homesick for her homeland, and the Pilgrim was the personality attempting to reconcile the two.

The opera was completed in autumn 1999 and premièred under Kent Nagano at the Salzburg Festival in August 2000.

Attending the rehearsals for my first opera was a tremendous experience for me. It was exhausting to be bombarded by the energies of strong artists for five weeks, compared with the largely solitary composing work interrupted only by occasional concert trips and world premieres. Now every note was weighed and interpreted, changes were demanded, solutions were sought, opinions clashed, and the mood was really quite tense at times. I sometimes felt guilty because of the grind the team was being put through on account of my music. I actually fell ill a couple of times, probably out of sheer anxiety. I spent many sleepless nights, and during those I wrote my solo cello piece *Sept papillons*.

However, after all that when I returned to my study in September 2000, it felt very difficult to start a new piece. The collaboration and its results, the wonderful premiere, weighed on my mind. While writing my Flute Concerto I had a new, strong feeling of isolation. For the first time, I realised just how lonely a pursuit composing is and how different my life was from that of performing artists who spent every day of their working lives in the midst of a network of human communications and the maelstrom of positive and negative energies with which rehearsals and performances are charged.

Act III

Adriana Mater

When Gerard Mortier was appointed director of the Opéra de Paris, he contacted me to ask about another opera. I hesitated for a long time. Firstly because I felt that a second opera would inevitably be weaker than the first. There was no rational basis for this argument, only the intuitive explanation that I prefer Berg's *Wozzeck* to his *Lulu* and Ravel's *L'enfant et les sortilèges* to his *L'heure espagnole.* It never even occurred to me that I might come to write more than two operas! Besides, why should I write another opera? Been there, done that. But on the other hand, collaborating with other artists, particularly Peter Sellars, had been so exciting and inspiring that I eventually decided to accept. In the context of stage works, my need for isolation was replaced by an increasingly strong need to open my music up to the world and to allow the world to influence my music. The need to write an opera that would reflect the world around it probably began to grow in me soon after the events of 11 September 2001. My conception of my music as a safe, closed world of my own was shattered. This process had actually already begun at the rehearsals for *L'amour de loin* in Salzburg, which was the first extended period of time ever that I had spent away from my composing and instead just sitting and listening to my music being rehearsed, morning to night, for five weeks. Peter Sellars's directing, which always seeks to make connections with today's world, also had an influence.

In accepting the commission from the Opéra de Paris, I also made a more far-reaching decision to continue exploring the potential of opera and also to continue writing concert music, above all chamber music. The latter of these guarantees that I can maintain an intimate and personal relationship with my music, while opera projects allow me to open up my horizons to external influences and cooperation. Nevertheless, writing music is and remains a solitary pursuit.

The team for *Adriana Mater* was a no-brainer: Amin Maalouf would write the libretto, and Peter Sellars would direct the production. Peter is also the dedicatee of the opera.

For the subject and musical material for my second opera, I went looking for something completely different from *L'amour de loin*. As a starting point, I suggested to Amin that the story should have something to do with motherhood: I told him what a huge experience it had been for me when pregnant with my first child to realise that there were two hearts beating in my body. Amin brought an equally personal element to the story: war and the violence that surrounds us.

In musical terms, I envisioned an idiom much darker and heavier than the translucent orchestration of *L'amour de loin.* I wanted to find voice types that I had not used before, such as a tenor. I eventually gave the title role to a low mezzo. Unlike *L'amour de loin*, where the two female roles were written for Dawn Upshaw and Lorraine Hunt (although Lorraine never made the production, having fallen ill), in this project I did not have any specific singers in mind when writing the vocal parts. This, too, was something that I wanted to do differently from the first project; I wanted to imagine the characters without reference to specific singers.

The synopsis for *Ariadna Mater* was written by Amin thus:

"*Adriana Mater* is set in a country at war. The country is not named, but it bears a strong resemblance to the Balkans in the late 20th century. Adriana, a young idealist woman, is raped. Finding herself pregnant, she refuses to have an abortion. 'The child is mine, not his,' she says to her sister, trying to convince herself, because the child of course has the blood of both: the victim and the offender. Will he be Cain or Abel? she thinks. Having reached adulthood, her son Yonas finds out that the man who begat him, who had fled the country after the war ended, has returned. Yonas swears to kill him but ultimately cannot. 'That man deserves to die, but you, my son, do not deserve to kill him,' says Adriana. *Adriana Mater* highlights perennial questions of humanity: Can one give life in a time of death? Should one always forgive? Is forgiveness cowardice or courage?"

Although the libretto is apparently completely different from the historical fairy tale of *L'amour de loin,* there are many similarities too: archetypal situations and emotions that have always touched the human soul. It was important for me to create rich characters that combined all kinds of personality traits, thoughts and feelings – good and bad – and to explore the actions prompted by these. It seemed important in this project to illuminate the endlessly complicated networks of interaction in which we all live and which sometimes inevitably lead to violence.

The idea of two hearts and their rhythmic polyphony was one of the first musical ideas that went into *Adriana Mater*, and accordingly it became a ubiquitous musical element. The tempo and rhythm relationships between the characters were of prime importance in writing the music; I had worked them all out in matrix form beforehand.

The four characters each have their own music, much like in *L'amour de loin.* The orchestration is dark and dramatic, and the harmonies are rich. Sister Refka has a harmonic texture that is vertically sparse but wide in range. Whereas Adriana often sings above her accompaniment, Refka's lines are embedded in the orchestration. Tsargo's music is rhythmical and greyer than the above, and his vocal line is often shadowed by low strings. Yonas's music is bright and energetic and coloured by trumpets and functions as a lightening element in Act II.

I began work on the opera in autumn 2002 and completed it in early spring 2005. The casting was done in the meantime, and Esa-Pekka Salonen was engaged as the conductor. Rehearsals began at the Bastille Opera one year later, in February 2006.

The rehearsal period for *Adriana Mater* was arduous and eventually ended with the premiere being cancelled because of a strike by the technical staff of the opera house. The decision to go ahead with the strike was made at the last moment: the singers were already in the opera house, and the international audience was milling around outside. The more than 120 foreign journalists who had showed up for the world premiere packed their bags and left, and not many of them could return for the subsequent performances. Arriving at the opera house, I could do nothing but stare at the bemused crowd outside through the bus window in shock and amazement. I tried to console myself by saying that this was not the worst thing that could happen to a composer, even if it felt like it. I tried to think of something even more terrible, and looking at the crowd I was reminded of the death of Janáček's daughter and how Janáček had notated her last words in his music notebook...

Act IV
La passion de Simone

In 2004, while I was in the middle of the three-year process of writing *Adriana Mater*, Peter Sellars approached me with another project that we had discussed ever since the rehearsals for *L'amour de loin* in Salzburg. I had noticed that Peter used texts by the French philosopher Simone Weil as material. Weil had always been an important philosopher, so much so that her book *La pesanteur et la grâce* was the only non-musical book that I packed when I went to Germany for further studies in composition. When I asked Peter in Salzburg why he used texts by Weil, he said he imagined that Amin Maalouf had been inspired by them when writing his libretto. When I took the matter up with Amin, it turned out that he did not know Simone Weil or her writings at all, but he developed an interest after our conversation. Now, in 2004, Peter wanted to commission me to write a piece about Weil for Vienna, specifically the New Crowned Hope Festival to be held in the Mozart anniversary year.

I completed *Adriana Mater* on 2 March 2005 and began work on *La passion* on the Saturday of the same week. Remarkably, beginning a new piece seemed quite effortless. The world of Simone Weil was very close to my heart, and I was glad to be able to write for Dawn Upshaw again. The work was completed about a year later, just before rehearsals for *Adriana Mater* began. It was important for me to write a concert work, not a work for the stage; after all, I was in the middle of writing an opera when this new idea emerged, and writing two stage works back to back seemed like an impossible proposition. (Both works were premièred in 2006.) However, quite early on Peter saw the production as being at least semi-staged, and he wanted to bring in a dancer. I initially resisted this, as I considered it important for the soprano to be alone on stage and the overall impression to be very abstract. Perhaps I was unconsciously going back to my old idea about a soprano and lighting. Throughout the composition process, I considered *La passion de Simone* a concert work that should work on its own, with no staging. Although Simone Weil is the central character, the soprano soloist does not represent her but instead speaks to her. Quotes from Weil herself are embedded in the electronics part, and my aim was to have the speaking voice as close to the listener in the performing space as possible, as if we were hearing her speak in our minds.

In my by now routine meetings with Amin and Peter, we sketched out the form and content of the work. Each of us had an angle on the life and work of Simone Weil. Peter emphasised her social activism, her compassion for the weak; Amin underlined the biographical elements; and I was interested as always in the passionate and uncompromising zeal that she had for seeking the truth as a philosopher, mathematician and author. All these views are represented in the final libretto.

As always with me, the first concrete step towards creating a new work was finding a solution to its overall shape – and this too was reached collaboratively. Simone Weil identified herself with Jesus, her great ideal, and in one of our conversations someone mentioned the structure of a passion play, based on the Stations of the Cross, i.e. the events leading up to the Crucifixion. We mapped Simone's life onto the 14 Stations of the Cross and grouped our main themes under those. It was on this basis that Amin wrote his libretto in 15 sections. Each section is an independent entity, but they form a linear progression. Amin Maalouf summarised the story thus:

"This young woman was 34 years old, almost the same age as Christ or Mozart when they died, when she decided to leave this world. This happened in August 1943, when the cruelty of man had reached its zenith. Simone Weil died, in silent protest as it were, in an English hospital. Her voluntary death was a renunciation of all forms of slavery: violence, hatred, Nazism and Stalinism, but also the industrial society that dehumanises human beings and plunges them into obscurity. Simone's writings, largely published posthumously, represent an attempt to point the way beyond obscurity. Her passion is a subtle and powerful compass for our trouble world.

'The Passion of Simone' is a fifteen-part musical path through her life and works. There is a woman on stage – Dawn Upshaw – who speaks to Simone and recalls her life with tenderness but not without admonishment. An outside voice, that of actress Dominique Blanc, speaks Simone Weil's own thoughts. Joining these two women's voices is the chorus, which functions as a third character."

I had four musical elements and all their subtle variations at my disposal: solo soprano, choir, orchestra and the electronic part, where actress Dominique Blanc reads texts written by Weil. I asked Amin to write a minimal libretto where the texts could be set alternately for the soloist and the choir and which would be of varying lengths.

La passion de Simone breathes through its changing orchestral textures, ranging from an airy, translucent texture to a more sombre rhythmic ostinato. The relationship between the soprano soloist and the orchestra varies from one section to another, and the choir parts are almost always settings of text. This is distinct from my operas, where the choir often merges into the orchestra and spans the gap between orchestra and soloists. In *La passion*, the choir dives into the orchestra's noisy machine imitation only in section V.

At the premiere in Vienna in late autumn 2006, the solo part was sung by Pia Freund, as Dawn Upshaw had fallen seriously ill. Susanna Mälkki conducted the Klangforum Wien orchestra and the Arnold Schönberg Choir. Peter Sellars created a wonderful production where dancer Michael Schumacher created a shadowlike angel figure that became such an inseparable part of the concept that by the time of this writing the work has only once been performed in a concert version. A semi-staged production is, after all, a very good solution for a performance in a concert hall. The performances following the premiere were sung in turn by Pia and Dawn, and the staging has been adapted to each venue. So is *La passion de Simone* an opera? It can certainly be regarded as one.

Act V
Émilie

My most recent opera, *Émilie*, was premièred only a few months before I wrote the present essay, and I find that the dust has not yet properly settled since then. My impressions are too chaotic and too emotional to be analysed, and it is too early to draw any conclusions.

As with all my opera projects, *Émilie* was the result of many years of rumination. The initiative for writing a monodrama for Karita Mattila came from Stéphane Lissner at the Aix-en-Provence Festival in 2001. Although the project did not take off back then, it took root in my mind. I worked out some ideas with Amin Maalouf under the working title *Elsa, la nuit*. Several years went by, during which I wrote *Adriana Mater* and *La passion de Simone*, but also a song cycle for Karita Mattila called *Quatre instants*. That was our first collaboration, and the incredible intensity that Karita brings to her performances inspired me both in writing the work and in hearing it performed.

A monodrama is of course an extreme art form, and as such eminently suitable for Karita. My original vision was quite radical: I imagined Karita alone on stage, surrounded only by an electronic background and a video or film projection. However, I began to suspect that this would represent an excessive challenge for any singer, even Karita, because the work was to last for more than an hour.

The opera as it finally emerged is divided into nine scenes, which illuminate the conflicting and complicated life of Émilie as a scientist, a lover, a mother and a wife.

What interested me in the character of Émilie was her rare intelligence combined with a woman's acute intuition, which contrasted with her profuse passion for men, gambling, clothing and jewellery – a passion that we might consider to have proven her ruin, as she died after giving birth to the child of her lover at the advanced age of 43. I envisioned a portrait of contradictions, like photos taken from very different angles that would nevertheless merge into a single image in the listener's mind.

In traditional opera, women are usually depicted as objects of love or as having suffered from love and being deceived in love. As a woman, I have naturally sought other perspectives. On the other hand, I am not interested in exploring the venal or hyperrealistic confessions of a woman (or a man) or of making scandalous revelations simply on the pretext of a feminine viewpoint.

Stories in Western culture are often quite straightforward tales of the struggle of good and evil, with no ambivalence. When depicting human beings or human emotions in my operas, I try to convey the plurality of humanity and emotions as we live and experience them in real life. I often use borderline states as metaphors, such as the border between light and shadow, and I am similarly interested in the nuances of the human mind, the often fragile borders between very different emotions. The drama that I explore in my operas is not in grand external events but in the movements of the mind. In this sense, *Émilie* is my most extreme opera, because it is entirely about Émilie's thoughts, and whether she is sitting at her desk in the beginning of the opera as she writes a letter is irrelevant, because the location does not matter. In this sense, my initial idea of a disembodied electronic accompaniment and no other set than video or film backdrops was perfectly logical. François Girard was not interested in using such elements in his productions, even though he is a film director (or because of that). Instead, he and the set designer François Seguin came up with a completely different idea based on the conception of the solar system in Émilie's day.

Speaking of video, two of the eight productions of *L'amour de loin* so far have used video projections. My idea of using video in *L'amour de loin* was to expand the sense of air and space, but in *Émilie* I envisioned video as having the opposite effect, creating an intimate feeling. The singer's voice is amplified as she whispers, and I imagined the same sort of effect to be created visually by using close-ups.

Although I rarely enter extra-musical ideas into my scores, they play an important role in my composing. In *L'amour de loin*, the visual, symbolic space, cold and warm colours and the scents of exotic spices had a direct bearing on the orchestration. With *Adriana Mater*, I was concerned with the psychological space, the personal relationships of the characters and how they change; this was reflected in my tempo matrix, the polyphony of the different heartbeats. In *Émilie*, I wanted the orchestra to breathe with the singer, to be an extension of her thoughts and mind.

Émilie is scored for a small orchestra that includes an amplified harpsichord. The voice of the soprano soloist is at times processed in real time. The sound of Émilie's quill pen is also amplified and used as a musical element. The orchestra is Émilie's mindscape, and the musical material shifts according to the subject discussed. A nervous harpsichord ostinato underpins her anxious thoughts, and an expansive microtonally tinted texture opens up when she begins to talk of the properties of beams of light or the nature of fire. The music box music in the childhood sequence incorporates reminiscences of the keyboard music of Scarlatti, which I have always been fond of.

Émilie has been compared to Schönberg's *Erwartung* and the opera *La voix humaine* by Cocteau and Poulenc, but this is only because they all feature a woman alone singing on stage. Parallels have been drawn on a similar basis between *L'amour de loin* and *Tristan und Isolde* or *Pelléas et Mélisande*. *Adriana Mater* has been traced back to the operas of Janáček, and so on. Such associations must be important for the listener, but for me the connections are very distant and vague. No doubt all the music that has had a profound effect on me has also remained with me, including the aforementioned masterpieces, all of which and many more I admire. Whenever I start an opera, I stare at a blank page, and historical models are of no help in overcoming that threshold. All ideas have some kind of a relationship with tradition – admission or denial, conscious or unconscious – and in writing my first opera I inevitably compared it with earlier works in the same genre. With my following operas, I saw them in relation to my first rather than to anything else.

Whether I will ever write another opera (or several) is something I cannot clearly answer at the moment. At this particular time, I do not feel writing an opera to be so compelling a thought as to find the proposals I receive from various opera houses to be attractive. On the other hand, every project I have undertaken so far has been a sum of encounters, and my operas have taken several years to mature in my mind. Sometimes I think of writing an opera to a libretto in Finnish. Sometimes I think of an opera that would have a great many small roles, quite the opposite of my operas so far. Sometimes I think of returning to my old idea of an abstract opera of lights. But time will tell.

This essay was written in 2010 and originally published in French. It is a condensed version of an essay in Finnish published in the compendium Hako, Pekka (ed.): *Aistit, uni, rakkaus. Kaksitoista katsetta Kaija Saariahoon.* [Senses, dreams, love. Twelve views of Kaija Saariaho.], pp. 253–283. LURRA Editions 2012.
Saariaho has finished her fourth opera, scheduled to be premièred at the Amsterdam Opera in March 2016.

Quo vadis, art of opera?

AULIS SALLINEN

Opera is theatre and music. Both art forms are as old as *homo ludens*. Thus, predictions about the demise of opera – because it is allegedly unnecessary and behind the times – have always been proven wrong. It is par for the course with this art form that it requires an institution to perform it, large or small. This is a life-and-death issue for opera but also its outlook for the future. Opera houses are compelled, for financial reasons, to stage classics that are certain to sell tickets, yet the people in charge of opera houses are fully aware of the risk of turning opera into a living museum. Therefore they also seek to stage contemporary opera, often at huge financial loss. But this is the crucial question for the present and future of opera: if new works are not performed, audiences will never come to know them, and they will never learn the grammar of contemporary art.

Despite the less than encouraging signs, new operas are being written all the time. Why? Being commissioned to write an opera means that performances are guaranteed, which is a considerable motivation for beginning such a huge task. However, it has no bearing on the creative work itself. For whom does one write music? For the audience (whom we do not know), for the critics (who are rarely reliable), or for one's colleagues (who would be only too happy to see a production fail)? For myself, I always write for the performer, the person(s) who will interpret the music, whether the work in question is a string quartet or a full-sized opera. There is talk of 'performer-friendly' music. If music connects with the performer, it has a chance of connecting with the audience too.

Because writing music is a craft, a seasoned professional can identify another professional after only a few minutes of listening to their music. This is true even if you do not really like what you are hearing. Therefore all good composers throughout history may serve as models; and if you mention only one of them, you are wronging the others. It is typical for a young composer to 'imitate' one or more old masters, in most cases his or her own teacher. When a composer's own voice emerges through maturation, it is useful for the composer to remember that he or she is doing something that no other creature in the entire universe is doing in quite the same way.

I have no idea where ideas come from. They are stealthy creatures that ambush you when you least expect it. My opera *Kullervo* contains a number called the 'Ballad of the Blind Singer', which is framed as the title character's dream and tells the universal tale of a man who unwittingly defiles his own sister. This is how it came about: On a square in a town in Provence there was a blind singer playing the accordion every Sunday. That is how it happened. Without ever knowing it, he became the model for the character in the opera. Inspiration is, I suppose, a state of mind that must be actively sought through work, and of course the mind must be alert. Perhaps that is why most of my ideas seem to emerge in the small hours.

People often imagine that any 'good subject', whether a best-selling novel or some other compelling narrative, will automatically work in music theatre. The subject is of course not unimportant, but what an opera libretto primarily needs are strong poetic elements. Also, the composer must be convinced that setting that particular subject to music will bring added value and the sort of richness that only music theatre can provide. Therefore I cannot consider the *Kalevala* to be a self-evident source for opera subjects. Its tales are of course gratifying because they are well-known and tried and tested, but that in itself is not enough. I chose to set the tale of Kullervo because Aleksis Kivi had already turned it into a powerful, Shakespearean drama. Besides, it remains regrettably relevant.

When I started out as an opera composer in the early 1970s, there was no such animal as an opera librettist in Finland – another indication of just how young and thin this tradition is in our country. Both of the texts supplied to me by Paavo Haavikko – *Ratsumies* (The Horseman) and *Kuningas lähtee Ranskaan* (The King Goes Forth to France) – were written as stage plays, and I had to condense them myself. When I began writing the libretto for *Punainen viiva* (The Red Line), I noticed that I was composing music while writing the text – not in detail, but as overall shapes. This process repeated itself with *Kullervo*, and I found it a great help for writing the music. The only libretto that I have ever received that was usable pretty much straight out of the box was *Palatsi* (The Palace) by Enzensberger and Dische, the product of experienced theatre professionals.

And what about the music? In order to keep a grip on the overall shape of the work through an extensive working process, I always draw a graphic representation of it: the overall shape with estimated durations, appearances of characters and their motifs, and how these pass from scene to scene. For reasons of coherence, I have always employed some kind of *leitmotif* technique. I have compared such a motif to a stone thrown into the water that produces rings that then affect their surroundings. Because symphonic thinking requires discipline of form and because I began my career as a symphonic composer, this requirement of coherence was transferred to my operas. My other work has influenced my operas rather than the other way around. Whatever the music or artwork a listener hears, the listener always takes away an overall impression, a conception of the shape of the work.

It is sad but true that many operas, even good ones, only ever get one production. The reason is that there are so few opera houses and their financial resources are scarce. And this is before we even consider all the works that never see the light of day outside the composer's study. And yet composers continue to write them. What is the use of all these efforts? Then again, we might ask what the point is of climbing the Himalayas or of sailing around the world.

It has been gratifying to note how small chamber opera companies have recently been commissioning and performing new works. This kind of activism helps compensate the rigidity of the established opera houses by responding more quickly to the ideas of young creators.

Aftermath of opera

TAPIO TUOMELA

It is more than 15 years since I wrote my opera *Äidit ja tyttäret* (Mothers and Daughters). In the introduction to his libretto, Paavo Haavikko wrote: "A story must be told from memory." Accordingly, I am now trying to recall that composing process and to observe how my working methods have changed since then.

In the 1990s, my experiences with vocal music consisted of my work as a Lied pianist, opera répétiteur and conductor. I was involved in all productions of contemporary operas at the Finnish National Opera and had learned at first hand what singers want from their vocal parts, at least in technical terms.

The libretto of *Äidit ja tyttäret* allowed ample scope for both *bel canto* and speech-like voice production, but it also invited an extension of vocal expression, for instance towards caricature. The women's ensemble singing traditions of eastern Europe found their way into the opera, and this inspired me to explore new folk music and, subsequently, traditional laments, yoiks and the folk music of the Kaustinen tradition. Ancient Finnish folk poetry, as recorded in *Suomen Kansan Wanhat Runot* (Ancient poems of the Finnish people), became a key element in many of my choral projects in the early 2000s.

Text articulation
Writing a vocal work usually begins with a reading of the text, searching inspiration in it and exploring its dimensions and potential.

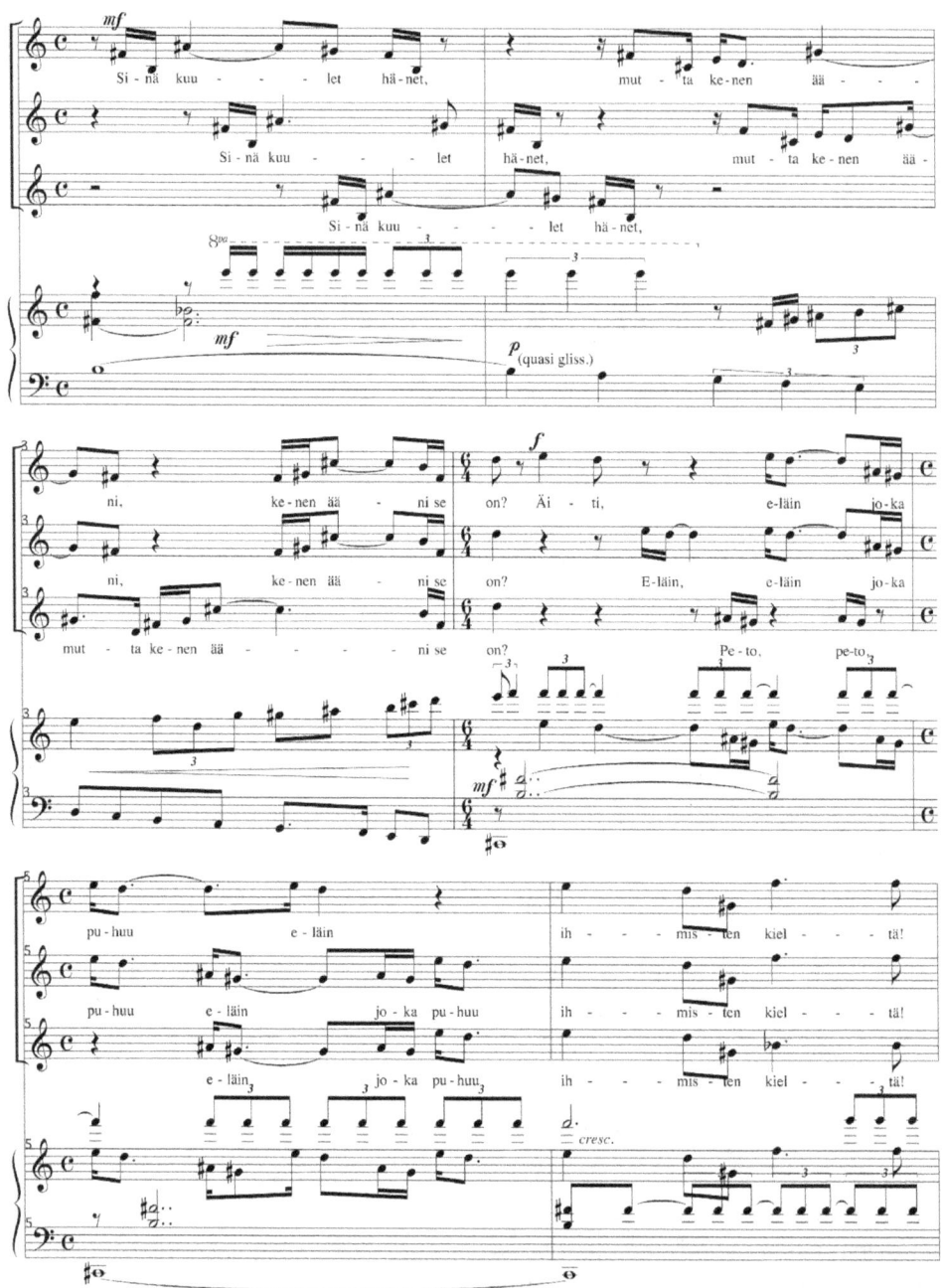

Example 1. Extract from the transition between Act I and Act II, measures 51–56.

The rhythmic character of a text is important for me, especially in a choral texture if the text is familiar and allows for layering and syllable fragmentation. Vowel colours and diphthongs can be used to good effect.

In solo songs and opera, vowel colours are a very different issue, especially for high women's voices. The comprehensibility of text becomes crucial: front vowels tend to be rounded the more the higher the tessitura is. On the other hand, a vocal part in the lower register will be obscured by the orchestra. Inevitably situations will occur where the most important or highest note in a phrase will have to be sung on a front vowel. In my most recent works, I have sometimes bypassed this problem by writing the syllable with the front vowel lower down on a grace note or by beginning the syllable on a lower note and continuing with a high melisma.

I am cautious about using superimposed texts when the listener is not familiar with the text and when understanding the text is important for following the story.

Paavo Haavikko's libretto was so clear and punchy that it was possible to inter-weave syllables when repeating text (Example 1).

In ensemble scenes, I made sure that no text obscured any other, even though it was often necessary to overlap lines slightly because of the natural pacing of the dialogue.

Example 2 (following page) is from the trio in Act I where we hear the thoughts of the characters weaving through each other.

Planning and execution in turn

Today, my composing is clearly divided into two phases, planning and execution. By execution I mean not only the producing of the material but also the technical processing that involves orchestration details, fixing the voice-leading and editing dynamics and articulations.

At the time of *Äidit ja tyttäret*, I used the computer only for writing out fair copy. Since then, as computers have evolved and my own IT skills have improved, the role of the computer in my work has grown; today, I also use it for sketching and playback. It is undoubtedly easier to keep track of proportions and the dimensions of gestures when you can 'road-test' your ideas, as it were.

I planned the continuum of scenes in *Äidit ja tyttäret* in parallel with writing the music.

After the first few scenes, I drew a diagram with numeric values and curves illustrating their changes for tempo, intensity/volume and the dissonance/consonance content of the harmony.

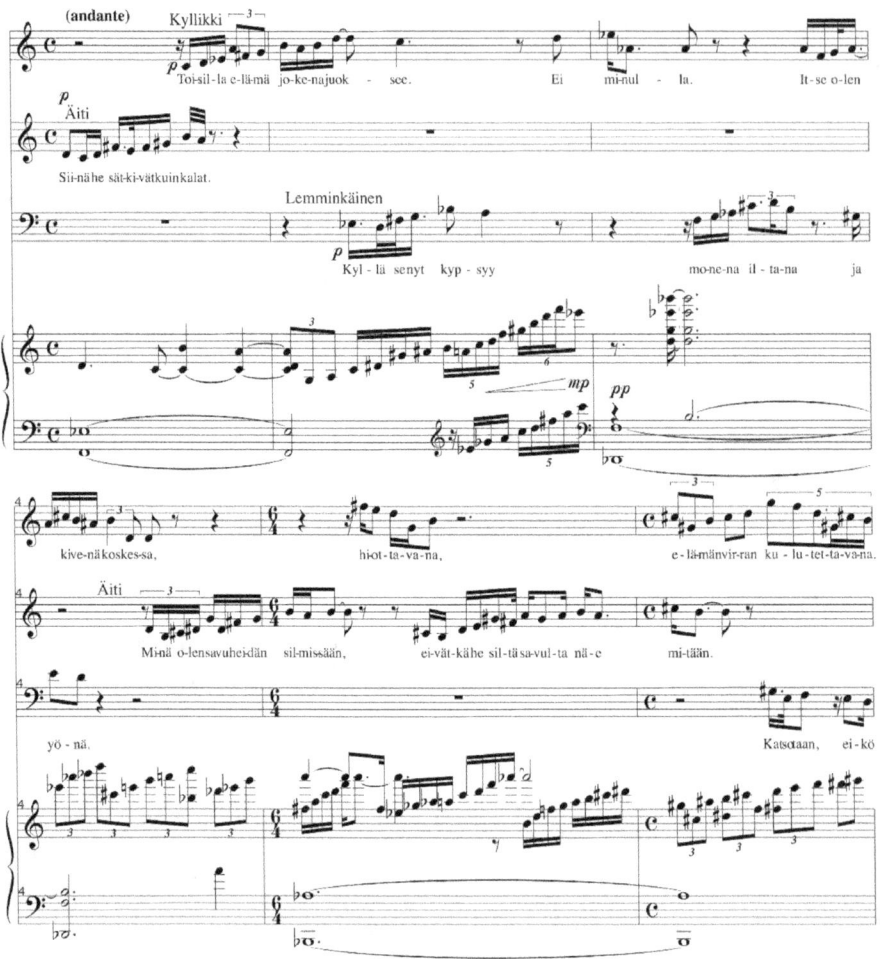

Example 2. Act I, opening of scene 4, measures 18–23.

Before writing out each scene, I made a rough outline of what the aforementioned values should be like in the scene and whether they should be static or change. Once I had written the scene, I revised the diagram according to the actual music. I felt that in this way I could better keep track of the overall structure and govern parameters such as information density, intensity of climaxes, use of registers, and so on.

From text to melody

For most scenes, I first wrote out the dialogue on grid paper, sometimes methodically with one square corresponding to one beat. I then sketched out a speech-like rhythm over the syllables, with approximate pitches, to shape each phrase and the relative pitches of the syllables in it. The lengths of the phrases and their arcs were now clearly visible.

The next stage was largely driven by intuition. Proceeding from the overall form of the work (mood, language of characters and gestures, consonant/dissonant harmonies, etc.), I began to sketch out harmonies that would suit each particular situation and utterance, sometimes working them out at the piano. I drew box-like harmony cells over the voice parts to show harmony changes in general terms, without exact pitches. The shape, outline or darkness of the boxes indicated something of their range, volume or internal texture: downward lines inside a box depicted downward movement or glissandi within a harmony, while a white box containing small circles depicted a consonant chord inside which there were staccato tones played on a vibraphone or a piano with pedal, and so on.

At this point, I generally went to the piano to hammer out the details.

I had begun work on Act I impatiently, without any particular harmonic plan, but after only a couple of scenes I felt a need to analyse the interval sets I had created in order to make the domestic realism of Act I differ from the fantasy world of Pohjola in Act II.

Some of the harmonies came from a harmonic map that I had prepared at the planning stage, where I had placed chords I had used before, in a rough order of increasing dissonance and organised by their lowermost interval.

The most interesting chords that emerged during the process of composition ended up at their relevant locations on the map, so that the harmonic matrix eventually evolved into a rather organised chord library diverse in sonority.

Act I is dominated by a scale formed of tones and semitones, often manifested in the melodic line as two major seconds separated by a leap of a sixth. The vocal texture is strictly syllabic.

In Act II, I read the lines of the Mistress of Pohjola as deliberately caricatured and provocative, which prompted an exaggeration of everything: the harmony is dissonant, the texture is jagged, and there are sharp, wide leaps and melismas.

The examples illustrating the process described above come from just before the interval, at the end of a rising wedge of intensity built up through three scenes. Lemminkäinen has just arrived at Pohjola, flirted with two of the homestead's daughters, been surprised by Louhi and gone off to perform tasks imposed by her, tasks that prove to be impossible.

The intensity is already high when the scene begins, as Lemminkäinen's Mother arrives to claim her son and she and Louhi end up in an altercation where Lemminkäinen's father is referred to (Example 3. P.E. = Mistress of Pohjola / Louhi).

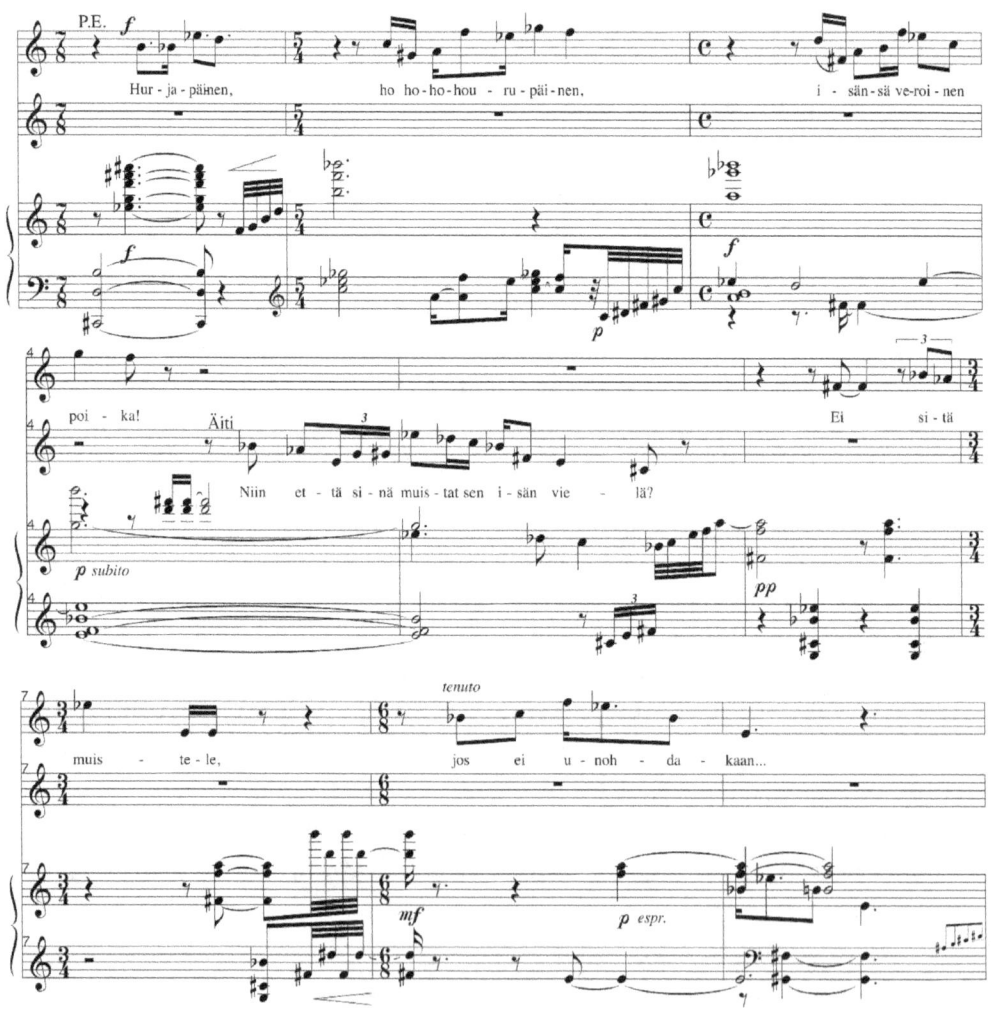

Example 3. Act II scene 3, measures 22–30.

The difference between the characters and voice types of the two women becomes clearer as the scene progresses, and towards the end (Example 4) Lemminkäinen's Mother is clearly more lyrical than Louhi.

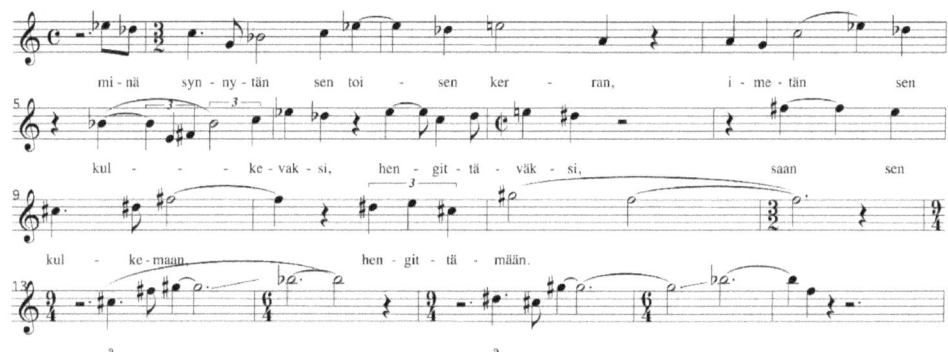

Example 4. Act II scene 3, measures 61–77.

From harmony to melody

An example of a different process may be found at the culmination of the opera in Act III scene 3. Here, the composition was guided by a vision stemming from the harmony and the tutti sound of the orchestra, the vocal texture being clearly subordinate to these: the key notes in the vocal part were directly derived from the already existing harmonic material. I controlled the width of the intervals and the text rhythm with a view to the voice type of the character. I filled in the spaces between the key notes with passing tones or scales (Example 5; HS means a tone derived from the underlying harmony).

More room

Example 6 contains an earlier sketch of the same vocal sequence. I had the opportunity to try out a few scenes from the opera with orchestra and singers at a brief orchestral rehearsal about six months before the premiere. The result was not surprising: transferring music to a concert hall requires more time than it does in the composer's head or his study. The piano score had been much more austere than the orchestration, but as the orchestra joined in, the vocal texture suddenly demanded more room.

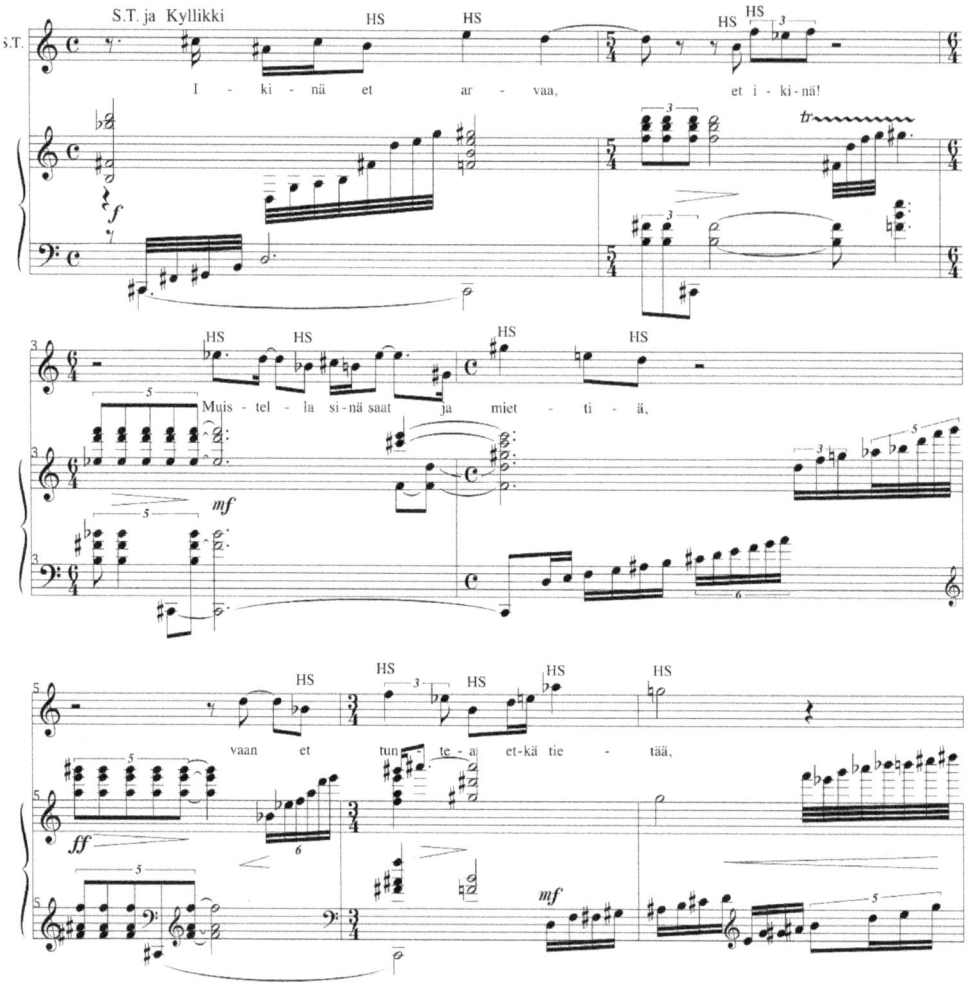

Example 5. Act III scene 3, measures 74–80.

It is not enough that the singer is audible; the text also has to be comprehensible. I already knew that if you want your text to be heard, it is not a good idea to have the singer and the orchestra blast out at the same time. It is interesting to compare Examples 5 and 6 from this perspective. In the preliminary rehearsal, it turned out that a natural diminuendo in the orchestra down to the level where a singer can become audible took more time than I had imagined.

The vocal phrases in measures 3 and 5 in Examples 5 and 6 eventually had to be pushed back by a beat or two to give the orchestra's tutti chord more space at the beginning of the measure and allow it to decay before the singer comes in.

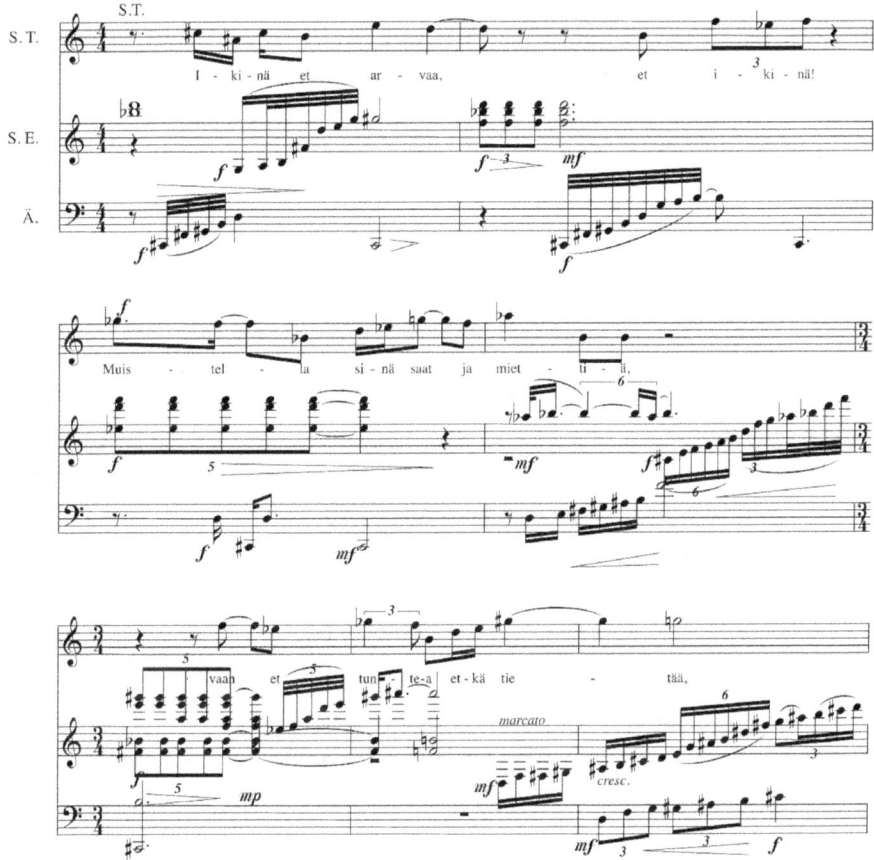

Example 6. An earlier sketch for the same scene.

Orchestration

I always first write out a piano score or short score of my orchestral works, with everything essential notated on a couple of staves. I initially only have a vague notion of orchestral colours and perhaps an idea for the principal instrumental solos. The orchestration and voice-leading do not become concrete until I begin to transcribe the short score into a full score. With *Äidit ja tyttäret*, I wrote the entire piano score using pencil and paper, in old-school style. However, no outsider could ever make head or tail of it, as it is scribbled over with corrections and voice-leading remarks. These days, I only use pencil and paper for initial sketches and then enter the material into the computer for post-processing.

In teaching orchestration at the Sibelius Academy, I have given much attention to how composers double vocal lines. My favourites in this are Mozart and Puccini for their sheer diversity. Mozart often doubles the vocal line motif by motif, in sections shorter than phrases and constantly changing the doubling instrument.

In *Äidit ja tyttäret*, I used rather little doubling of the vocal lines in the first half, for instance, Lemminkäinen's Mother principally sings without instrumental doubling in Act I, as does Louhi, the Mistress of Pohjola. This was a conscious choice, as both parts contain a lot of text that must be carefully articulated and are therefore very precisely notated to resemble speech. An instrumental part doubling all that – especially if it were in the same register – would be at risk of inaccuracies, which in turn would undermine the comprehensibility of the text. A singer can best find support in the orchestral harmony or melody at phrase boundaries, where taking a breath allows him or her to listen momentarily with more focus than during singing. One singer I know reported that singing a phrase in a contemporary piece on stage (at worst physically far removed from the orchestra) is like diving into a tunnel, where you scarcely hear or see anything else. Maybe a good analogy would be to think of a singer as a diver, who only has contact with the outside world when coming up for air. During the rehearsal period, I mentally took my hat off multiple times to Ritva Auvinen and Taru Valjakka, who in the big roles of Lemminkäinen's Mother and Louhi did a great job far outside their comfort zones.

I became increasingly aware of the doubling conundrum, and as the work progressed I aimed to make the accompanying texture translucent and harmonically clear enough for the singer to find the reference points needed. I only used the warm sound of violin doubling, which is very common in Italian opera such as Puccini, where it was specifically motivated. Because of its rarity, the string doubling of the vocal line should create a strong effect, as in the events leading up to the Daughter of Saari drowning herself (Example 7).

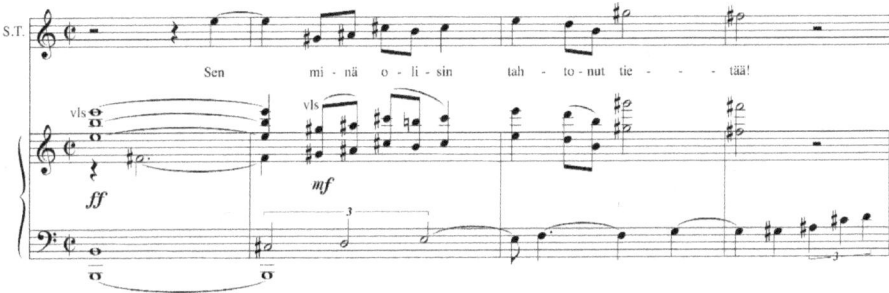

Example 7. Act III scene 3, measures 41–44.

The scoring of *Äidit ja tyttäret* was determined by the fact that Mozart's *Die Entführung aus dem Serail* was playing on the main stage at the same time, and I was allowed to use the musicians who were not needed for that: a sinfonietta-size string section, double woodwinds (but only one bassoon), two horns, a trumpet, a trombone, a tuba and two percussionists. I initially planned to add a kantele, but it would have had to be amplified, so I ended up giving sampled kantele sounds for the keyboard player to play. This proved particularly effective in the scenes featuring new folk music that step outside the narrative and comment on it. I also used it as a glissando colour (Example 8, measures 2 and 4) and to shade static harmonies where the pulse disappears.

A rugged sense of timelessness combines with Haavikko's incisive text perhaps most effectively in the opening chorus, where director Erik Söderblom with great inventiveness had the trio emerge from a coffin (the same coffin which the Daughter of Saari enters at the end). A distancing effect is achieved with a hurdy-gurdy, which has the practical function of providing a harmonic reference for the singers (Example 9).

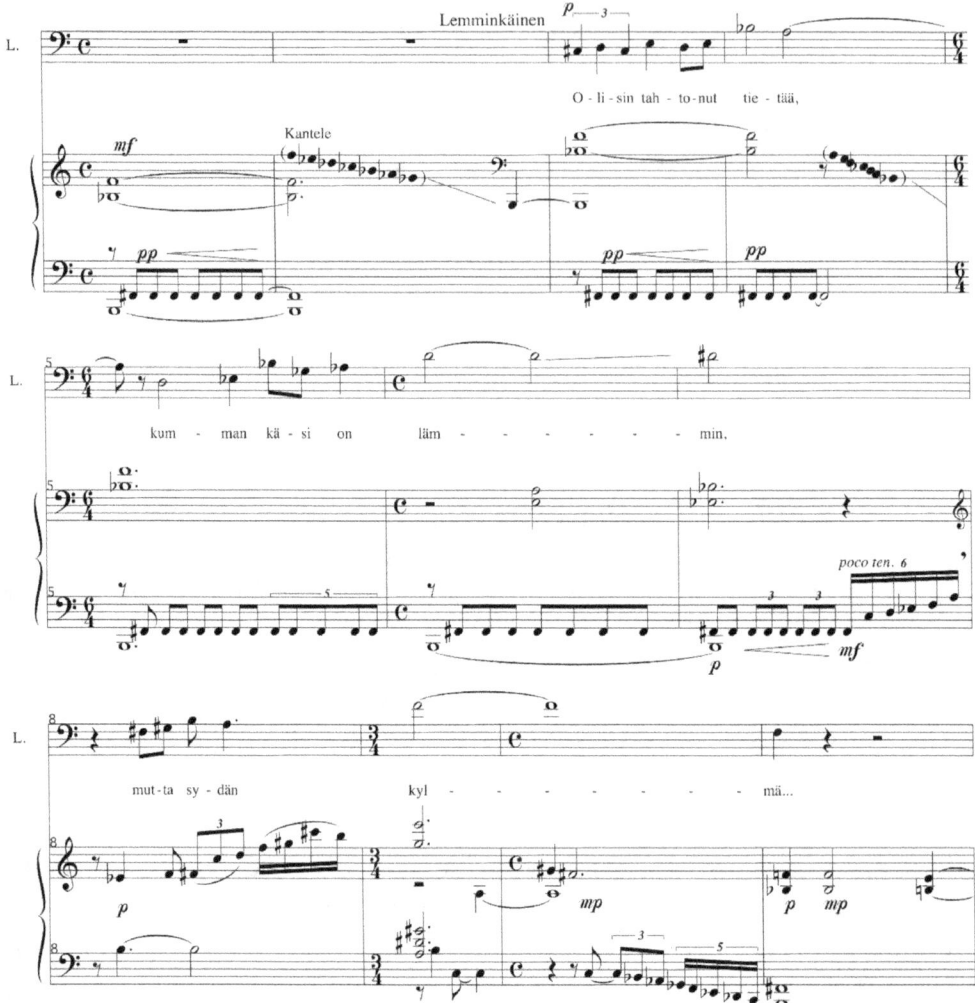

Example 8. Act III scene 3, measures 89–99.

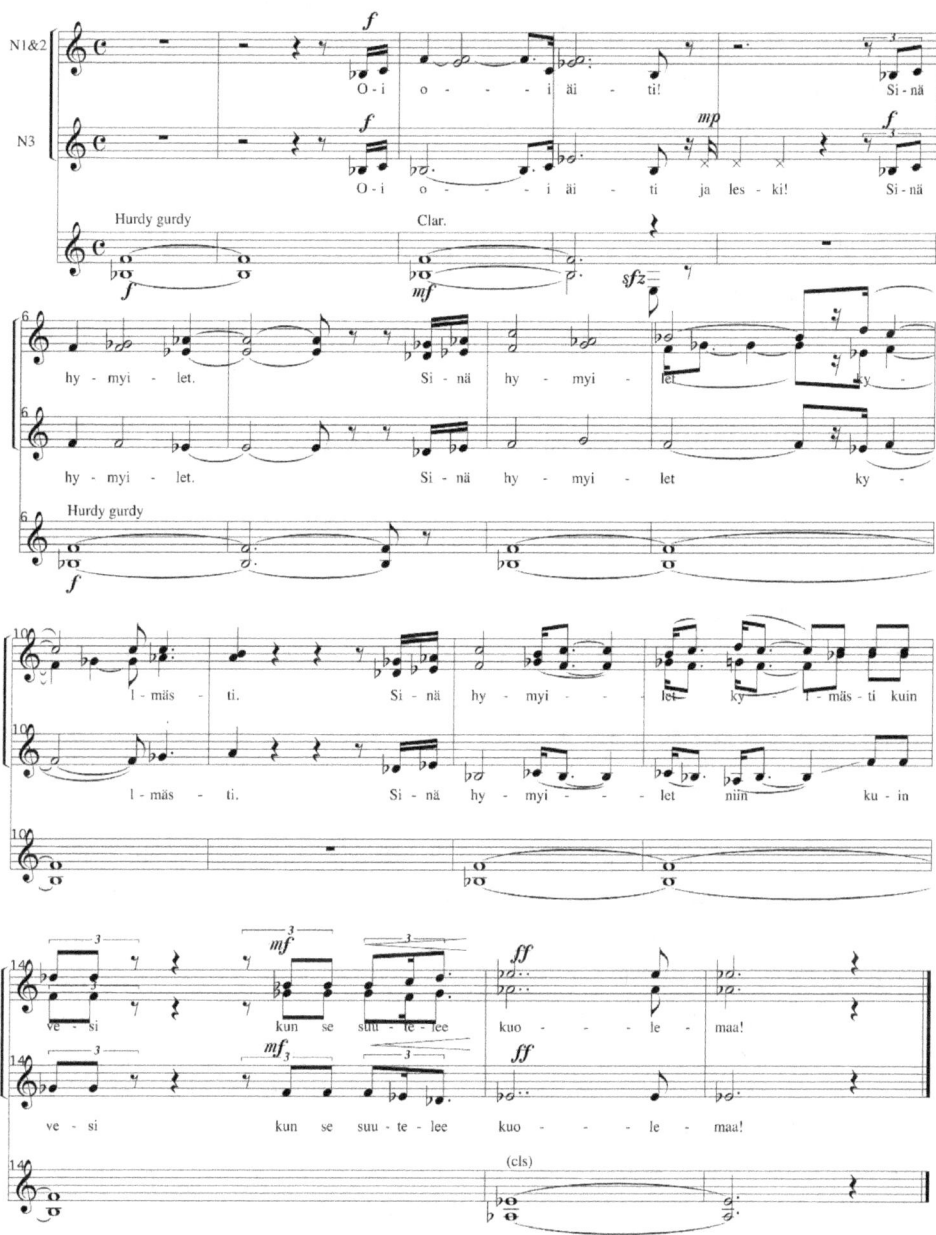

Example 9. Opening chorus, measures 41–56.

The libretto and how it was adapted

Among the most memorable experiences in this opera project were the couple of meetings I had with librettist Paavo Haavikko. The first draft of the libretto, with fewer than ten pages, was dated May 1997. It was subsequently augmented along the way, and Haavikko agreed to my interpolating folk poetry for the folk music scenes.

At the director's request, a monologue for Lemminkäinen was added after the drowning of the Daughter of Saari, and Haavikko gave permission to use text from his script for the TV series *Rauta-aika* (The Age of Iron).

I got into the habit of faxing questions concerning minor changes to Haavikko from France – which is where my family and I were living while I was writing Act I – until finally he said: "Look, it's your opera, so you don't need to ask permission for every little change."

I once met him at the Art House publishers' office. He was sitting at the back of a large room in dim light, crouched over a small desk with a pile of invitations that he was signing in assembly-line fashion. After I had watched this for a while, standing in the doorway, Haavikko invited me to sit down on the only other chair, which was by the door – we were still some 10 metres apart. He asked me where exactly I needed changes. I could only marvel at the speed at which he dictated text to me for the locations I had named and then immediately asked me: "Did you get all that?"

One passage in particular stuck in my mind. In the scene between Lemminkäinen and his mother, I needed a pair for the line "The man left, the boy grew up," as the music required it. Without a moment's hesitation, Haavikko quipped: "The man left, the boy grew up. The boy grew up, the man left." I was on my way home before I realised how ingenious that pithy remark actually was. Lemminkäinen's Mother is first talking about her husband, who left her when her son was a small child, and then about Lemminkäinen himself, who grew up and then left her.

Haavikko's language is fantastic from a composer's point of view: concise, fresh, colloquial, clear but sometimes very ambiguous. I made the mistake of asking him for his interpretation of certain very aphoristic sentences. Of course there can be no single unambiguous interpretation; in some cases, the author was simply amused by something he had come up with for a character to say, such as "A mother is a predator, an animal who speaks the language of humans" or "A woman is poor merchandise. You cannot buy it and pay for it, the interest accumulates all the time."

When the opera was revived three years later, I discovered that my interpretation or understanding of certain sentences in the libretto had changed, but of course I did not go back and change the music.

In retrospect

Although many years have gone by and I have accumulated all kinds of experience since the opera project, I would probably not write a very different opera to that particular text even today. Some details would be different, but that is all. I have later discovered a handful of errors in syllable length in the opera. (In the Finnish language, vowel length carries meaning; if you lengthen a vowel in a vocal line, this sometimes changes the meaning of the word.) The vowel length should therefore be checked before composing any text for voice. Today, I would probably plan out the harmonies and their similarities or differences beforehand, not while I was already writing the music. The most obvious difference now would be in the orchestral colour: I have expanded my colour palette towards noise, especially in string textures.

My musical aesthetic has not changed substantially since those days, although I am probably now more context-aware. My ideal would be to take into account the needs of the commissioning party and of the audience, whom I want to be able to provide a meaningful experience. The audience at a contemporary music concert is completely different from an opera audience or a TV audience.

Homogeneity is not as much of a virtue for me as it used to be. In the early days of my career, I imagined that a composer must above all prove that he can write music with symphonic unity. However, large-scale works in particular become so heavy through this approach that they cannot manage to communicate or to sustain the listener's interest throughout. A Swedish critic once wrote in an otherwise positive review that I had not completely managed to escape the Finnish *svårmodighet* – a Swedish word that may be rendered as 'melancholy' but literally (and illustratively) translates as 'heavy-mindedness'. Soon after that, I read the exhilarating book *Norrlands Akvavit* by Swedish author Torgny Lindgren, which the author described using the German word *Heiterkeit* ('excitedness' but perhaps more accurately 'good spirits') as opposed to the dullness or melancholy of everyday life. At the time I wished I had that kind of absurd courage to abandon myself – and very soon after that epiphany I wrote my *Fiddler* string quartet, where folk music made a comeback into my musical idiom.

The composers and their operas

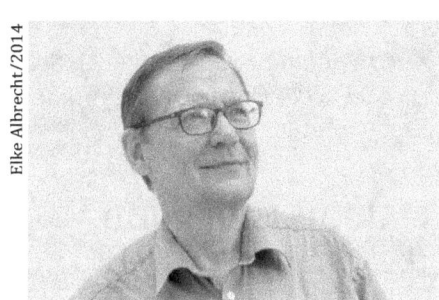

Elke Albrecht/2014

KALEVI AHO
(b. 9 March 1949)

Avain (The Key). One-act dramatic monologue for baritone and 13 instrumentalists. FP 4 Sep 1979, Helsinki Festival/Finnish National Opera.

Hyönteiselämää (Insect Life). Opera in two acts. FP 27 Sep 1996, Finnish National Opera.

Salaisuuksien kirja (The Book of Secrets). Opera in one act (four scenes). Third part in the opera trilogy *Aika ja uni* (The Age of Dreams). FP 15 Jul 2000, Savonlinna Opera Festival.

Ennen kuin me kaikki olemme hukkuneet (Before We All Have Drowned). Opera in two acts. FP 8 Feb 2001, Finnish National Opera.

Frida y Diego (Frida and Diego). Fresco operístico, opera in four acts. FP 17 Oct 2014, Sibelius Academy, Helsinki.

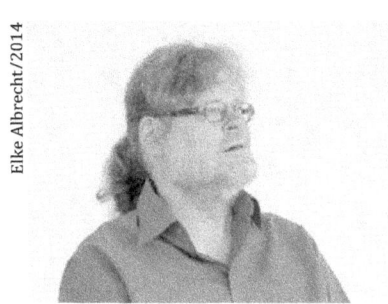

Elke Albrecht/2014

ATSO ALMILA
(b. 13 Jun 1954)

Kolmekymmentä hopearahaa (Thirty pieces of silver). Opera in three acts. FP 17 Jun 1988, Ilmajoki Music Festival.

Ameriikka (America). Opera in two acts. FP 12 Jun 1992, Ilmajoki Music Festival.

Isontaloon Antti (Antti Isotalo). Folk opera in four acts with a prologue. FP 14 Jun 2000, Ilmajoki Music Festival.

Pohjanmaan kautta (Ex!). Comic opera in two acts. FP 13 Jun 2002, Ilmajoki Music Festival.

Auringonkukat (Sunflowers). School opera. FP 14 Oct 2009, Finnish National Opera.

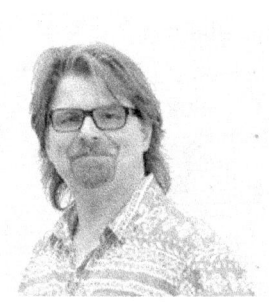

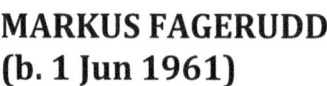

Elke Albrecht/2014

MARKUS FAGERUDD
(b. 1 Jun 1961)

Gaia. Opera in four acts for young audiences. FP 24 Mar 2001, Finnish National Opera.

Kerjäläiset (The Beggars). School opera. FP 17 Mar 2003, Finnish National Opera.

Heinähattu, Vilttitossu ja suuri pamaus (Strawhat, Feltslipper and the Big Bang). Children's opera. FP 23 Aug 2003, Helsinki Festival.

Sotajoulukuu (War December). School opera. FP 28 Feb 2007, Vantaa (Finnish National Opera).

Seitsemän koiraveljestä (Seven Canine Brothers). Opera for the whole family in one act. FP 12 Jul 2008, Savonlinna Opera Festival.

Free Will. Community Opera. FP 21 Jul 2012, Savonlinna Opera Festival.

Välilasku (Stopover). Chamber opera. FP 2 Feb 2012, Kapsäkki, Helsinki.

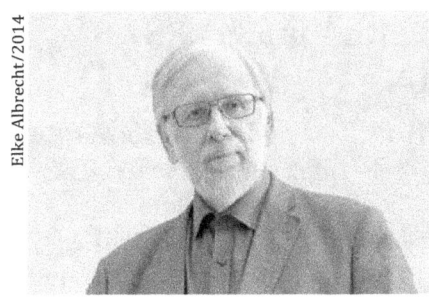

PAAVO HEININEN
(b. 13 Jan 1938)

Silkkirumpu (The Damask Drum). Concerto for singers, instrumentalists, movements, images, words... Opera in one act. FP 5 Apr 1984, Finnish National Opera.

Veitsi (The Knife). Opera in two acts. FP 3 Jul 1989, Savonlinna Opera Festival.

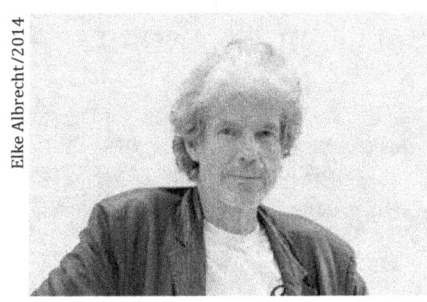

MIKKO HEINIÖ
(b. 18 May 1948)

Riddaren och draken (The Knight and the Dragon). Church opera in two acts. FP 9 Nov 2000, Turku.

Kärmeen hetki (The Hour of the Serpent). Opera. FP 15 Sep 2006, Finnish National Opera.

Eerik XIV. Opera. FP 22 Nov 2011, Logomo Turku (Turku Music Festival & Turku European Cultural Capital 2011).

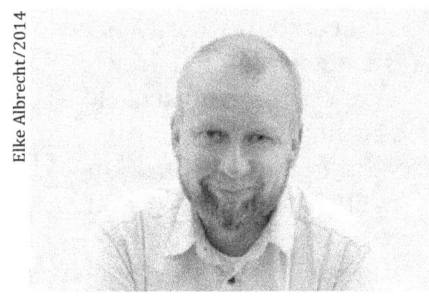

HEINZ-JUHANI HOFMANN
(b. 20 Feb 1973)

Ihmissydän (The Human Heart). Monologue opera. FP 8 Sep 2011, Espoo.

Ahti Karjalainen – elämä, Kekkonen ja teot (Ahti Karjalainen – Life, Kekkonen and Works). Seven scenes. FP 31 May 2012, West Coast Kokkola Opera.

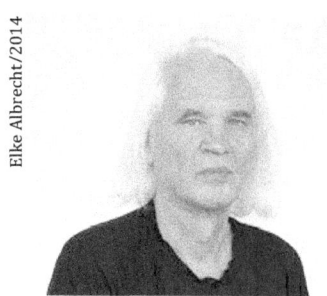

Elke Albrecht/2014

PEKKA JALKANEN
(b. 5 Sep 1945)

Tirlittan. Children's opera in two acts. FP 31 Jan 1987, Helsinki (City of Helsinki Culture Department).

Seitsemän huivia (Seven Veils). Opera in three acts with prologue and epilogue. FP 19 Oct 1990, Kokkola.

Dominus Krabbe. Monologue opera. FP 24 Aug 2012, Helsinki Festival.

Elke Albrecht/2014

OLLI KORTEKANGAS
(b. 16 May 1955)

Short Story. Opera in one act. FP 15 Oct 1980, Sibelius Academy, Helsinki.

Grand Hotel. TV opera in one act. FP 12 Sep 1987, YLE TV 1.

Joonan kirja (The Book of Jonah). Opera in one act. FP 6 Oct 1995, Finnish National Opera.

Marian rakkaus (Maria's Love). Opera with prologue and ten scenes. Second part of the opera trilogy *Aika ja uni* (The Age of Dreams). FP 15 Jul 2000, Savonlinna Opera Festival.

Messenius ja Lucia (Messenius and Lucia). Opera in two acts. FP 16 Sep 2005, Oulu.

Isän tyttö (Daddy's Girl). Opera in two acts. FP 7 Jul 2007, Savonlinna Opera Festival.

Yhden yön juttu (One Night Stand). Opera in one act. FP 15 Oct 2011, Sibelius Academy, Helsinki.

Jannen salaisuus (Janne's Secret). Children's opera. FP 27 Mar 2015, Finnish National Opera.

Oma vika (Own Fault). Monologue opera. FP 31 Oct 2015, Opera Archipelago, Turku.

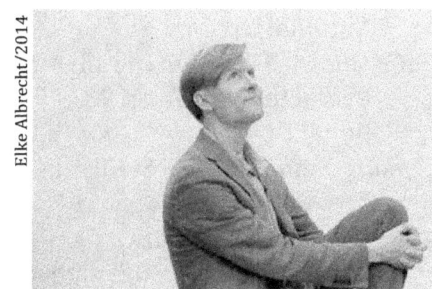

Elke Albrecht/2014

JUHA T. KOSKINEN
(b. 26 Oct 1972)

Velhosiskot (The Witch Company). Opera for six singers and ensemble. FP 18 Sep 1996, Ooppera Skaala, Helsinki.

Madame de Sade. Chamber opera. FP 8 Jul 1998, Aix-en-Provence Festival, France.

Eukko – pidättekö vainajista (The Old Woman – Are You Fond of Dead People?). Chamber opera. FP 4 Mar 2000, Finnish National Opera/Musica nova Festival/Ooppera Skaala.

Brunelda – Amerikan sydän (Brunelda – The Heart of America). Opera ritual. FP 6 Nov 2002, Ooppera Skaala, Helsinki.

Scrabble vs. Komet. From the sci-fi opera saga *Kommander Kobayashi.* FP 14 Jan 2005, Opera Stabile, Hamburg, Germany.

Tumps! Stand-Up Opera with Pasi Lyytikäinen and Adam Világi, FP 12 Oct 2005, Ooppera Skaala, Helsinki.

Markiisitar de Sade (Madame de Sade). Chamber opera. FP 11 Aug 2010, Ooppera Skaala, Helsinki.

Lusia Rusintytär. Monologue opera. FP 7 Aug 2015, Oulunsalo Soi Festival.

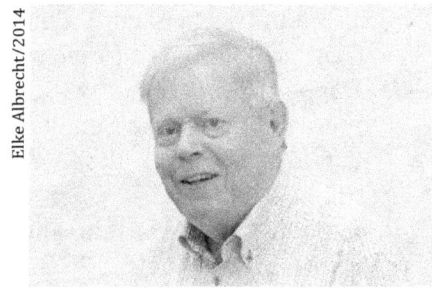

Elke Albrecht/2014

ILKKA KUUSISTO
(b. 26 Apr 1933)

Muumiooppera (Moomin Opera). Children's opera in two acts. FP 7 Dec 1974, Finnish National Opera.

Miehen kylkiluu (The Rib of a Man). Opera in three acts. FP 2 Feb 1978, Finnish

National Opera.

Sota valosta (War for the Light). Opera in five acts. FP 2 Apr 1981, Finnish National Opera.

Jääkäri Ståhl (Jaeger Ståhl). Opera in six acts with an epilogue. FP 3 Jun 1982, Vaasa (Vaasa Opera).

Pierrot eller nattens hemligheter/Pierrot ja yön salaisuudet (Pierrot or the Secrets of the Night). Youth opera in two acts. FP 5 Apr 1991, Kauniainen Music School

Postineiti (The Postmistress). Opera in two acts. FP 10 Jun 1992, Joensuu Song Festival.

Fröken Julie/Neiti Julie (Miss Julie). Opera in two acts. FP 5 Jan 1994, Vaasa (Vaasa Opera).

Gabriel, tule takaisin! (Come back, Gabriel!). Chamber opera in four acts. FP 11 Feb 1998, Finnish National Opera.

Isänmaan tyttäret (Daughters of the Fatherland). Opera in three acts. FP 11 Jun 1998, Ilmajoki Music Festival.

Kiljusten Kalevala (Kalevala after the Kiljunen Family). Family opera (children's musical) in two acts. FP 23 Mar 1999, Finnish National Opera.

Nainen kuin jäätynyt samppanja (A Woman like Frozen Champagne). Chamber opera in two acts. FP 29 Feb 2000, Helsinki (Finnish Chamber Opera).

Kuninkaan sormus (The King's Ring). Opera in two acts with a prologue. FP 12 Apr 2002, Vaasa (Vaasa Opera).

Pula! Ooppera konikapinasta (Shortage! An opera of the horse rebellion). Opera in two acts with epilogue. FP 10 Jun 2004, Nivala.

Matilda ja Nikolai (Matilda and Nikolai). Opera in two acts. FP 22 Oct 2004,

Pori (Pori Opera).

Vapauden vanki (Prisoner of freedom). Monologue opera in two acts. FP 1 Jul 2007, Huittinen (Finnish Chamber Opera).

Kohti kotia (Homeward bound). Church opera in two acts. FP 23 Oct 2009, Isokyrö (Vaasa Opera).

Taipaleenjoki (Taipale River). Opera. FP 16 Jun 2010, Ilmajoki Music Festival.

Aino Ackté. Opera. Unperformed.

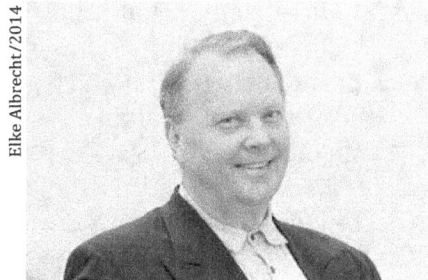

TIMO-JUHANI KYLLÖNEN
(b. 1 Dec 1955)

Roope – poika joka ei uskaltanut pelätä (Roope, the boy who did not have the courage to be afraid). Opera for the whole family. FP 15 Nov 2007, Vantaa

Tango solo. Monologue chamber opera in 13 scenes. FP 12 Jan 2011, Espoo.

El Libro de los Reyes (Kuninkaiden kirja/ The Book of Kings). Opera for the whole family in five acts (17 scenes). FP 19 Mar 2009, Cádiz, Spain.

Érase que era, una niña (Miksi juuri minä?/ Why Me?). Opera for the whole family in 13 acts. FP 6 Oct 2012, Lima, Peru.

Norppaooppera (The Seal). Opera for the whole family in five acts. FP 20 Jul 2013, Savonlinna Opera Festival.

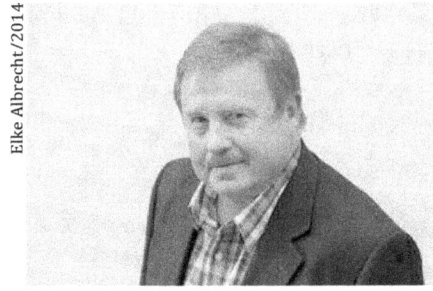

JUKKA LINKOLA
(b. 21 Jul 1955)

Elina. Opera in two acts. FP 20 Feb 1992, Finnish National Opera.

Lieran poika (Liera's Son). Folk opera in two acts. FP 10 Jul 1993, Ruovesi.

Angelika. TV opera. FP 6 Dec 1993, YLE TV 1.

Täyttyneiden toiveiden maa/Matka (The Journey). Opera in three acts. FP 27 Mar 1998, Kotka (Kotka Opera Society).

Joppe Jokamies (Everyman). Chamber opera. FP 1 Oct 2004, Malmitalo, Helsinki.

Hui kauhistus (One Spooky Night). Opera for the whole family in one act. FP 17 Jul 2006, Savonlinna Opera Festival.

Hallin Janne (Janne Halli). Folk opera. FP 15 Jul 2007, Jämsä.

Rockland. Opera in two acts. FP 15 Jul 2011, Pine Mountain Music Festival, Michigan, USA.

Robin Hood. Opera for the whole family. FP 14 Jan 2011, Finnish National Opera.

Hölmöläiset (The Dummies). Opera. FP 14 May 2013, Finnish National Opera.

Myrkkyhuntu (Poisonous Veil). Opera. FP 26 Oct 2014, Helsinki.

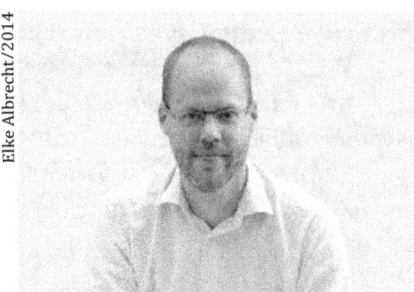

Elke Albrecht/2014

ULJAS PULKKIS
(b. 22 Jul 1975)

Viisi naista kappelissa (Five women in a chapel). Chamber opera. FP 1 Sep 2012, Espoo (Helsinki Festival).

Kekkonen – ooppera suurmiehestä (Kekkonen – an opera about a great man). Opera. FP 7 Jun 2013, Ilmajoki Music Festival.

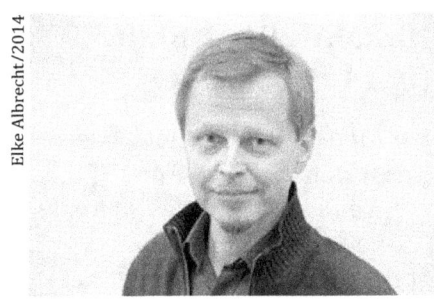

Elke Albrecht/2014

VELI-MATTI PUUMALA
(b. 18 Jul 1965)

Anna Liisa. Opera in three acts with prologue. FP 18 Aug 2008, Helsinki Festival.

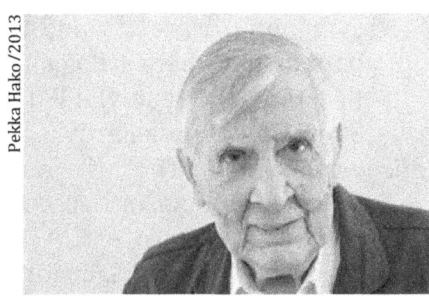

Pekka Hako/2013

EINOJUHANI RAUTAVAARA
(b. 9 Oct 1928)

Kaivos (The Mine). Opera in three acts. FP
10 Apr 1963, YLE Radio & TV.

Apollo contra Marsyas. Comic opera musical in three acts. FP 30 Aug 1973,
Finnish National Opera.

Runo 42 „Sammon ryöstö" (The Myth of
Sampo). Choir opera in one act. FP
8 Apr 1983, Helsinki.

Marjatta matala neiti (Marjatta, the Lowly
Maiden). Mystery play in one act. FP
3 Sep 1977, Espoo.

En dramatisk scen (A dramatic scene).
Chamber opera in one act. Unperformed.

Thomas. Opera in three acts. FP 21 Jun
1985, Joensuu Song Festival.

Vincent. Opera in three acts. FP 17 May
1990, Finnish National Opera.

Auringon talo (The House of the Sun). Tra-
gedia buffa, chamber opera in two
acts. FP 25 Apr 1991, Lappeenranta
(Finnish National Opera).

Tietäjien lahja (The Gift of the Magi).
Christmas tale, chamber opera. FP
23 Dec 1996, YLE TV 1.

Aleksis Kivi. Opera in three acts. FP 8 Jul
1997, Savonlinna Opera Festival.

Rasputin. Opera in three acts. FP 19 Sep
2003, Finnish National Opera.

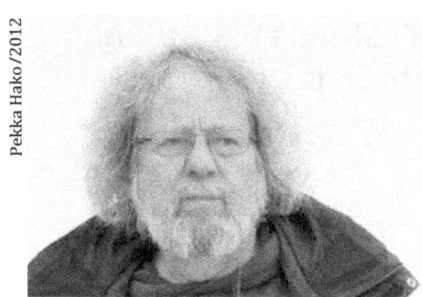

Pekka Hako/2012

HERMAN RECHBERGER
(b. 14 Feb 1947)

Zin Kibaru. Youth opera based on an African tale. FP 15 Apr 1978, Kajaani.

Die Nonnen (The Nuns). Musikspiel in one act. Unperformed.

Laurentius. Opera in two acts. FP 24 Aug 1994, Vantaa.

...nunc et semper... Fresco for large choir, symphony orchestra and tape. First part of the opera trilogy *Aika ja uni* (The Age of Dreams). FP 15 Jul 2000, Savonlinna Opera Festival.

Mielinkielinliemi (The Notion Potion). Children's opera in two acts for ages 8 to 80. Unperformed.

Noitasapatti (Black Sabbath). School opera. FP 29 Sep 2000, Helsinki (Finnish National Opera).

Das Opernschiff (The Opera Ship). Children's opera in three acts with entr'acte and epilogue. Unperformed.

Abenteuerliche Schwalbenreise (The Adventurous Journey of the Swallows). Children's opera. Unperformed.

Helike Athanatos (Immortal Helike). Extracts performed in concert.

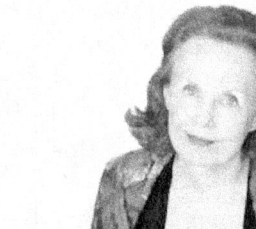

Maarit Kvtöhariu/2014

KAIJA SAARIAHO
(b. 14 Oct 1952)

L'amour de loin. Opera in five acts. FP 15 Aug 2000, Salzburg Festival, Austria.

Adriana Mater. Opera in two acts (7 tableaux). FP 3 Apr 2006, Opéra National de Paris, France.

La Passion de Simone. A musical path in 15 parts – oratorio for soprano solo, choir, orchestra and electronics. FP

26 Nov 2006, New Crowned Hope Festival Vienna, Austria.

Émilie. Opera in one act with nine scenes. FP 1 Mar 2010, Opéra de Lyon, France.

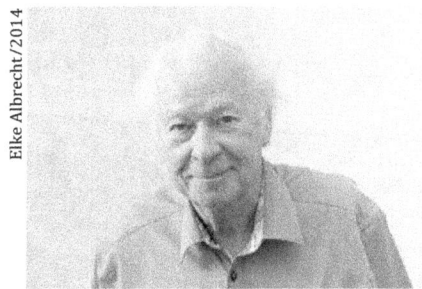

AULIS SALLINEN
(b. 9 Apr 1935)

Ratsumies (The Horseman). Opera in three acts. FP 17 Jul 1975, Savonlinna Opera Festival.

Punainen viiva (The Red Line). Opera in two acts. FP 30 Nov 1978, Finnish National Opera.

Kuningas lähtee Ranskaan (The King Goes Forth to France). A chronicle for the music theatre of the coming Ice Age, opera in three acts. FP 7 Jul 1984, Savonlinna Opera Festival.

Kullervo. Opera in two acts. FP 25 Feb 1992, Dorothy Chandler Pavillon, Los Angeles, USA.

Palatsi (The Palace). Opera in three acts. FP 26 Jul 1995, Savonlinna Opera Festival.

Kuningas Lear (King Lear). Opera in two acts with a prologue. FP 15 Sep 2000, Finnish National Opera.

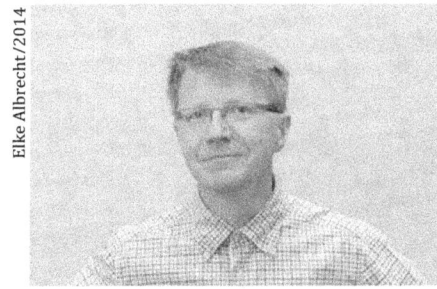

TAPIO TUOMELA
(b. 11 Oct 1958)

Korvan tarina (The story of the ear). Conceptual soap opera. FP 23 Sep 1993, Finnish National Opera.

Äidit ja tyttäret (Mothers and Daughters). Chamber opera in three acts. FP 6 Nov 1999, Finnish National Opera.

For more information on composers and their works,
please visit the Music Finland website: www.musicfinland.fi

Performances of Finnish operas outside Finland

Year (FP)	Composer	Opera	Location
1856 (1852)	Pacius, Fredrik	*Kung Karls jakt* (The Hunt of King Charles)	Stockholm, Sweden
1926 (1924)	Madetoja, Leevi	*Pohjalaisia* (The Ostrobothnians)	Stadttheater Kiel, Germany
1927 (1924)	Madetoja, Leevi	*Pohjalaisia* (The Ostrobothnians)	Kungliga Teatern, Stockholm, Sweden
1927 (1910)	Merikanto, Oskar	*Elinan surma* (The Death of Elina)	Estonia Theatre, Tallinn, Estonia
1930 (1924)	Madetoja, Leevi	*Pohjalaisia* (The Ostrobothnians)	Stora Teatern, Gothenborg, Sweden
1931 (1924)	Madetoja, Leevi	*Pohjalaisia* (The Ostrobothnians)	Radio broadcast, Berlin, Germany
1938 (1917)	Launis, Armas	*Kullervo*	Radio broadcast, Nice, France
1938 (1924)	Madetoja, Leevi	*Pohjalaisia* (The Ostrobothnians)	Det Kongelige Teater, Copenhagen, Denmark
1940 (1917)	Launis, Armas	*Kullervo*	Nice, France
1943 (1924)	Madetoja, Leevi	*Pohjalaisia* (The Ostrobothnians)	Magyar Állami Operaház, Budapest, Hungary

1949 FP!	Sonninen, Ahti	*Merenkuninkaan tytär* (The Sea-King's Daughter)	Prix Italia Competition, Italy
1950 FP!	Pylkkänen, Tauno	*Sudenmorsian* (The Wolf's Bride)	Turino, Italy
1950/1951/ 1952/1953/ 1957 (1924)	Madetoja, Leevi	*Pohjalaisia* (The Ostrobothnians)	FNO guest performances: Stockholm/Sweden, Copenhagen/Denmark, Malmö/Sweden, Oslo/Norway, Reykjavik/Iceland, Leningrad/Russia
1953 (1951)	Hannikainen, Väinö	*Aino-taru* (The Aino Legend)	Tournee of the Chamber Choir Helsinki: Hannover/Germany; Salzburg, Bad Ischl, Wien, Graz/ Austria
1973 FP!	Rydman, Kari	*Slåttsmordet* (The Castle Murder)	Hässelbystrandsskolan, Vällingby, Stockholm, Sweden
1975 FP!	Marttinen, Tauno	*Psykiatri* (Der Psychiater)	Stadthalle Bayreuth, Germany, Int. Jugendfestspieltreffen (guest performance)
1975 (1975)	Kentala, Aaro	*Morsiustaivas* (Bridal Firmament)	Umeå, Sweden
1976 (1963)	Merikanto, Aarre	*Juha*	Städtische Bühnen Hagen, Germany
1976/1979/ 1981/1983 (1975)	Kokkonen, Joonas	*Viimeiset kiusaukset* (The Last Temptations)	FNO guest performances: Stockholm/Sweden and Oslo/Norway, London/Great Britain, Wiesbaden/Germany and Zürich/Switzerland, Ost-Berlin/ Germany and New York/ USA
1977 (1974)	Kuusisto, Ilkka	*Muumiooppera* (Moomin Opera)	Graz, Austria
1979/1980/ 1981/1982/ 1983 (1978)	Sallinen, Aulis	*Punainen viiva* (The Red Line)	FNO guest performances: London/GB, Stockholm/Sweden, Wiesbaden/Germany and Zürich/Switzerland, Moscow, Leningrad/Russia, Tallinn/ Estonia and New York/USA

1980 (1975)	Sallinen, Aulis	*Ratsumies* (The Horseman)	Bühnen der Landeshauptstadt Kiel, Germany
1980 (1978)	Sallinen, Aulis	*Punainen viiva* (The Red Line)	Stora Teatern, Gothenborg, Sweden
1981 (1979)	Aho, Kalevi	*Avain* (The Key)	FNO guest performances: Warschau and Poznań, Poland
1982 (1979)	Aho, Kalevi	*Avain* (The Key)	Hamburgische Staatsoper, Germany
1984 (1979)	Aho, Kalevi	*Avain* (The Key)	Nordic Music Festival, Copenhagen, Denmark
1984 FP!	Nordgren, Pehr Henrik	*Den svarte munken* (The Black Monk)	Kungliga Operan, Stockholm, Sweden
1984 (1977)	Rautavaara, Einojuhani	*Marjatta, matala neiti* (Marjatta, Lowly Maiden)	Tournee of the Tapiola Choir, Austria, Hungary
1984 (1984)	Vuori, Harri	*Kuin linnun jalanjäljet taivaalla*	Ung Nordisk Musikseminar, Malmö, Sweden
1985 (1963)	Merikanto, Aarre	*Juha*	Theatre of the Northwestern University School of Music, Evanston, Illinois, USA
1985 (1978)	Sallinen, Aulis	*Punainen viiva* (The Red Line)	FNO guest performances: Osnabrück and Dortmund, Germany
1986 (1984)	Sallinen, Aulis	*Kuningas lähtee Ranskaan* (The King Goes Forth to France)	Bühnen der Landeshauptstadt Kiel, Germany
1986 (1984)	Sallinen, Aulis	*Kuningas lähtee Ranskaan* (The King Goes Forth to France)	Santa Fé Opera Festival, USA
1987 / 1989 (1963)	Merikanto, Aarre	*Juha*	FNO guest performances: Edinburgh Festival/GB and Essen/Germany
1987 (1984)	Sallinen, Aulis	*Kuningas lähtee Ranskaan* (The King Goes Forth to France)	Royal Opera House Covent Garden, London, Great Britain
1989 (1924)	Madetoja, Leevi	*Pohjalaisia* (The Ostrobothnians)	Mikkeli Opera guest performances: Plzen & Teplice, Czech Rep.

1989 (1896)	Sibelius, Jean	*Jungfrun i tornet* (The Maiden in the Tower)	Pfalztheater Kaiserslautern: Kaiserslautern, Saarlouis and Landau, Germany
1990 (1978)	Kuusisto, Ilkka	*Miehen kylkiluu* (The Rib of a Man)	Tarto, Pärnu & Tallinn, Estonia
1990 (1924)	Madetoja, Leevi	*Pohjalaisia* (The Ostrobothnians)	Statni Divadlo Usti Bad Labem Opera, Czechoslovakia
1991 (1975)	Kokkonen, Joonas	*Viimeiset kiusaukset* (The Last Temptations)	Kuopio Opera guest performances: Gothenborg, Sweden
1991 (1990)	Rautavaara, Einojuhani	*Vincent*	Bühnen der Landeshauptstadt Kiel, Germany
1991 (1975)	Sallinen, Aulis	*Ratsumies* (The Horseman)	Ystad Opera, Ystad, Sweden
1991 (1975)	Sallinen, Aulis	*Ratsumies* (The Horseman)	Estonia Theater Tallinn, Estonia
1991 (1990)	Rautavaara, Einojuhani	*Vincent*	Theater Hagen, Germany
1992 FP!	Sallinen, Aulis	*Kullervo*	Dorothy Chandler Pavilion, Los Angeles, USA
1992/1993 (1992)	Chydenius, Kaj	*Figaron häät* (The Marriage of Figaro)	KOM Theatre guest performances in Poland, Germany and Chile
1992 (1991)	Rautavaara, Einojuhani	*Auringon talo* (The House of the Sun)	Kungliga Teatern, Stockholm, Sweden
1994 (1985)	Rautavaara, Einojuhani	*Thomas*	Theater Hagen, Germany
1994–1995 (1991)	Rautavaara, Einojuhani	*Auringon talo* (The House of the Sun)	Theater Vorpommern, Germany: Greifswald and Stralsund (1994–1995), Mönchengladbach (1995)
1995 (1992)	Sallinen, Aulis	*Kullervo*	Nantes Opéra, France
1998 (1990)	Rautavaara, Einojuhani	*Vincent*	Tiroler Landestheater, Innsbruck, Austria

1998 FP!	Koskinen, Juha T.	*Madame de Sade*	Aix-en-Provence Festival, France
1998/1999 (1997)	Rautavaara, Einojuhani	*Aleksis Kivi*	SOF guest performances: Strasbourg & Mulhouse, France & Cosenza, Italy
1999 (1995)	Bergman, Erik	*Det sjungande trädet* (The Singing Tree)	FNO guest performance: Berlin, Germany
1999 (1999)	Padilla, Alfonso	*A la luz de la oscuridad* (From Darkness to Light)	Guest perfomances: Caracas, Venezuela; Lima and Cuzco, Peru
1999 (1997)	Rautavaara, Einojuhani	*Aleksis Kivi*	Minnesota Opera Theatre and Orchestra, Minneapolis, USA
1999 (1995)	Sallinen, Aulis	*Palatsi* (The Palace)	Theater Vorpommern: Festival Nordischer Klang, Greifswald, Germany
2000 (2000)	Kuusisto, Ilkka	*Nainen kuin jätynyt samppanja* (A Woman Like Frozen Champagne)	Finnish Chamber Opera guest performances: Tarto, Estonia
2000 FP!	Saariaho, Kaija	*L'amour de loin*	Salzburger Festspiele, Austria
2000–2001 (2000)	Saariaho, Kaija	*L'amour de loin*	Stadttheater Bern, Switzerland
2001 (2000)	Saariaho, Kaija	*L'amour de loin*	Théâtre du Châtelet, Paris, France
2001 (2001)	Fagerudd, Markus	*Gaia*	FNO guest performances: Utrecht, The Netherlands
2001 (1992)	Sallinen, Aulis	*Kullervo*	Theater Lübeck, Germany
2001 (1992)	Sallinen, Aulis	*Kullervo*	University College Opera, London, Great Britain
2001 (2000)	Sallinen, Aulis	*Kuningas Lear* (King Lear)	Pfalztheater Kaiserslautern and Theater Trier, Germany
2002 (2001)	Aho, Kalevi	*Ennen me kaikki olemme hukkuneet* (Before We All Have Drowned)	Theater Lübeck, Germany

2002 (2002)	Sivén, Jani	*Troijan naiset* (The Trojan Women)	Guest perfomances of the Helsinki Conservatory: Berlin, Germany
2002 (2000)	Saariaho, Kaija	*L'amour de loin*	Santa Fé Opera Festival, Santa Fé Opera, USA
2002 (2000)	Saariaho, Kaija	*L'amour de loin*	Barbican, London, Great Britain
2003 (2000)	Saariaho, Kaija	*L'amour de loin*	Staatstheater Darmstadt, Germany
2004 (1991)	Rautavaara, Einojuhani	*Auringon talo* (The House of the Sun)	Walton Arts Centre, Fayetteville, Arkansas, USA
2004 (1991)	Rautavaara, Einojuhani	*Auringon talo* (The House of the Sun)	Musikwerkstatt Wien and Konservatorium Wien, Austria
2004 (2000)	Tikka, Kari	*Luther*	FNO guest performances: Wittenberg and Berlin, Germany
2005 FP!	Koskinen, Juha T.	*Scrabble vs. Komet*	Opera stabile, Hamburg, Germany
2005 (1975)	Kokkonen, Joonas	*Viimeiset kiusaukset* (The Last Temptations)	Tampere Opera guest performance: National Theatre, Prague, Czech Republic
2005 (2003)	Rautavaara, Einojuhani	*Rasputin*	FNO guest performances: St. Petersburg, Russia
2005 (1990)	Rautavaara, Einojuhani	*Vincent*	Theater Heidelberg, Germany
2005 (2000)	Hakola, Kimmo	*Marsin mestarilaulajat* (The Mastersingers of Mars)	Festspielhaus St. Pölten, Austria
2005 (2000)	Saariaho, Kaija	*L'amour de loin*	FNO guest performances: Holland Festival, Muziekgebouw, Amsterdam, The Netherlands
2006 (2003)	Rautavaara, Einojuhani	*Rasputin* (Lübeck version)	Theater Lübeck, Germany
2006 (1975)	Sallinen, Aulis	*Ratsumies* (The Horseman)	SOF guest performances: Bolshoi Theatre, Moscow, Russia

2006 (2000)	Saariaho, Kaija	*L'amour de loin*	Al Bustan Festival, Lebanon
2006 (2000)	Saariaho, Kaija	*L'amour de loin*	MärzMusik, Berlin, Germany
2006 (2000)	Saariaho, Kaija	*L'amour de loin*	Théâtre du Châtelet, Paris, France
2006 FP!	Saariaho, Kaija	*Adriana Mater*	Opéra National de Paris, France
2006 (1992)	Sallinen, Aulis	*Kullervo*	Stadttheater Bern, Switzerland
2006 (2000)	Saariaho, Kaija	*L'amour de loin*	Conservatoire de Strasbourg, France
2007 (1992)	Sallinen, Aulis	*Kullervo*	Saarländisches Staatstheater, Saarbrücken, Germany
2008 (2003)	Fagerudd, Markus	*Heinähattu, Vilttitossu ja suuri pamaus* (Strawhat, Feltslipper and the Big Bang)	Kapsäkki guest performances in Germany, Sweden and the USA
2008 (2006)	Saariaho, Kaija	*Adriana Mater*	Barbican, London, Great Britain
2008 (2006)	Saariaho, Kaija	*Adriana Mater*	Santa Fé Opera, USA
2008 (2000)	Saariaho, Kaija	*L'amour de loin*	Bergen International Festival, Norway
2008 (2000)	Saariaho, Kaija	*L'amour de loin*	La Comedie de Clermont, Clermont-Ferrand, France
2009 FP!	Kyllönen, Timo-Juhani	*El libro de los Reyes*	Gran Teatro Falla, Cádiz, Spain
2009 (1984)	Sallinen, Aulis	*Kuningas lähtee Ranskaan* (The King Goes Forth to France)	Guildhall School of Music and Drama, Barbican Centre, London, Great Britain
2009 (2009)	Fagerlund, Sebastian	*Döbeln 1809*	West Coast Kokkola Opera guest performances: Stockholm & Umeå, Sweden

2009 (1978)	Sallinen, Aulis	*Punainen viiva* (The Red Line)	FNO guest performances: St. Petersburg, Russia
2009 (2000)	Saariaho, Kaija	*L'amour de loin*	Volkstheater Rostock, Germany
2009 (2000)	Saariaho, Kaija	*L'amour de loin*	English National Opera, Coliseum, London, Great Britain
2010 FP!	Saariaho, Kaija	*Émilie*	Opéra de Lyon, France
2010 (2010)	Saariaho, Kaija	*Émilie*	Het Muziektheater, Amsterdam, The Netherlands
2010 FP!	Linjama, Jyrki	*Die Geburt des Täufers* (The Birth of the Baptist)	Carinthischer Sommer, Ossiach, Austria
2010 (2000)	Saariaho, Kaija	*L'amour de loin*	Vlaamse Opera, Antwerp & Ghent, Belgium
2011 (2006)	Saariaho, Kaija	*Adriana Mater*	Theater Osnabrück, Germany
2011 (2010)	Saariaho, Kaija	*Émilie*	Spoleto Festival, Charleston, USA
2011 FP!	Linkola, Jukka	*Rockland*	Pine Mountain Music Festival, Michigan, USA
2011 (1992)	Sallinen, Aulis	*Kullervo*	Oper Frankfurt, Germany
2012 (2000)	Saariaho, Kaija	*L'amour de loin*	Canadian Opera Company, Toronto, Canada
2012 (1994)	Kuusisto, Ilkka	*Fröken Julie* (Miss Julie)	Montforthaus Feldkirch, Austria
2012 (2010)	Saariaho, Kaija	*Émilie*	Lincoln Center Festival, New York, USA
2012 FP!	Kyllönen, Timo-Juhani	*Érase que era, una niña*	Teatro Británico, Lima, Peru
2013 (2011)	Hyytiäinen, Miika	*Pierrot lunaire und drei Schattenträume*	Wondersite Festival, Tokyo, Japan
2013 (2010)	Saariaho, Kaija	*Émilie*	Lisbon & Porto, Portugal
2013 FP!	Hyytiäinen, Miika	*La figure de la terre*	Sophiensäle, Berlin, Germany

2014 (2000)	Saariaho, Kaija	*L'amour de loin*	Den Norske Opera, Oslo, Norway
2014 FP!	Hyytiäinen, Miika	*Aikainen* (Early)	Berlin, Germany
2014 (2010)	Saariaho, Kaija	*Émilie*	Salzburger Landestheater, Salzburg, Austria
2014 (2014)	Hyytiäinen, Miika	*Aikainen* (Early)	London, Great Britain
2014 FP!	Hyytiäinen, Miika	*You are here*	Glyndebourne Opera House, Great Britain
2014 (2000)	Saariaho, Kaija	*L'amour de loin*	Trondheim Chamber Music Festival, Norway
2015 (2000)	Saariaho, Kaija	*L'amour de loin*	Landestheater Linz, Austria
2015 (2000)	Saariaho, Kaija	*L'amour de loin*	Tokyo Opera City Concert Hall, Japan
2015 (2000)	Saariaho, Kaija	*L'amour de loin*	Grand Theatre de Quebec, Quebec City, Canada

FNO = Finnish National Opera, FP = first performance (world premiere), SOF = Savonlinna Opera Festival

Select bibliography

Alho Olli (ed.). *Finland, a cultural encyclopedia.* Finnish Literature Society, Helsinki 1999.

Aho Kalevi et al. *After Sibelius – Finnish Music Past and Present.* Finnish Music Information Centre, Helsinki 1992.

Hako Pekka. *Finnish Opera.* Finnish Music Information Centre, Helsinki 2002.

Hillila Ruth-Esther & Hong Barbara Blanchard. *Historical Dictionary of the Music and Musicians of Finland.* Greenwood Press, Westport 1997.

Jaakkola Jutta & Toivonen Aarne (eds.). *Inspired by tradition. Kalevala poetry in Finnish music.* Finnish Music Information Centre, Helsinki 2005.

Korhonen Kimmo. *Inventing Finnish Music. Contemporary Composers from Medieval to Modern.* Finnish Music Information Centre, Helsinki 2003.

Savonlinnan Oopperajuhlat & Savonlinnan Maakuntamuseo (eds.). *Oopperaa Linnassa. Savonlinnan Oopperajuhlien 30-vuotisjuhlanäyttely. Opera in the Castle. Exhibition in honour of the 30th anniversary of the Savonlinna Opera Festival.* Savonlinna 1997.

Richards Denby. *The Music of Finland.* Hugh Evelyn, London 1968.

Wilmer S E & Koski Pirkko. *The Dynamic World of Finnish Theatre.* Like, Helsinki 2006.

Discography

Almila, Atso
- *Ameriikka* (America). Kamaristudio CS Records CSCD 114 (CD/1993).

Bergman, Erik
- *Det sjungande trädet* (The Singing Tree). Ondine ODE 794-2D (2 CD/1992).

Chydenius, Kaj
- *Lapualaisooppera* (Lapua Opera). Siboney SIBCD 7 (CD/1996).

Crusell, Bernhard Henrik
- *Den lilla slavinnan* (The Little Slave Girl). Classica CL 144 (CD/2000).

Ekat oopperat – Viisi animaatiota (First operas – Five animations):
- Jarkko Hartikainen: *Aurinko ja kuu* (The Sun and the Moon).
- Kimmo Kuokkala: *Geenimanipuloidun omenan kirjeenvaihtoilmoitus* (A GM Apple).
- Matti Laiho: *Lehmä ja pilvi* (The Cow and The Cloud).
- Ari Romppanen: *Lehmä karkaa* (The Runaway Cow).
- Adam Világi: *Kalastaja, joka rikkoi toisten verkot* (The Fisherman who Tore up the Other's Nets).

„Ekat oopperat – Viisi animaatiota" (First operas – Five animations"). DVD made in collaboration with Oop! – the Finnish National Opera's department for children and young people, Sibelius Academy's Department of Composition and Music Theory, Mikkeli Art Museum, Regional Arts Council of Southern Savo and selected schools. (DVD/2007). [Subtitles: English, Finnish]

Fagerudd, Markus

- *Heinähattu, Vilttitossu ja suuri pamaus* (Strawhat, Feltslipper and the Big Bang). Ooppera- ja teatteriseurue Kapsäkki: KAPS-1 / Fuga: FUGA9173 (CD/2003).

Heininen, Paavo

- *Silkkirumpu* (The Damask Drum). Finlandia Records FACD 106 (CD/1989).

Heiniö, Mikko

- *Riddaren och draken* (The Knight and the Dragon). BIS-CD-1246 (CD/2001).
- *Eerik XIV.* Turku Music Festival Foundation (DVD/2011). [Subtitles: English, Finnish, Swedish]

Hofmann, Heinz-Juhani

- *Ahti Karjalainen – elämä, Kekkonen ja teot* (Ahti Karjalainen – Life, Kekkonen and Works). Alba ABCD 381 (CD/2015).

Kokkonen, Joonas

- *Viimeiset kiusaukset* (The Last Temptations). Deutsche Grammophon 2740 190 (3 LP/1978), re-released as Finlandia Records FA 104 LP3 (3 LP/1984), re-released as Finlandia Records FACD 104 (2 CD/1990).

Kortekangas, Olli

- *Grand Hotel.* Ondine ODE 749-2 (CD/1990).
- *Messenius ja Lucia* (Messenius and Lucia). Ondine 1073-2D (2 CD/2006).

Kuusisto, Ilkka

- *Pierrot eller nattens hemligheter/Pierrot ja yön salaisuudet* (Pierrot or the Secrets of the Night).
  [1] Grankulla musikskola GM CD 3 (CD/1991) (Swedish version),
  [2] Kauniaisten musiikkikoulu KM CD 2 (CD/1991) (Finnish version).
- *Pula! Ooppera Konikapinasta* (Shortage! Opera about the horse rebellion).
  [1] Macedonia MACD 006 (2 CD/2005)
  [2] Macedonia MADVD 005 (DVD/2005).
- *Vapauden vanki* (Prisoner of freedom). Fuga FUGA9279 (DVD/2009). [Subtitles: English, Finnish, German, Swedish]
- *Nainen kuin jäätynyt samppanja* (A Woman like Frozen Champagne). Fuga FUGA9312 (DVD/2011). [Subtitles: English, Finnish, German, Swedish]

Kuusisto, Jaakko

- *Prinsessan och vildsvanarna* (The Princess and the Wild Swans). FSRCD14 (CD/2005).

- *Koirien Kalevala* (The Canine Kalevala). Ondine ODV 4007 (DVD/2008). [Subtitles: English]

Launis, Armas
- *Aslak Hetta.* Ondine ODE 1050-2D (2 CD/2005).

Linjama, Jyrki
- *Die Geburt des Täufers* (The Birth of the Baptist). Alba ABCD 370 (CD/2014).

Linkola, Jukka
- *Täyttyneiden toiveiden maa/Matka* (The Journey). Alba ABCD 200 (2 CD/2004).
- *Hui kauhistus* (One Spooky Night). Ondine ODV 4006 (DVD/2009). [Subtitles: English]
- *Robin Hood.* Alba AB-BR-DV 1 (DVD Video & blu-ray/2013). [Subtitles: English, Finnish, Swedish]

Madetoja, Leevi
- *Pohjalaisia* (The Ostrobothnians).
  [1] Finnlevy Stereo SFX 22B24 (3 LP/1975), re-released as Finlandia Records 511002 (2 CD/1992).
  [2] Finlandia Records 3984-21440-2 (2 CD/1998).
- *Juha.* Ondine ODE 714-2 (2 CD/1988).

Melartin, Erkki
- *Aino.* BIS-CD-1193/94 (2 CD/2002).

Merikanto, Aarre
- *Juha.*
  [1] Finnlevy Stereo SFX 1B2B3 (3 LP/1972), re-released as Finlandia Records FA 105 LP3 (3 LP/1985), re-released as FACD 105 (2 CD/1988)
  [2] Ondine ODE 872-2D (2 CD/1996).

Pacius, Fredrik
- *Kung Karls jakt* (The Hunt of King Charles). Finlandia Records FACD 107 (2 CD/1991).
- *Die Loreley.* BIS-CD-1393/1394 (2 CD/2003).
- *Princessan af Cypern* (The Princess of Cyprus). BIS-CD-1340 (CD/2004).
- *Kaarle-kuninkaan metsästys* (The Hunt of King Charles; Finnish language version). Naxos 8.660122-23FIN (2 CD/2004).

Palmgren, Selim

- *Daniel Hjort.* Finlandia Records 0630-14912-2 (2 CD/1996).

Panula, Jorma

- *Jaakko Ilkka.* Levytuottajat GDL 2014 (LP/1979).
- *Jokiooppera* (River Opera). Jorma Panula Säätiö JPSLP 001B003 (2 LP/1983).
- *Haavurikukko* (The Country Surgeon). Medipolar (2 LP, edited version/1980) (not distributed commercially).

Pethman, Esa

- *Ulstadius.* Turun Tähtituotanto FFCD1035 (2 CD/2002).

Pohjola, Seppo

- *Arabian Jänis* (The Arabian Rabbit). Alba ABCD 228 (CD/2006).
- *Kaappi* (The Closet) und *Rakkaimpani* (My Dearest). Alba ABCD 263 (CD/2008).

Pokela, Marjatta

- *Mörköooppera* (Bugbear Opera). Discophon RCA PL 40189 (LP), RCA PK 40189 (cassette/1980), extracts released on CD in 1990 as Kerberos KECD 686 (CD).
- *Mörri-Möykyn suvi* (The Summer of Grumpy Griping). Discophon Kerberos KEL 653 (LP), KEC 653 (cassette/1983).
- *Mörkö se lähti laivaan* (Mörköooppera 2) (The Bugbear Goes On Board, or Bugbear Opera 2). Discophon Kerberos KEL 667 (LP), KEC 667 (cassette/1985), extracts released as Kerberos KECD 686 (CD/1990).
- *Karamelliooppera* (Sweets Opera). Fazer Musiikki 4509-97611-2 (CD/1994).

Puumala, Veli-Matti

- *Anna Liisa.* Ondine ODE 1254-2D (2 CD/2015).

Pylkkänen, Tauno

- *Mare ja hänen poikansa* (Mare and her Son). Ondine ODE 1055-2D (2 CD/2005).

Rautavaara, Einojuhani

- *Kaivos* (The Mine). Ondine ODE 1174-2 (CD/2011).
- *Runo 42 "Sammon ryöstö"* (The Myth of Sampo). Ondine ODE 842-2 (CD/1995).
- *Marjatta matala neiti* (Marjatta, the Lowly Maiden)
  [1] BIS LP-132 (LP/1979), re-released as BIS-CD-94 (CD/1995).
  [2] Finlandia FACD 921 (CD), re-released as Finlandia 3984-26586-2 (CD/1999).
  [3] Ondine ODE 1169-2 (CD/2011).
- *Thomas.* Ondine ODE 704 LP2 (2 LP/1986), re-released as ODE 704-2 (2 CD/1988).

- *Vincent.* Ondine ODE 750-2 (2 CD/1990).
- *Auringon talo* (The House of the Sun). Ondine ODE 1032-2D (2 CD/2003).
- *Tietäjien lahja* (The Gift of the Magi). Arthaus Musik 100 419 (DVD/2005). [Subtitles: English, French, German, Spanish]
- *Aleksis Kivi.*
  [1] Ondine ODE 1000-2D (2 CD/2002).
  [2] Ondine ODV 4009 (DVD/2011). [Subtitles: English, Finnish]
- *Rasputin.* Ondine ODV 4002 (DVD/2005). [Subtitles: English, Finnish, French, German]

Rechberger, Herman
- *Laurentius.* MILS Musiikki OY MILS 9761 (CD/1997).

Saariaho, Kaija
- *L'Amour de loin.*
  [1] Deutsche Grammophon DVD-VIDEO NTSC 073-402 6 (DVD/2005).
  [Subtitles: English, French, German, Spanish]
  [2] Harmonia Mundi HMC801937.38 (2 CD/2009).
- *La Passion de Simone.* Ondine ODE 1217-2 (CD/2013).

Saastamoinen, Ilpo
- *Velho-trilogia* (Wizard Trilogy): *Velho* (The Wizard). *Riekko* (The Willow Grouse). *Käärme* (The Snake). Santa Claus Medias SCMCD-01 (2 CD/2000) (The Best of Velho trilogy on the disc Velhon aika, Time of the Wizard).

Sallinen, Aulis
- *Ratsumies* (The Horseman). Finlandia Records FA 101 LP3 (3 LP/1979), re-released as FACD 101 (1576-511012) (2 CD/1991).
- *Punainen viiva* (The Red Line).
  [1] Finlandia Records FA 102 LP3 (3 LP/1980), re-released as FACD 102 (1576-51102-2) (2 CD/1990).
  [2] Ondine ODV 4008 (DVD/2010).
- *Kullervo.* Ondine ODE 780-3T (3 CD/1992), re-released as ODE 1258-2T (2014).
- *Palatsi* (The Palace).
  [1]Savonlinna Opera Festival SOJ 01 (2 CD/1996), also released as an appendix to Classica magazine, CL 118 (2 CD/1996).
  [2] Arthaus Musik 102 091 (DVD/2006), recorded from the Savonlinna Opera Festival 1995. [Subtitles: English, Finnish, French, German, Italian, Spanish]
- *Kuningas lähtee Ranskaan* (The King Goes Forth to France). Ondine ODE 1066-2D (2 CD/2006).

- *Kuningas Lear* (King Lear). Ondine ODV 4010 (DVD/2015). [Subtitles: English, Finnish]

Sibelius, Jean
- *Jungfrun i tornet* (The Maiden in the Tower)
  [1] BIS-LP-250 (LP/1984), re-released as BIS-CD-250 (CD/1984).
  [2] Virgin Classics 7243 5 45493 2 8 (CD/2002).

Tikka, Kari
- *Frieda*. Profile Records PROCD-020 (CD/1997) (Four scenes from the opera on the disc *Siinä on rakkaus* - Kari Tikan lauluja, containing songs by Kari Tikka).
- *Luther*. Ondine ODV 4001 (DVD/2004). [Subtitles: English, Finnish, German, Swedish]

Tuomela, Tapio
- *Äidit ja tyttäret* (Mothers and Daughters). MusiKado GmbH aulos AUL 66156 (2 CD/2007).

Glossary

Fennomania Swedish had been the language of administration and education in the Swedish era and remained the only official language in Finland well into the Russian era, Finnish – the language of the common people – not being considered worthy of official status. Church services, however, were held in Finnish since the Reformation in the 16th century. A movement towards improving the status of the Finnish language, connected with the quest for a national identity, led to the establishment of an ideological movement known as Fennomania in the 1840s. Its members advocated the superiority of the Finnish language; they founded the Finnish Party and in 1847 established the first regular Finnish-language newspaper, *Suometar*, aimed at an educated and cultured readership. Philosopher, journalist and later statesman Johan Vilhelm Snellman was a prominent Fennoman. He complained in the press about the Finnish people being culturally and materially underprivileged compared to other nations and argued that this was because of Finland's underdeveloped national identity. Snellman eventually appealed directly to Tsar Alexander II, who in 1863 issued a decree declaring the Finnish language to have equal status with Swedish. For all that Finland's nationalist movement and the national identity issue were a joint national effort, the language dispute between Finnish and Swedish – the historical status of the latter firmly supported by the *Svecomania* movement – represented a deep and at times violent divide. Indeed, the language dispute persists at a lower level to this day, especially in the regularly arising political debate concerning compulsory Swedish lessons in all Finnish schools.

Finlandia Hall Designed by the celebrated architect Alvar Aalto and opened in 1971, this concert and conference centre was home to the Helsinki Philharmonic Orchestra and at times the Finnish Radio Symphony Orchestra until the inauguration of the Helsinki

Music Centre in 2011. The poor acoustics of the main auditorium prompted much heated public debate ever since the building was completed, fuelling continuing demands for a purpose-built concert hall. Subsequent improvements, both structural and electronic, never succeeded in improving the acoustics beyond marginally adequate.

Finnish history   The concept of Finland as a region and later a more definite political entity was slow to emerge, and the concept of Finland as a nation in her own right developed later still. The following is a brief timeline of Finnish history, focusing mainly on events leading up to and following Finnish independence (1917).

pre-1100: Prehistory, arrival of the ancestors of the Finns in several waves over several centuries; the Sámi are pushed towards the north.

1154: Crusade to Finland by Erik IX, King of Sweden, commonly held as the beginning of almost 700 years of Swedish rule. The term 'Finland' initially only referred to the south-western corner of modern Finland.

1323: The border between Sweden and the Principality of Novgorod was officially agreed for the first time by the Treaty of Nöteborg. Later, the eastern border of Sweden (i.e. of Finland) would be pushed back towards Russia on several occasions as Sweden evolved into a regional superpower by the 17th century.

1475: Olavinlinna Castle, today in the city of Savonlinna, was built as a border stronghold.

1522: Gustav Vasa, King of Sweden, abandoned the Catholic Church and established the Lutheran Church as the state church.

1700–1721: Great Northern War, in which Sweden lost her superpower status and much of her eastern territories to Russia. Finland was twice occupied by Russia in the early 18th century but was restored to Sweden by treaty on both occasions. The south-eastern part of Finland (hence known as 'Old Finland') was ceded by Sweden to Russia in 1743.

1809: As a result of an agreement between Napoleon and Tsar Alexander I, Russia captured Finland from Sweden in the Napoleonic Wars. Thanks to deft manoeuvring by Finnish politicians and the desire of the Tsar to pacify the borderlands of the Empire, Finland was created an autonomous Grand Duchy: most importantly, Finland's Swedish-era legislation and administration were retained largely intact, and Swedish remained the official language of government. 'Old Finland' was restored to the Grand Duchy.

1812: Finland's capital, Turku, was considered by the Russians to be too close to Sweden for comfort, and the small town of Helsinki was appointed the capital city.

1863: The Finnish language was given equal official status with Swedish by Imperial Decree.

1917: Russian Revolution, leading to the establishment of Soviet Russia.

6 December 1917: Finland declared independence. The Bolshevik government was the first to recognise Finland.

1917–1918: Civil War in Finland between the Russian-minded Reds who advocated revolution and the German-supported Whites who preferred the existing social order. The Reds initially held large parts of southern Finland but were eventually overwhelmed by the military superiority of the Whites.

1919: Finland became a parliamentarian republic.

30 Nov 1939 – 13 Mar 1940: Winter War (against the Soviet Union)

25 Jun 1941 – 19 Sep 1944: Continuation War (against the Soviet Union)

15 Sep 1944 – 27 Apr 1945: War of Lapland (to drive former German allies out of Finland) In the Second World War, Finland was obliged to cede a large portion of southern Karelia to the Soviet Union, leading to a massive influx of Karelian refugees; between 350,000 and 400,000 were resettled elsewhere in Finland after the war.

1995: Following a referendum, Finland became a Member State of the European Union.

Finnish language   Finnish belongs to the Finno-Ugric language family along with Hungarian, Estonian and the Sámi languages, as opposed to the Indo-European language family to which the majority of European languages belong. Finnish was declared a national language with equal status to Swedish in 1863. The Sámi languages are today recognised as minority languages in the Sámi homeland in Lapland. Finnish is a heavily inflected language, with 15 noun cases and a number of enclitic suffixes, which together with an elaborate verbal system and features such as consonant gradation make it a daunting prospect for learners. On the other hand, Finnish is extremely easy to pronounce, as it has one of the highest sign-to-sound ratios of all world languages: basically each letter corresponds to one and only one sound.

Finnish National Opera (Suomen Kansallisooppera)   The opera company founded at the initiative of Edvard Fazer in 1911, the Domestic Opera (Kotimainen ooppera), was renamed the Finnish Opera in 1914 (Suomalainen ooppera) and the Finnish National Opera in 1956. The FNO obtained its own orchestra in 1963, that duty having previously been performed by the Helsinki Philharmonic. The opera company was initially based at the Alexander Theatre, built in 1880 as the theatre of the Russian garrison in Helsinki. This was intended as a temporary home, as it was far too small and cramped for the proper staging of grand opera and ballet, but it was not until the 1970s that a movement to build a proper opera house got under way, mainly due to the efforts of Alfons Almi (1904–1991), an opera singer who held leading administrative positions at the FNO from 1953 to 1971. After many delays, the new Opera House was eventually inaugurated on

30 November 1993 with a performance of *Kullervo* by Aulis Sallinen. The studio stage of the Opera House, Almi Hall, is named after Alfons Almi. Between 1975 and 2010, the FNO gave the world premieres of 28 Finnish operas.

Directors and artistic directors referred to in this book:

1911–1938	Edvard Fazer	1984–1992	Jorma Hynninen
1911–1912	Aino Ackté	1992–1996	Walton Grönroos
1938–1939	Aino Ackté	1997–2001	Juhani Raiskinen
1973–1974	Leif Segerstam	2001–2007	Erkki Korhonen
1974–1984	Juhani Raiskinen	2007–2013	Mikko Franck
1984–1992	Ilkka Kuusisto		

Kalevala The *Kalevala* is a collection of myths and tales from an orally transmitted tradition of the Finns and related peoples that can be traced back some 2,000 years. This poetry was traditionally recited by singing or chanting in a style known as *runo* singing. The *Kalevala* was compiled by physician and linguist Elias Lönnrot (1802–1884), who collected a great deal of folk poetry himself from old singers in Karelia and elsewhere. Lönnrot was convinced that there had to be a single underlying narrative from which this ancient folk poetry was derived. He had a Homeric vision of reconstructing this national epic, and in view of this he proceeded with remarkable integrity, refraining from editing his material and from inserting his own additions except for a number of linking passages. The first edition of the *Kalevala* was published in 1835 to great success, and the second and now definitive version was published in 1849; it contains 22,795 lines arranged into 50 *runos*, or cantos. The *Kalevala* remains one of the key works of Finnish literature and has inspired numerous artworks in other genres, above all in visual arts and music. The Finnish word for 'hero' (*sankari*) is derived from the Swedish word for 'singer' (*sångare*), reflecting the importance of the singing of spells and the knowledge of words in the tales of the *Kalevala*: if one knows the right words, one can control anything. As an example, a confrontation between the old sage Väinämöinen, the central character in the epic, and a young hothead named Joukahainen ends up with Väinämöinen 'singing Joukahainen into the bog' with the power of words alone.

The following is a list of key characters and concepts in the *Kalevala* that are referred to in the pages of this book:

Aino: Sister of Joukahainen whom Väinämöinen desires to marry; she drowns herself rather than marry the old man.

Ilmarinen (also *Seppo Ilmarinen*): A master blacksmith who can make virtually anything out of metal. He fashions the wondrous mill known as the Sampo.

Joukahainen: A young man from Lapland who taunts and challenges Väinämöinen to a duel of words and when bested by him pleads with him to spare his life, offering his sister in marriage.

Kalevala: The home of the people of Kaleva, the main characters in the epic.

Kullervo: A tragic character who is sold into slavery and kills the wife of his owner (Ilmarinen the smith). Having escaped, he unwittingly seduces his own long-lost sister, who drowns herself on discovering this. Kullervo then kills the clan who had killed his parents and finally falls on his own sword out of shame.

Lemminkäinen: A young womanising hero who has a passion for both women and war. He is killed attempting to win the hand of the Daughter of Pohjola and brought back from the dead by his mother.

Louhi: The Mistress of Pohjola, a malevolent figure of power who becomes the chief enemy of the people of Kaleva.

Marjatta: The central character of the final tale in the *Kalevala*, a Nativity legend. She becomes pregnant after eating a berry and gives birth to the King of Karelia, leading to the departure of Väinämöinen.

Pohjan neiti (also *Pohjolan tytär*): One of the daughters of Pohjola, eagerly courted by Väinämöinen and Lemminkäinen but eventually won by Ilmarinen by making the Sampo.

Pohjola: The 'northern land', a realm separate from Kalevala that initially appears as foreign and sinister and subsequently becomes an enemy. The geographical locations of Kalevala and Pohjola have been much debated but never definitively established; one theory has it that Pohjola represents the richer and more advanced civilisation of Constantinople.

Saaren tytär: Literally 'daughter of the island', one of the conquests of Lemminkäinen.

Sampo: The Sampo, made by Ilmarinen the smith, is described a wondrous mill that can produce gold, grain and salt in endless quantities, but the description is too vague to determine whether it represents an artefact from another, more advanced civilisation (such as Constantinople) or whether it is merely a manifestation of the universal mythological concept of the cornucopia or horn of plenty.

Väinämöinen: The central figure in the *Kalevala* – a demigod, hero, shaman, singer and builder of the first kantele.

For more information on the *Kalevala* and its contents, visit the website of the Finnish Literature Society: http://neba.finlit.fi/kalevala/

Kantele (also **kannel**)   A zither-like instrument without a fretboard. The original instrument had five strings; nowadays there are larger instruments with tuning mechanisms that allow the performing of concert harp repertoire, and also electrically amplified kanteles. The kantele is mentioned in the *Kalevala*, being associated with traditional *runo* singing in general and with the character of Väinämöinen in particular.

Kaustinen A small community in Ostrobothnia in western Finland renowned for its folk fiddler tradition, and also the location of Finland's premiere folk music festival, organised annually since 1968. The nearby community of Haapavesi is also an important centre of folk music.

Kivi, Aleksis (1834–1872) Originally Alexis Stenvall, Aleksis Kivi is regarded as the father of modern Finnish literature. He wrote the first and one of the most important novels in the Finnish language, *Seitsemän veljestä* (Seven Brothers), the widely performed play *Nummisuutarit* (Cobblers on the Heath) and a great deal of highly original and influential poetry. Though he achieved a measure of success in his lifetime, he was precipitated into mental instability and an early death by vicious attacks on his prose and poetry, considered too realistic for the Romantic sensibilities of the day. It was only much later that he came to be hailed as Finland's national author.

Ilmajoki Music Festival (Ilmajoen musiikkijuhlat) A festival in Ostrobothnia that began in 1975 with a guest performance by the Finnish National Opera of the opera *Pohjalaisia* (The Ostrobothnians) by Leevi Madetoja. The performance was repeated in 1977, and the festival was permanently established. Conductor and composer Jorma Panula played a leading role in the establishment of the festival. His 'folk operas' *Jaakko Ilkka* and *Joki-ooppera* (River Opera) were premièred there in 1978 and 1982, respectively. New works by Atso Almila, Ilkka Kuusisto, Pekka Kostiainen, Uljas Pulkkis and Jaakko Kuusisto have since been premièred there. The Ilmajoki festival profiles itself as a more folk-like, lower-threshold event than the high-brow Savonlinna Opera Festival.

Musiikkitalo The Helsinki Music Centre, commonly referred to by its Finnish name, was inaugurated in 2011. It houses the Finnish Radio Symphony Orchestra, the Helsinki Philharmonic Orchestra and the Sibelius Academy, the latter having teaching and administrative facilities on one side of the building. In addition to the main concert hall, whose acoustics are generally agreed to represent a remarkable improvement on Finlandia Hall, the building houses a smaller chamber music hall (Camerata), a multi-purpose theatre (Sonore), a studio for amplified music (Black Box) and a hall with four small organs in different styles (Organo).

Numminen, M.A. Mauri Antero Numminen (b. 1940) is a singer, composer, entertainer, author and filmmaker. He is known for his peculiar, opinion-dividing twangy singing style, which he has applied with a cheerful disregard to genre divisions to styles as diverse as German 1920s Schlagers and Schubert's Lieder. His writings include a book on Finnish beer bars and a novel about the tango.

Savonlinna Opera Festival (Savonlinnan oopperajuhlat)   Olavinlinna Castle was built as a border stronghold in 1475 but lost its significance after Finland was captured by Russia in 1809. Opera singer and administrator Aino Ackté realised the potential of the by then half-ruined castle as a setting for opera performances and organised the first opera festivals there in 1912–1914 and 1916. After these early efforts, it was not until 1967 that the annual Savonlinna Opera Festival was founded. Bass singer Martti Talvela was the festival's artistic director in the 1970s and was a central figure in its development into a festival of international prominence. Of all Finnish composers, Aulis Sallinen is the most firmly connected to the festival, as no fewer than three of his six operas were given their world premiere in Savonlinna and two others were also produced there, to a total of 62 performances of his operas to date. Directors or artistic directors of the Savonlinna Opera Festival referred to in this book:

1986–1991	Pentti Savolainen	2002–2012	Jan Hultin
1992–2002	Jorma Hynninen	2013–	Jorma Silvasti

Retretti   An art centre in the municipality of Punkaharju, about 30 km from Savonlinna. Before going bankrupt in 2012, it was one of the largest art centres in northern Europe and was known not only for its prominent exhibitions but also for its exhibition space, which consisted largely of artificial caverns excavated into the bedrock. In these caverns there was also a concert hall where many performances of chamber operas were staged by the Savonlinna Opera Festival.

Sello Hall   A concert hall in the city of Espoo, to the west of Helsinki in the Helsinki metropolitan area.

Sibelius Academy   The only music university in Finland. Founded as the Helsinki Conservatory in 1882, it was named after Jean Sibelius in 1939. Sibelius himself studied at the institution in his day and taught there from 1890 to 1892. In 2013, the Sibelius Academy was merged into the University of the Arts Helsinki together with the Academy of Fine Arts and the Theatre Academy.

Singing competitions The major competitions for solo singers in Finland are the Lappeenranta singing competition (since 1960), the Timo Mustakallio competition in Savonlinna (since 1974) and the International Mirjam Helin Singing Competition (since 1984).

Taisto Communism (Taistolaisuus) A political label applied to the opposition faction within the Finnish Communist Party in the 1970s and 1980s. The term was coined by editors of the newspaper *Helsingin Sanomat* after the name of the leader of this opposition, Taisto Sinisalo. Members of the faction never accepted the name. They were also referred to as Stalinists, although it was controversial whether this was strictly accurate. In any case, they saw themselves as 'the healthy core' of the Communist Party and had prominent supporters among stage directors, actors, musicians and students, leading to a heavy politicising of the arts in the 1970s. The faction was also noted for their unquestioning and dogmatic idolisation of the Soviet Union.

Index